James Woodall has written on music, theatre and literature for, amongst others, *The Times*, the *Daily Telegraph*, the *Observer* and GQ magazine. He has written a book on flamenco, and his biography of Jorge Luis Borges, *The Man in the Mirror of the Book*, was published in 1996. He lives in Berlin.

By the same author:

In Search of the Firedance: Spain through Flamenco

The Man in the Mirror of the Book:
A Life of Jorge Luis Borges

For my mother and father

Eu vou fazer uma canção pra ela
Uma canção singela, brasileira

I'm going to make a song for her,
A simple Brazilian song

Caetano Veloso

Song lyrics

Contents

Galeão Airport

Guanabara Bay

RIO-NITERÓI BRIDGE

NORTH ZONE

SÃO CRISTÓVÃO

NITERÓI

Madureira (Império Serrano)

National Museum

CENTRO

Mangueira

Maracanã Stadium

Sambadrome

SANTA TERESA

8 Bob's house

RIO DE JANEIRO

FLAMENGO

Pico do Papagaio

Pico da Tijuca

Parque Nacional de Tijuca

BOTAFOGO

7 Zuila's house

6 Canecão

A

SOUTH ZONE

Lagoa Rodrigo de Freitas

AVENIDA ATLANTICA

N

COPACABANA

GÁVEA

5 Chico's house

3 Ana's flat

4 Plataforma

LEBLON

2 João's flat

1 Ipanema Inn

IPANEMA

BARRA DA TIJUCA

A Pão de Açúcar (Sugar Loaf), with cable car

B Corcovado, with funicular

Atlantic   Ocean

0   5   10 km

1 Ipanema Inn   **5** Chico's house
2 João's flat   **6** Canecão
3 Ana's flat   **7** Zuila's house
4 Plataforma   **8** Bob's house

Acknowledgements

My first thanks go to Liz Calder for introducing me to the work of Chico Buarque. A few months later, Blake Morrison enabled me to meet him in Paris.

Edna Crepaldi at London's Brazilian Contemporary Arts was supportive of my explorations of Brazil from 1993 to 1995, financially and in many other ways. And I mustn't forget Bitti, who cried. My brother Andrew, meanwhile, patiently recorded, from records and CDs on to cassette, Chico Buarque's and Caetano Veloso's music for me on several occasions.

When mentioning a Latin American music label on his World Service show, John Peel reminded me – unwittingly, of course – of the name of a Soho shop I had quite forgotten and been searching for for months (see Chapter One), for which I am grateful. Thanks also to Adrian Evans.

My agent Gillon Aitken was exemplary in his tolerance for what might have appeared my rather wayward enthusiasm for a species of Latin American pop when I was supposed to be researching a classic Latin American author. The publisher of this book, Richard Beswick, has been continually understanding and supportive; his colleague, Antonia Hodgson, has also been tirelessly diligent in text preparation and proof checking. I have, too, to thank Ingrid Mersel in Amsterdam.

In Brazil, thanks are due to many.

On my first visit to Rio de Janeiro, Paulo Mamede was an indispensable contact from the moment I stepped off the plane, and then with his wife Mimine provided charming hospitality for Carnival 1994.

Luiz Schwarcz, Chico Buarque's publisher in São Paulo, generously gave me a copy of the best book available on him; I must here acknowledge my debt to this – *Chico Buarque: letra e música 1* (second edition, Companhia das Letras, 1994), with a text by Humberto Werneck – as it is an essential source for facts and details about Chico's life, from which I have drawn freely. I have also gleaned much from Charles A. Perrone's *Masters of Contemporary Brazilian Song* and Claus Schreiner's *Música Brasileira*, not least of all over the English words for some of Chico's and Caetano's songs; both are openly thanked here as sources for translation, as is Arto Lindsay for Caetano Veloso's lyrics for 'Haiti' and 'Branquinha'. It would be churlish, moreover, not to mention the continual background help I've had from forays into *Brazil: The Rough Guide*. (See Some Books, p. 303, for further details.)

Also in São Paulo, I owe a very great debt of thanks to John Coope and his colleagues at Cultura Inglesa, without whom my final research trip to Rio, and therefore the completion of this book, would not have been possible.

In Salvador da Bahia, I must thank Patricia Lorens, Billy Arquimimo and Juana Elbein dos Santos; in Rio, Márcia Elwis, Zuila Miranda and Bob Nadkarni.

Also in Rio, Ana Miranda and Emir Sader came to my rescue in February 1996, and helped make Carnival week unforgettable. In Berlin, I would like to thank, as always, Bill Dean and the British Council.

In 1993 and 1994, Bob and Moo Broughton in London – but particularly during 1994's Carnival in Rio – helped in so many ways that I do not know where or how to start thanking them. Suffice it to say that Chapters Four and Five of this book would not exist without them.

I have, finally, to thank Caetano Veloso and Gilberto Gil for agreeing to be interviewed several times, once each in person, and also over the phone; and Gal Costa, for precious time she gave me in Portugal in July 1995.

My greatest thanks of all go to Chico Buarque.

Author's Note

All of the music discussed here, as well as many of the incidents which accompanied my discovery of it, was experienced in a state of uncommon emotional optimism. Such certainties are by nature fragile and, as was bound (by a law of human averages) to happen, optimism had been replaced by its opposite when the book came to be written. Before putting pen to paper, I thought I would write about magic. Instead, I have tried to write about consolation.

Music is consolation for many. My simple Brazilian songs will always be there after human feeling proves how fallible it is. They will be there long after this narrative has lost any topicality it may possess. And music listened to and enjoyed by millions makes one rise above personal sorrow.

The unique melodies, irresistible rhythms and undying poetic wisdom of Chico Buarque and Caetano Veloso comprise, in my view, a gift to the world – like García Lorca's, Osip Mandelstam's and Jacques Brel's.

If this book can convey something of the true but entirely distinct genius of these two Brazilian musicians, then as far I'm concerned that will be consolation enough.

Some of the names of people who play a part in this story have been changed.

One

'London, London'

In the late spring of 1992, I was at my desk leafing through various publishers' catalogues. One of them was Bloomsbury's. A half-page announced a novel by a Latin American I'd never heard of. The novel was called *Turbulence*; its author was Chico Buarque.

'Leafing through publishers' catalogues' is journalese for 'looking for a job'. So-called literary journalists like myself rely for more than half the material they want to write about on information culled from these biannual booklets, put out by publishers to flog their lists.

As I say, Chico Buarque's name meant nothing to me, though I made a mental note from the blurb that he was a 'popular musician' in his native Brazil, and had been 'involved in politics'. The book seemed to be about Rio de Janeiro. I'd never been to Latin America and knew nothing about Brazil – other than, very roughly, where it was, that Brazilians spoke Portuguese, adored football and had terrible governments. The only Brazilian I knew was an old family friend whose daughter had been one of my first girlfriends.

Chico Buarque, meanwhile, might make a possible feature. On the other hand, he might not. At that stage, I was still guessing.

A few weeks later, I was invited to a publishing do close to my home in Highbury – drinks in a windy Islington garden. The party was in honour of a Dutch publisher, Maarten Asscher, who was over in London and happens to be a friend of mine. Coincidentally, the Dutch edition of Buarque's novel was also in his catalogue for publication in Amsterdam that summer.

Bloomsbury's publishing director, Liz Calder, was there too. I knew her by reputation only. The independent company she had co-founded in the mid-1980s was a rare success story in a decade when London publishing became money-grubbing and faceless. To this day, she remains one of the most liked and charismatic editors in the business.

Liz didn't know me at all. Somewhat pushily, I introduced myself. I said straightaway that I was interested to know more about Chico Buarque. This was disingenuous; what I meant was that I was hoping to 'work on him' on the basis of scant Latin American credentials (my first book, on Spain, seemed to have led people to believe that anything 'Latin' was my domain – it was not), and then land a newspaper commission.

Liz's reaction was rather extraordinary. She warmed to me instantly, and said she was avid to get some coverage for this man, and that we should keep very, *very* closely in touch about it if I got anywhere. She didn't quite hug me, but when we finished talking about possibilities, I felt as though she had.

Only later did I learn that I had inadvertently tapped

into a deep seam in Liz Calder's life: one, she would say, she's never really left behind.

As a young mother, she spent four years in the mid-1960s in Brazil with her first husband, who worked for Rolls Royce. Needing a break from housewifery, she did some modelling in São Paulo. Through it, she got a taste of Brazilian (as opposed to ex-pat) life, and responded to the cultural impulses of the time: the military had taken over in 1964, but full-scale repression was still some years off. This was the swinging era of architect Oscar Niemeyer, *cinema novo*, the bossa nova – and a young singer-songwriter called Chico Buarque de Hollanda.

Chico Buarque became a national hero in 1966 with a song called 'A banda' ('The Band'). Liz heard it, and along with legions of Brazilians, whose lifeblood is music, became a fan. Chico (short for Francisco) had a velvet voice, tropical good looks, and wrote songs of exquisite poetry. At the age of just twenty-two, this lithe and engaging musician was soon the heart-throb of a nation of over a hundred million. Liz did meet him once, very briefly. In 1968, she left Brazil when the regime began to harden, but had followed his career ever since.

The reason for her excitement in 1992 was that she was about to publish Chico Buarque's first novel (*Estorvo* in Portuguese) over a quarter of a century after becoming, conceivably, his first British fan. It would be a bit like a Brazilian who'd lived in London during the 1960s and been a Beatles fan publishing a first novel by Paul McCartney.

★   ★   ★

Some weeks after the party, Liz sent me a proof of *Turbulence*. A few weeks after that, I took it with me on holiday to Scotland.

It's a strange tale. A man narrates twenty-four hours of his life in a city that could be but is never named as Rio de Janeiro. As I'd never been there, I was no wiser than most gringo readers about the location. For all I knew, it could have been Mexico City or Tokyo. Aspects of Rio I had heard about – fenced-off condominiums, arbitrary violence, tropical landscape, awful buses – *were* all in this text, but I'm damned if I knew on first reading what it was about.

The man has a sister; he steals her jewels; he has a bladder problem; he then comes up against some urban guerrillas. That's to sell the novel short, but it was about all I could make of it that September. Its setting was glutinously obscure, its pace leisurely, its plot threadbare. No music or politics so far as I could tell. I wasn't sure I liked it – and nothing could have been further from the deep-green hillsides around me, the sea loch at the bottom of the glen, the salmon river rushing past the drive in front of the house where I was staying . . . These crystal-clear surroundings, along with my more devoted attention to a famous oyster bar down the road, no doubt accounted for my finding *Turbulence* quite impenetrable. Perhaps I should have read it in bed with flu, or in a sweaty north London pub, or on the Tube.

Still, a month and a half later, I was having dinner with Chico Buarque in Paris. I was interviewing him for the *Independent on Sunday* Review, which was to run a feature to tie in with the publication of the novel. In other words,

I'd got the job, though I'd had to move several mountains to secure the commission.

It was a typical freelance improvisation. Richard Williams, then in charge of the Review, procrastinated for weeks. Every time I rang him (if I got through), he'd say he'd like to do it. And then did nothing. Every time I rang Bloomsbury's publicity director, the line was engaged. When I did on occasion speak to her, she persuaded me that Williams was 'really keen'. When I got back to Williams (if I got through), he began to sound less keen than perplexed. Who was this freelancer he didn't know (I could hear him thinking), pestering him about some Latino nobody really wanted to read about? (This is the sort of thing you hear most British newspaper editors thinking when you splutter a foreign name or word down the line.) He continued, nonetheless, to say he'd like to 'do' it.

The crunch came when I said *I* could not do the story without meeting the subject – in Paris. Buarque has a pad there, and Paris was the only place I could see him to beat the deadline – i.e. to get the piece done well before he was in London for publication, and make it an exclusive.

By this time, the idea had been mysteriously shunted from arts to books, and Blake Morrison, the paper's literary editor, had taken it over. My astonishment when he rang me to confirm the commission rose to incredulity when I heard him agreeing to a flight and a hotel in Paris. He'd obviously been warned that there were strings attached to the story. Cannily, he also saw that an exclusive with a star of Chico's standing – making a books piece of it at that – was too good to miss. (They were happier times for the

Independent; Blake, sacked from the Sunday paper in 1995, was one of its true *éminences grises*.)

So why not use a Paris stringer or staffer? I suspect that's where my Latin 'expertise' came in. The fact that I spoke Spanish, was clued up about flamenco and knew a bit about books was on paper a help – though in truth quite irrelevant: as was, it seems, the fact that I knew not a word of Portuguese and had never been anywhere near Latin America, let alone Brazil.

Blake's style was as generous as it was brisk and perceptive. I suspect on this occasion he thought he'd get the right piece from someone fired up about the subject, and not just a run-of-the-mill profile from someone who'd read cuttings the night before.

Was I fired up at this point? Not exactly. Liz Calder had lent me some records and CDs, and I'd listened in a desultory sort of way. Chico had a charming voice and sang in an incomprehensible tongue. There was a certain magnetism in his music, perhaps a deceptive simplicity, though it hadn't yet stopped me from listening to Radio 3. It still had about it a tinge of 'geriatric beach music', as my brother called it when I later asked him for the umpteenth time to record some Chico albums (borrowed, naturally, from Liz Calder). I was dead keen on the commission though. A couple of days in Paris never did any harm. I had a few of Chico's tunes buzzing around in my head, and had done some reading. I'd even interviewed Liz.

But I was also apprehensive. Should Chico be a tricky sort of customer and behave like pop stars are supposed to behave – fractious, megalomaniac and substance-abusing –

I'd be floored. I'd never interviewed a huge star before: though of course Chico was only really huge in one place, about which most Britons were as ignorant as me. That was part of the problem. The *Independent on Sunday* Review was not a fanzine. I'd have to build him up from nothing. And if we ran out of conversation, I'd actually have nothing to say about Brazil – except to tell him that I knew nothing about it.

Did he speak English? Apparently. French certainly; his flat was in the first *arrondissement*, and he was based there doing PR for the French edition of *Turbulence*. In fact, he was travelling all over Europe, as the book was appearing in many countries. He was, it seemed, pretty well known in Italy and Spain. This was absolutely no help to me at all.

I took the precaution of rereading *Turbulence* before meeting its author. This time, the book worked better. Its atmosphere of a supercharged city, by turns sublime and foul, elegant and threatening, did weave a kind of spell. The streets in the story have a pulse of their own, roaring with pollution, sweat, brash commerce. The people who teem down them have to fend for themselves and sometimes dive for safety – as if being chased indoors by a swarm of bees.

The narrator is the vessel through which the city 'thinks'. Distinctive juxtapositions of phrase and imagery came alive, maybe because I was working harder at the book. It was still a strange one, but I thought I began to see what Buarque was getting at. If *Turbulence* was Rio de Janeiro, I wanted to know more about it.

We met at nine at the Escargot Montorgueil, near Les

Halles. The plush, dimly lit restaurant was also near his flat, convenient for him of course, but it wasn't just that. Chico was on crutches.

I'd been warned. He'd been playing football in Rio and broken his ankle. He'd been laid up for many weeks and would be hobbling around for quite a few more. He'd walked, in so far as he could walk anywhere, to the restaurant alone.

I didn't make much of his incapacity at the time, although I mentioned it in my piece. What I failed to comprehend was its real implication. Here was one of Latin America's major stars doing the publicity rounds for his European publishers more or less physically handicapped, and prepared to come out on a miserable October night to meet an unknown English journalist to talk about, among other things, Brazil and Brazilian music – of which this English journo was (though Chico had, I suspect, been primed to the contrary, if Bloomsbury were doing its job) woefully ignorant. At least it wasn't as bad as Chico's author tour in Norway: everyone there was astonished to learn that he was 'also' a professional musician.

Chico is a very polite man and, as I was to discover, almost painfully modest. He was publicising his book because his publishers had asked him to. If he was bored during our dinner, he didn't let on at any point – and didn't blanch when some way into our conversation I said that it was important to 'get across to British readers something about Brazil, which is not somewhere most of us know much about, so can we talk about that?' This was downright patronising, but Chico didn't take it that way.

Apart from the crutches, there were three things that

struck me on meeting him: he was remarkably good-looking, and remarkably slim; he seemed incredibly young (he was forty-eight); and he did not remotely resemble a pop star.

He wore a well-cut jacket, white shirt, dark trousers. His clean-shaven face was olive-coloured, lean, and had an essential seriousness, a sombre look, to it; it lit up when he smiled. His smile bared his teeth, which I remember were – are – perfect. His full head of dark-brown hair was tightly curled, and somehow boyish. He smoked a lot – every five to ten minutes – and obviously liked wine, red wine. We shared a bottle of fine Burgundy. We may have had brandy to finish.

We started with snails. As we ate, Chico listened to my questions intently, looking at me with his enormous turquoise eyes, smiled quietly, and whether speaking French or English (his French is better) was never less than lucid. Often, he got animated, nervous even, though it was the nervousness – nerviness, perhaps – of intellectual animation, never of confusion. He gesticulated freely with his hands, usually with a long cigarette held in his fingers. He had an immense amount to say, and said it – unless I was vastly mistaken – willingly, with pleasure.

The pleasure for me was in what I learnt.

He is the son of a prominent Brazilian intellectual of the 1930s and 1940s, Sérgio Buarque de Hollanda. Sérgio died in 1982, aged seventy-nine. Chico's mother, Maria Amélia, now eighty-seven, lives in Rio de Janeiro, her home city. Sérgio was from São Paulo.

Chico was supposed to graduate in architecture at the

University of São Paulo; instead, he picked up a guitar when he first heard the bossa novas of João Gilberto in the late 1950s, headed for Rio, and never looked back.

João Gilberto? Bossa nova?

'White samba,' said Chico, by way of eloquent definition. I didn't persist in my ignorance and ask what samba was: that, I knew in a vague way, was the music of the Brazilian blacks.

I did know that Chico had become famous for 'A banda', and asked him about it.

'It really isn't my favourite song,' he said. 'I don't know why it caught on.' He said this without fuss. He hasn't performed 'A banda' for years. Oddly, I didn't get around to hearing the song myself for another year and a half.

Chico was far from recalcitrant. In fact, he generally talks a lot, and rather fast. Amongst the many other things he told me during that dinner – about his family, his three daughters, Brazilian politics, the writing of *Estorvo* – I found one story, and two observations, especially riveting.

The story concerns the manner in which Chico went into exile from Brazil in 1968.

In March 1964, Brazil was rocked by a military coup. It was bloodless, and though ushering in years of undemocratic rule by generals, the regime that took power was, initially, benign. However, with the rise of leftist guerrilla activity in the mid-1960s, the predictable bogeyman, communism, became the military's first target: anyone suspected of anti-state sentiment could be branded a 'communist' subversive, and accused of any number of failings – from being a supporter of Fidel Castro to offending the Church and family values. All political parties were abolished in 1965.

For artists, the real blow fell with the government's imposition in December 1968 of something called the 'Ato Institucional No.5' (or 'AI-5') – the Fifth Institutional Act – enshrining state censorship. Chico had never been openly political, and his songs in the two-year periods either side of 'A banda' had been lyrical, sophisticated, poetic, but not confrontational. But anyone who knew him was aware that he had no time for non-democratic politics, and that his sympathies were of the left.

That was not, in itself, the problem. A play, *Roda viva* (*Rat Race*), written by Chico in 1967 and premièred in Rio de Janeiro in January 1968, was.

Roda viva was an exuberant and violent satire on the show-biz ethic, something which since his precocious success in 1966 Chico had eschewed. The play, starring amongst others his new wife, an actress called Marieta Severo, was vibrantly, colourfully anti-establishment. Its aggressive imagery – a huge Coca-Cola can next to a statue of St George, lamb's blood washing over the stage, simulated copulation – and pessimism (the protagonist commits suicide) did much, in the first instance, to alter the public's view of the 'A banda' boy as a goody two-shoes.

It had also caught the eye of the authorities. After Rio, *Roda viva* went to São Paulo, a city then alive with the sounds and activities of student agitators and the counter-culture: on 17 July 1968, the theatre where *Roda viva* was playing, the Teatro Galpão, was invaded by a group from the sinisterly named 'Command for the Hunting-Out of Communists' – Brazilian brownshirts, basically. They destroyed the scenery, and beat up the actors.

Two and a half months later, in Pôrto Alegre in southern Brazil, *Roda viva* had one further performance, on 3 October; on the 4th, two actors were abducted, beaten up and dumped in undergrowth miles from the city. All the players were eventually ejected from their hotel and sent back by bus to São Paulo. *Roda viva*'s life came to an undignified end.

Then there was the Passeata dos Cem Mil, the March of the Hundred Thousand. In the month before the violent attack on *Roda viva* in São Paulo, students, artists and intellectuals, even the clergy, had organised a huge protest in Rio de Janeiro against government repression. The focal point of the demonstration was the Avenida Rio Branco, in the heart of Rio's commercial and administrative district. '*Uma beleza*', the poet, diplomat and boss-nova lyricist Vinícius de Moraes called it – 'quite beautiful'. One of the Passeata's protestors was the twenty-four-year-old Chico Buarque.

At seven o'clock on the morning of 18 December 1968, five days after the announcement of the 'AI-5', Chico was visited by the military police. He was taken to the Brazilian Army's headquarters on the Avenida Presidente Vargas, close to where he had demonstrated six months before – against the government in whose name these unbidden captors worked. Marieta, six months pregant, followed in a car behind, barely seeing where she was going: she had forgotten to put in her contact lenses.

After interrogation – peaceful, but startling and lasting the whole day – in which *Roda viva* and the Passeata were cited as examples of things which would flout the new law, Chico was set free; however, if he wanted to leave the city, he would have to get permission from a certain Colonel Atila.

A fair for the record industry was taking place in Cannes in January 1969, for which Chico had already made travel plans. He obtained his licence to leave, and with Marieta flew out of Rio de Janeiro on 3 January. Originally, they'd planned to be away only for a few weeks. They didn't return until over a year later.

The reason was simple: friends advised them to stay out of Brazil. Other musicians and artists were being rounded up, imprisoned, sent into exile. In time, more anonymous agitators and flouters of the regime's laws were being tortured; some disappeared altogether.

Brazil's repression at this time was, it has to be said, on nothing like the scale of Argentina's or Chile's in the 1970s. Tens of thousands disappeared in those two countries in a simultaneous fascist convulsion that recalls Nazi Germany. Brazil – partly, I believe, because of a more equable and tolerant strain in its people than in many Hispanic Latin American societies – escaped true barbarity.

But when I heard, and saw, Chico Buarque telling me in Paris the story of his experience at the hands of *his* rulers, it was obvious that the pain of it had struck deep: his features tightened when he remembered the police visit, and saddened when he moved on to describe his enforced period away from Brazil.

He and Marieta ended up in Rome. Their first daughter Silvia was born there in March 1969. Vinícius de Moraes, an old friend of Chico's father Sérgio and who was also in Rome, was her godfather.

Chico's main problems were work and money. Apart from supporting himself and his family in Rome, there was their flat in Rio for which he was still paying and which he now risked losing. In Italy, there was a degree of interest in the *cantante brasiliano*, but not enough. Chico made an indifferent record in Italian, and ended up together with his friend, a Brazilian singer called Toquinho, as a support act for Josephine Baker, 'glorious at the age of sixty-three', says Humberto Werneck – which was also, says Chico, 'the approximate age of her public'.

Professionally, it was a dismal year – 'humiliating', Chico said as we dined, referring to his shadowy rôle behind Baker, who had not the slightest idea of who he was. Brazil, his homeland, was the source and inspiration of all that he knew best: music, poetry and football. His homesickness was intense. The relative emptiness of exile was, for a young man whose Brazilian career in 1966 appeared to be stretching before him on a golden road, all the more demeaning. Towards the end of 1969, he signed a recording deal with Philips, and resolved to return home.

Philips' Brazilian director, André Midani, persuaded Chico that things *were* improving in Brazil. It was a curious line to take given that, in 1969, a particularly vicious general, Emilio Garrastazu Medici, had taken over the reins of power. But Chico went, and arrived with his wife and daughter at Rio's Galeão airport in March 1970.

Things, as Chico soon found out, were by no means improved in Brazil. If anything, they were getting worse. In Rome, Vinícius had told Chico: 'When you return, return with a bang.' The bang Chico made was 'Apesar de você' ('In Spite of You'): to hell with the regime, it cried, exquisitely, courageously. It remains one of the most infectious and defiant pop songs ever written.

Of the two observations I remember Chico making as we dined, one was that Brazilians don't make a distinction between 'pop' and 'serious' music: culture, he pointed out, isn't as graded as it is in Europe. Music is music, and in Brazil Chico Buarque (of course he didn't say this himself) is considered a great composer.

The other thing he said, when we talked generally of the obstinate financial and political mess Brazil had landed itself in during the last half-century, was that a country that can invent the bossa nova can't be all bad.

Then, I could neither agree nor disagree. I took the statement on trust. I knew little enough about Brazil, even less about the bossa nova. Unsure of my ground, I chose not to put these words into my article. Now, like a mantra, I hear the words every time I think of Brazil – and if I had any say in the matter, the country would adopt them as its motto. The bossa nova is one of the seminal musical inventions of all time. Chico Buarque de Hollanda, though I was shockingly ill-informed about this when I sat opposite him in the Escargot Montorgueil, is one of the bossa nova's greatest and most thrilling exponents.

I was having dinner with Brazil's Schubert. Or at *least* its Paul McCartney: a Brazilian Beatle, with politics. Not silly politics. Real politics. Chico Buarque is a poet-singer who has won a battle with history.

Back in London, I settled down to Liz Calder's CDs

and records – and found that my recording of dinner with Chico was defective: my travel-worn dictaphone had picked up far more restaurant noise, particularly from a table of Japanese businessmen next to ours, than it had of Chico's deep, mellifluous but somewhat under-enunciated musings. Memory and a degree of journalistic licence came necessarily into play.

More significantly, so did his music. From Mr Bongo, a shop in Berwick Street specialising in Latin American records, I purchased a double album: *A Arte de Chico Buarque*.

It was quite a find, and full of some of his best songs from the late 1960s and early 1970s, though not, crucially, either 'A banda' or 'Apesar de você', about both of which I wrote (based on what Chico had told me) in my article. The latter song I didn't get to know for another year either. Mr Bongo's manager, John Cooper, also agreed to a short-term loan of his battered personal copy of one of Chico's most important albums, *Construção* (*Construction*), from 1971.

I mention this not so much for my purchases and borrowings as for the fact that Chico himself paid Mr Bongo a visit a few weeks later when he was in London for his book launch. He'd heard that his records could be bought there, and was fascinated to know what was on offer. If there was one place in London which knew his name and music, he was naturally keen to see it.

John's amazement when Chico appeared – still hobbling, with a stick – in this tiny Soho basement was total. John told me as much when I returned his copy of *Construção*. Chico Buarque in *his* shop?

I invited John to the launch party – quite beyond my remit, but I didn't think anyone else would mention it to him. I left him the address: the Groucho Club. Unsurprisingly, John didn't turn up, and when I went back some months later (having already returned his album) to visit Mr Bongo, it had moved. John had also disappeared. The new premises in nearby Lexington Street were charmless and so, it has to be said, were Mr Bongo's new managers. There wasn't a Chico record in sight.

In those chilly November weeks of 1992 as I worked on the article, and after it appeared, Chico's music flooded my front room. In the normal course of events, I might have returned to Radio 3. There were new articles to work on, new projects to begin, new music perhaps to listen to, plenty of other things to get on with that had nothing to *do* with music, Brazilian or otherwise. Liz would get her CDs and records back, I'd get my cheque for the article, Chico would put a dreaded book tour behind him, and none of us would be the worse for wear.

Except it wasn't quite like that. Between dinner with Chico in Paris and the beginning of 1993, something happened to my musical nervous system. *A Arte de Chico Buarque* was never off my turntable. Liz didn't get her CDs and records back for months. I began to have an intense interest in Portuguese, a language I could just about read but not yet, when sung or spoken, comprehend. It didn't matter. The sensual cascade of syllables, sibilant consonants and lingering vowel sounds, the mix of alien diphthongs and honeyed inflections in Chico's songs were all I needed to be convinced that Portuguese was the language, surely, God created for music.

And what music: bright and melancholy in the same phrase, constantly modulating from major to minor, melodically inventive, rhythmically intricate. It uplifts, yet makes one feel the fragility of light-heartedness, regret the loss of a kind of euphoria before it's gone.

Liz had given me a word for this: *saudades* ('sauw-da-jies'), something to do with longing, memory, need, nostalgia, love. Music that rolls all these sensations into one had to be worth nurturing. Chico had also used the word when talking about his year of exile in Italy.

The concept of 'Carnival', meanwhile, the very idea of Rio de Janeiro – more imagined than understood, but endlessly celebrated in Chico's songs – became seductive. The whole notion of Brazil was suddenly fascinating. And the name 'Chico Buarque' took on the resonance it had had, and still has, for millions in Brazil. It was a name I began to love as much as I began to love the songs it lay alongside on the record sleeve.

I became, at the age of thirty-two, an unrepentant pop fan – Brazil-style. It was like being fifteen again. It was like starting an affair.

The following summer, I took a friend to a concert at the Royal Festival Hall in London. The concert was part of a celebration of Latin American music, a biennial event called 'Gran, Gran Fiesta'. It was a hot Sunday evening in July, and the man performing was Caetano Veloso.

I knew nothing about him either, except that he and

Chico Buarque were good friends. I didn't know Caetano's music at all. I thought I'd better try it. It didn't seem possible that another Brazilian could be as exciting as Chico.

The RFH was packed, as it rarely is. The whole of Brazilian London had turned out. I met the impresario Michael Morris briefly as we went in.

'He's huge in Brazil,' he announced, 'they adore him there.' More than Chico? I wondered, eyeing him suspiciously.

In the auditorium, the crowd was buzzing. Brazilian flags were draped over the fronts of boxes. People were bringing in beer in plastic cups. Slow handclapping started up when the clock hit 7.45. The temperature rose.

I realised I hadn't been to a pop concert since Peter Gabriel's *So* tour in 1987. And the expectation in the air, though in a much smaller venue than Earl's Court where I'd seen Gabriel, was similar: the bulk of the audience was, I felt, awaiting some kind of superstar . . .

The figure who emerged on stage to roars of adulation (followed by a band of six – cellist, bassist, guitarist and three percussionists) was slight, willowy, androgynous. He was dressed in a tight white polo-neck top and loose linen trousers, and wore Jesus boots. He was clean-shaven and grey-haired. Occasionally during the concert he would hitch his trouser legs up at the thighs as he stood at the microphone, in a kind of nervous tic, as if he were using them as worry beads.

If he was nervous (and from time to time it showed), it mattered little. Caetano Veloso, the same age as Chico, sang with the most beautiful voice I have ever heard live: high, poised, graceful, and not once out of tune. You can't say that for the world's finest tenors. There was tangible poetry in Caetano's singing, effortless intensity and commitment: his voice gleamed. As he sang, he stretched out his arms which, mesmerically, began to resemble wings. I thought he might start to fly. Even if one didn't know what the songs were about (and I didn't), again it mattered little: Caetano was, for nearly three hours, by turns elegant show- man and bashful lyricist. His presence was magnetic, his music relentlessly exuberant and questioning. Everything about him made the spine fizz.

This was without doubt a performer of genius. It was his first London show. As far as I could see, he had come from an enchanted world. And he couldn't be more different from Chico.

I say Caetano's was the most beautiful voice I had ever heard live. His stage personality was also one of the most candid. During a quiet acoustic section of the concert, he explained various things: among them that coming to London was especially moving for him, as he'd lived there between 1969 and 1972, in exile – like Chico, only for longer – from General Medici's regime.

At that time, a major musician back in Brazil had asked him to compose a song for Brazilians. Caetano obliged, and now said, nearly twenty-five years on, that it was 'as if Elvis Presley had asked John Lennon to write a song from New York' – which was received with gales of laughter from, I presume, the audience's British constituency.

I cringed. At the microphone, Caetano asked: 'What's

so funny? I don't see what's so funny.' There was an embarrassed hush. For a moment, this most intelligent of singers seemed to have forgotten where he was. John Lennon? Britain? Elvis? Not even a Brazilian genius mucks around with that formula.

Caetano moved on. He had also composed a song in English, short, wistful, and entitled 'London, London'. He wanted to sing it now. Seated, he twirled his guitar on its bottom with one finger on the tip as he recounted the writing of the song. The guitar slipped and fell with a crash to the floor. (This is what I mean by nervousness.) Caetano recovered, though when my friend Gail and I looked at each other it was as if to ask, What will he do next? Slip over and unseat the cellist?

Minutes later Caetano's clangers were forgotten. As he went through 'London, London', every single Brazilian member of the audience, knowing the song by heart, sang along – in English – word for word. The Brits could only turn their heads in wonder. I'd never heard anything like it.

He then sang a song called 'Coração vagabundo' ('Vagabond Heart'), a bossa nova of such lilting softness that tears, pathetically and without warning, leapt into my eyes. When I turned to Gail to enthuse over its perfection, she clearly wondered what sort of person she'd come to the concert with. By that stage, I wasn't sure I knew either.

Gail belonged to a newspaper. Arts. Twenty minutes later, she'd seen enough. Encores were being called for. She was concerned to get her car out before the crowds. She wasn't clapping. I think she thought it was a bit undignifed, as an arts editor, to join the braying masses. She left. I have seen more than one arts editor behave like this.

(The only other person who abandoned me in such a way was one of my oldest friends, who upped and went in the middle of Mike Leigh's film *High Hopes*. At least she hung around so we could argue about it afterwards. I have since learnt never to go to anything you badly want to see or hear with someone you like, *ever*.)

What Gail missed was Caetano's party piece. The song was a wry ballad, 'Alegria, alegria' ('Happiness, Happiness'), an anthem from the late 1960s. Those who knew it and plenty who didn't rushed immediately to the front of the stage with the first chords, and danced to the song. They danced six deep, and asked for more. And Caetano had more – three encores in total. His fans at the front didn't want to let him go, and nor – though I remained seated – did I.

I was transfixed.

The next day, I went to Tower Records in Piccadilly Circus to see what I could plunder from the Brazilian section. To my delight, I found not only a CD of Caetano's (*A arte de . . .* , with many of the songs I'd heard the night before, including 'Coração vagabundo') but also one of Chico's from 1989 I'd been looking for for months, quite without success. Now I had it.

Was I foolish to feel that this sudden addiction to two Brazilian magicians came with unusual luck?

For the next four months, theirs were the only two

voices that filled my front room. Something had broken
inside my head.

'London, London' (1971)

I'm wandering round and round, nowhere to go
I'm lonely in London, London's lovely so
I cross the streets without fear
Everybody keeps the way clear
I know I know no one here to say hello
I know they keep the way clear
I am lonely in London without fear
I'm wandering round and round here, nowhere to go

While my eyes
Go looking for flying saucers in the sky
While my eyes
Go looking for flying saucers in the sky

Oh Sunday, Monday, autumn pass by me
And people hurry on so peacefully
A group approaches a policeman
He seems so pleased to please them
It's good at least to live and I agree
He seems so pleased at least
And it's good at least to live in peace and
Sunday, Monday, years and I agree

While my eyes, etc.

I choose no face to look at
Choose no way
I just happen to be here
And it's OK
Green grass, blue eyes
Grey sky, God bless silent pain
And happiness
I came around to say yes
And I say

While my eyes, etc.

Two

Where the Music Starts

I have no musical talent whatsoever.

Like many, I had piano lessons, and proved unequal to the task. Aged eleven, I passed Grade Two with the lowest possible pass mark: 100. The best I could manage in the years ahead was to ask my piano teacher at public school to play me the fast movement of the 'Moonlight Sonata', which I liked to listen to but had a chance of about one in three million of playing. I stopped lessons, to his and my relief, aged fourteen.

One of my brothers, an enthusiastic drummer as a boy, is now aged thirty-four and reteaching himself the piano. The other brother got a Distinction at Grade Eight trombone, and is currently ambitious to crack Hindemith's sonata for the instrument. Noble and as yet unfulfilled ambitions, I should add, but there's music somewhere in the genes. Today, all I can play are C and E major on the guitar.

Yet without music, I don't see how life is bearable.

I should now swiftly move on to the next chapter. But I won't, because there is a story, of sorts, to tell.

My first obvious ability was with a pencil. My parents took me, aged four, to a fair, and when we got home my father suggested I try and draw what I'd seen. When he saw the result he announced, By God, the boy can draw.

This pencil discovery also came with the realisation that I had a mental block over tying my shoelaces, and, all too soon, an astonishing resistance to telling the time. Did clocks fly across the playroom when for the eighth time in any given session James registered complete bafflement over the concept of one longish hand pointed at twelve and one slightly smaller hand at six? I think so.

This may have gone on for a few years. But there were compensations for the eldest's burgeoning innumeracy (my father was good at figures, my mother – if it's possible – worse than me). Mum is a real music fan, and has always loved opera. For my father, Mozart and Schubert and Gilbert & Sullivan did quite nicely, thank you. When he met her in the mid-1950s, his future wife was in the grip of Maria Callas fever, and I think she did much to educate him in sounds from beyond the 1820s and the D'Oyly Carte.

So by the time I was five, their record collection was quite substantial, opera included. One LP was highlights from *Aida*. I couldn't leave this album alone. One reason was because I responded to the famous 'Triumphal March'. The tune and rhythm were and are unmistakable, and wonderfully primitive.

I used to be allowed to march up and down the sitting room in my dressing gown to its soaring trumpet theme before going to bed. I loved the whole performance. So, I think, did my parents. All failures with figures and over tasks that required minimal mathematical understanding were forgiven. The march became a ritual. It was the first tune I really knew by heart.

My parents, it has to be said, inducted me into Verdi at around the time the Beatles were moving out of their teenyboppy MBE 'She Loves You' phase into the proto-weirdness of *Revolver*. Like the Queen, many Brits who'd enjoyed the Beatles' *nice* songs were a bit perplexed when they stopped touring, went into the studio, and came up with things like 'Tomorrow Never Knows' and 'Strawberry Fields Forever'. Wasn't it the Queen who is supposed to have said, after the Beatles (John Lennon actually) had made that infamous comparison to Christ and then indulged in some seriously counter-cultural gestures, 'The Beatles are getting awfully strange these days' . . . ?

In Brazil at this time, Chico Buarque sang 'A banda', and wooed a nation. Waiting in the wings was Caetano Veloso, to shock the same nation a year later.

My musical tastes as a boy were a mix of the snobbish and the obvious. On the one hand, because of my parents' influence, I could genuinely claim an attraction to Mozart and Beethoven (Verdi eventually dropped down the hit-list). When I was sent to prep school in 1969, classical symphonies and other respectable bits and pieces were my staple diet. Curiously, I didn't get beaten up for this.

On the other hand – and this is slightly embarrassing – I was also a bit of a Beach Boys fan. Perhaps it was my mother who approved of them; she'd even bought a

'Best of . . .'-type album – probably for dancing at a party (my parents were thirty-four and thirty-one respectively in 1965, the year my *Aida* fixation began). I nicked the album, and played it constantly.

I did not know what 'Surfin' Safari' meant, or the delicious-sounding 'Sloop John B'. A 'little Deuce Coope' could have been anything from a beer (as in 'Ind') to a spaceship. But still, by the age of eight, the Beach Boys were my band. I sang along, understanding little, but lapping up those big, high, harmonised choruses and bright tunes.

Eventually a rather sophisticated prep-school friend of mine, Christian, to this day my oldest chum, suggested I was on the wrong track. He showed me an album which was black, and had four large square photos on one side, with smaller photos and a list of tracks and credits on the reverse. On the front, above the photos, were three words in white: 'LET IT BE'.

'The Beatles are far better than the Beach Boys,' he said, with dark authority. I disagreed completely. There was no justification for this, as I didn't know any Beatles songs (apart from the obvious ones). That was not the point. My territory was the Beach Boys, and that was that.

Christian was of course right. *His* only problem was that later he began to think that Elvis was even better, and by the time I'd converted from the Surfers to the Fabs I couldn't see what he was on about at all: Elvis has never meant anything to me.

Christian nonetheless was the linchpin in the first major cultural event of my life. I must have seen his copy of *Let It Be* some time in the spring of 1971, a year after its UK release. He must have played it to me then. At the time, I probably scoffed, and suggested we groove to 'Surfin USA' instead.

Yet by the summer, I had persuaded my mother to buy me a copy of *Abbey Road* – perhaps because I now thought it was the coolest thing, aged ten, to have a copy of a record by this band called the Beatles. Mum knew exactly who they were, though whether she knew or cared that they had broken up by the time she forked out £2 for their last recorded album, I had no idea.

She's never said as much, but I think she rued the day she introduced her eldest to the Beatles. For the next two years, until shortly before puberty, nothing else counted. OK, I did my prep, played cricket very badly, got good marks at French, proved transcendentally awful at maths, came home for the holidays, and was perfectly nice – as nice as any average pre-pubescent boy is likely to be – but this was all ancillary to real life. Real life was the Beatles.

Why was this? Simple, really: their music answered a deep and wholly unarticulated need in my virgin nervous system. It made me dance. Their stories and sounds and atmospheres and rhythms unlocked my imagination. I'm certain no other group or musician of their time could have done the same – not the Rolling Stones, the Who, the Kinks, nor even Led Zeppelin (they wouldn't have been allowed); and the American Hendrix, Joplin, Dylan and the Doors were off-limits for a ten-year-old who had no older sibling to learn from.

So I memorised the words of dozens of Beatles songs, and got a friend at prep school who played the guitar to accompany me in the music room, or if that failed, the music master to play the piano for me: 'Can't Buy Me Love', 'Yesterday', 'Paperback Writer', 'I Am the Walrus', 'Lady Madonna', 'Revolution', 'You Never Give Me Your Money', 'Let It Be'. The list doesn't stop. I had a sweet enough voice.

I drank in everything, from the heart-throb crooning of 'All My Loving' to the demonism of 'Helter Skelter' (this became my show-off dance number): the music room had a record player, and I and other friends had the records – most Beatles albums I had either bought, been given, or odd-jobbed for. I became fascinated by John Lennon, and doodled thousands of portraits of his inimitable features – round specs, thin nose, hippie hair – during and outside classes. My first real ambition was to be like him: to be a Beatle. I was obsessed, and in love.

It was a bit sad, really, as the Beatles were of course no more. The brilliant sixties had moved into the corpse-like seventies. Paul began a kitsch band called Wings. George went seriously sub-Continental. John made a nice but mixed album called *Imagine*, and then, like Ringo, seemed to vanish.

Everything that had had a veneer of hope in the sixties seemed to go sour very soon in the succeeding decade. Vietnam was the great catastrophe of its early years, if only because for people of my parents' generation the United States was what the modern world *was*.

I remember Vietnam. I couldn't understand it, nor I think could my parents; how often did they try and explain the war to me?—and yet it wasn't ever really called 'a war'. But a great country was going to pieces in those dreadful pictures we'd seen day after day on TV in the late sixties.

In the early seventies, something that meant a lot to my parents, and to everyone who remembered 1945, seemed to die: America was going down the tubes.

Yet *I* was still intoxicated when in 1972 Mum relented and gave me *Revolver* as a present – her second Beatles album. And the Beatles music that *really* mattered to me, which I could (and can still) sing myself to sleep to, was everything – every single song – from *Revolver* on.

I was a boy still enjoying a dream millions had lived with until the Beatles broke up in 1970, one year into my prep-school career. After the Beatles, everything went wrong. I know that now. Aged twelve, I didn't know. Before sex, before my first kiss, before the predictable humiliations of a mad public school, I was still besotted by the Beatles: a love of pure innocence.

Most people's adolescence is embarrassing to recall let alone read about. So I'll skip mine. Musically, the most significant date in a dreary decade was 1976–7: the year of punk. It finished off any residual interest I had in rock and pop. (And how many of the post-Beatles British rock bands I and thousands like me had listened to stopped producing anything worthwhile well before spit-and-mohican mania? Yes, Genesis, Pink Floyd, Deep Purple all crumbled musically in or before 1975, leaving punk to deliver the mortal blow – pop historians say necessarily so.)

I also went, for motives that have long eluded me, to the first open-air Knebworth concert in the summer of that year. I was fifteen. Top of the bill were the Rolling Stones, about whom I felt and still feel mere resignation.

I enjoyed 10CC, who came on penultimately, far more. That probably says it all.

Knebworth was important because of how horrible it was. I think I'd been persuaded by some friends to go. (My mother, who picked me up the next morning, would claim that *I* was determined to go, whatever the cost . . . I do remember that we had an argument in the car on the way back about Mick Jagger. I said he was exciting because he had bisexual appeal. That didn't go down too well. In those days, I argued with my mother about more or less anything.)

Apart from these 'friends' disappearing at some point into the crowd of 250,000 (amongst the same friends, one was an extremely nubile blonde of fourteen I'd known for years, so coolly mature that she went off to smoke dope all day with a couple of obnoxious seventeen-year-olds from Ampleforth), my main memories of this dismal event are, firstly, of when at eight p.m., two hours late, the Stones had still not appeared (they did so after four), a naked man got up on stage and masturbated, to the crowd's whooping amusement; and secondly, because it was also a hot day, of the stench of 250,000 people. It was the smell of twelve hours worth under an August sun, drinking beer, smoking dope, sweating, urinating, and having sex under sleeping bags. I have never forgotten that stench. It smelt, as King Lear would have it, of mortality.

The occasion was not designed to endear an intellectually stuck-up teenager, already giving up on pop, to his fellow men. My adolescence turned stormier. I soon reverted to my pre-Beatles classical tastes. Throughout introspective years at Oxford I cultivated a pretty heavy-duty enthusiasm for a number of composers: Mahler, Ravel, Bartók and, for some reason, Franz Liszt.

In Spain, meanwhile, which I visited in the long summer vacation of 1980, I heard on a car radio guitar-playing of a kind that was quite novel. The performer was Paco de Lucía.

Now this really was something else. Flamenco became a new obsession, lasting a decade and ending in a book on the subject. I should probably have just written about Paco de Lucía, and perhaps one day will. I met him only once, to shake his hand after a concert in Seville. I asked him then if I could interview him, and he said yes, of course. I never have.

Paco de Lucía is one of the towering musical geniuses of the century. He unites deep artistic sensibility with complete melodic freedom. Like Picasso with brush and canvas, Paco de Lucía invents new space and new dynamics with his instrument every time he picks it up. Listening to him over many years, I seriously believed there was nothing better in the world, anywhere.

Then Brazil came along.

Three

From Samba to Sunburn

(*Carioca*: the word used for a native of Rio de Janeiro.)

I should not have been there. Rio de Janeiro may be in the same hemisphere as Buenos Aires, it may only be two hours away by plane, but they are distinct, irreconcilable universes.

Rio is a city that dreams are made on. Someone – God, perhaps – seems to have picked up a pile of primeval rock and thrown it into the warmest bit of the Atlantic with a view to creating a bejewelled miracle of nature; the fallout is a charmed circle of lush mountains surrounding one of the most exhilarating, and lawless, cities on earth.

Buenos Aires by contrast, though also enormous, is rigid, enclosed, physically repetitive – and today more or less law-abiding. It's supposed to be a port, but unless you live at the top of a high-rise you wouldn't know it.

Buenos Aires, like the Argentine, wants to be European:

most Argentines would barely call themselves South American. The trouble is, neither the city nor the people are quite interesting enough to be anything else. By trying but failing to be Paris or Rome, Buenos Aires ends up feeling like New York gone wrong (and Claude Lévi-Strauss said this, admittedly, about Rio de Janeiro: nothing worse than a French intellectual on the Third World . . .).

Buenos Aires has a really unspeakable recent past, and this fact kept preying on my mind when I found myself there on a research trip in October 1993. I had a ghoulish feeling that every day I was tramping on the bones of thousands of unknown *porteños*, murdered by the government in the 1970s.

The 1970s. It's not as if all that happened 'in the war', as we say in Europe: Argentina's Dirty War occurred during my adolescence, at the same time as Pol Pot's Cambodian genocide – a different order of horror, of course, but similar in intent. In Argentina, I could not work out how it was possible to go to a nominally civilised nation, mix with nominally civilised people, and yet find the subject of their half-century (until 1983) of social and political catastrophe almost taboo. But taboo it is.

It's easy to feel trapped in Buenos Aires, as I did in those early (southern-hemispherical) summer weeks of 1993. I knew almost no one, and had to rely for social diversion on contacts made through my research project: a life of the writer Jorge Luis Borges.

The subject had chosen me – in appropriately Borgesian manner – not I it. Somehow his life, obscure at the best of times, felt like Argentine ancient history; having to concentrate on this blind old librarian meant I missed out on the realities of the modern city. The terrible years from 1970 and the return of democracy in 1983 seemed a far more interesting subject. Borges, a political incompetent, more or less ignored them. Still, unknowns like me with epic overdrafts can't be choosers, and I'd accepted a contract six months previously to write a life of JLB.

Due to fly back to London via New York at the beginning of November, I saved Rio up until my last weekend in South America. An act of self-indulgence, possibly, but by that stage I'd have given a lot to leave Borges and his city behind by several continents, let alone one country.

In fact I had what I thought was the best possible reason to go to Brazil: Chico Buarque, knowing I'd be in Argentina, had said, Come along.

We have to go back to July 1993, to the weeks just after Caetano Veloso's RFH concert. One afternoon, I got a call from someone called Roger Preston. He had some extraordinary news: Chico Buarque was going to play in London at the end of the month, his first ever concert there. I practically fell off my chair.

Roger was extremely well spoken, gravelly toned in voice, languorous even, from a different era; he sounded more like one of my father's City friends after a good lunch than a pop impresario. I don't think Roger would describe himself as that, but impresario on this occasion he was: he was responsible for raising the money to bring Chico over, for one concert, at the London Palladium. (An excellent start, at least: the Palladium was where I'd last heard Paco de Lucía play in London.)

Roger's connection with Brazil is non-musical. For years he was head of a multinational in Rio, and is now retired. He and his wife Rachel were great supporters of the arts while in Brazil, and were now doing the same from the UK end: the people they knew and know reads like a *Who's Who* of Brazil's *personnes dorées*. Chico is a friend of theirs. Roger was after press coverage and had got my name through Liz Calder.

Apart from Caetano's concert, this was the most exciting thing to have happened all summer. For Chico to be playing in London just three weeks after Caetano was too good to be true. The charm was taking unexpected form.

So I wrote a piece about Chico for the London *Evening Standard*. There were three significant things about this. The first two concern the way I sold it. I stressed, first of all, that Chico Buarque was 'Brazil's Beatles' – absolute nonsense, but the editor liked it (the Beatles do have an odd connection with Brazil, I soon learnt, but not with Chico). The second thing was true: Chico was as mad about football, I said in CAPITALISED *ITALICS*, as he was about music – Brazil, World Cup, Pelé, *songs* about Pelé, etcetera. Go for the obvious. No Portuguese or politics. It did the trick.

The third thing concerned Chico's looks. In the opening paragraph of my *Independent on Sunday* piece, I'd described him as having 'slightly monkeyish features'. Chico, typically, took it as just a bit of journalistic playfulness, which is what it was, though it seems his second daughter, Helena, who was travelling with him during the *Estorvo* tour, took mortal offence. Eyebrows had been raised elsewhere, mainly amongst London's ex-pat Brazilian females: this,

I gathered, was *not* how they were used to having their country's best-looking man talked about. A friend of mine, Martin, said it was racist.

Nothing of course could have been further from my thoughts. So I put things to rights in the *Standard*. I roped in Liz Calder to provide some A-grade schmaltz:

> . . . 'He's really a poet, a kind of golden Renaissance man you don't meet every day,' she says.
>
> He is also very good looking. 'It's his eyes, which are aquamarine, almost translucent,' purrs Calder.

This is actually a polite version of something rather different Liz said when I got to know her better: along the lines of being alone in her sweetest dreams on a tropical island with her Brazilian Adonis . . .

The occasion of Chico's first concert in London was made much of by the Brazilian community. Banco do Brasil held a reception at their City headquarters, where I met Roger and Rachel Preston for the first time, both charming and on this occasion, I thought, somewhat reticent. Little did I know.

Liz was there, as were *Turbulence*'s translator, Peter Bush, and legions of Brazilian women. In fact, it took me a while to spot Chico, who was surrounded by women, all of them beautiful and immaculately dressed: a mob scene. The adoration only added to Chico's almost outrageous charisma. Once located, there seemed to be no one else in the room.

He came over and kissed Liz firmly, warmly, on both

cheeks. He then took my hand, looked me straight in the eye, and laughed: 'So, I'm good looking now, eh?' I could only laugh with him, at my own embarrassment.

Roger and Rachel had invited Liz and me to have dinner with Chico and Marieta, after the reception, at their home in Vauxhall.

At nine, Liz drove me across London with Chico's great 1984 anthem 'Vai passar' ('On Its Way'), written to celebrate the imminent end of military rule in 1985, blasting through her speakers.

Both of us were excited, mainly about the concert the following night, but I was in a particular spin: Liz had seen Chico perform a month earlier in Lisbon, and known nothing about his London date (secured at the last minute and partly because he felt buoyed up by Caetano's success). And Liz was Chico's *publisher*, after all, and therefore needed to maintain professional decorum at all times. I was just a besotted journo. About to have dinner with Chico, again.

In the dining room at the Prestons' opulent house, I sat opposite Marieta – dark, handsome, with determined, aquiline features, and pretty, bobbed jet-black hair. She and Chico, married for thirty years, are today regarded by the media and the public in Brazil in the same way as royalty is in other countries. They look the part. Roger was to my right, at the head of the table, conducting dinner – which didn't start until eleven – – in Portuguese. Rachel at the other end was also fluent.

Chico and Liz sat either side of Rachel, and exchanged a

lot of cigarettes and knowing looks throughout a delicious dinner. To my left was a forbidding Brazilian theatre critic called Barbara Heliodora Carneiro de Mendoça. I managed to talk to her briefly about Shakespeare (she was an expert) and then was silenced by a long-ish discussion in Portuguese about the state of Brazilian theatre.

Chico, a published and performed playwright too (Liz's 'golden Renaissance man'), had some decided views on the matter. I switched to admiring Roger's remarkable Portuguese cheese, scooped out like double cream from the middle of a round, rind-covered wodge, and drank a great deal of his wine as the Portuguese flowed. I didn't understand a word.

Liz drove me back to Highbury at three, and we both wondered at the Prestons' assembled company. Chico and Marieta had been treated not only to his publisher, the theatre critic and me, but to a very, *very* quiet lady to the critic's left, and for some extraordinary reason to an ex-British ambassador to Saudi Arabia. Nice guy, and, well, patently right-wing. Roger and Rachel themselves seemed the epitomé of affluent, upper-middle-class Englishness; impossible they could vote anything other than Tory. And here was Chico Buarque *staying with them*. We couldn't work it out.

The concert the next night was a midsummer miracle.

I took the friend who'd reckoned my *Independent* 'gaffe' about Chico's features was racist. Martin already knew something about my new obsession: he has endured quite a few of them over the years, but couldn't get a handle on this one, as he didn't know any Brazilian music. He thought I'd gone a bit soft in the head. I thought I'd see if I couldn't convert him.

We were due to meet Liz in or outside the Café Royal: she was in neither location, though some others who were also 'due to meet her' were, including a rather cross editor from Penguin Books.

'That Liz!' she hissed.

Martin and I ended up drinking margaritas in a Mexican bar just off Regent Street. All of Liz's party were supposed, eventually, to gather there: she'd bought about two dozen tickets and sold them to friends and colleagues to enlarge the London branch of the Buarque fan club. It was Liz's temporary absence that seemed to have caused a sense-of-humour failure in the Penguin editor. 'Who is this Brazilian crooner anyway?' she demanded.

In the bar, Martin and I got talking to another such target of Liz's zeal, a languid, pretty editor from *Vogue*.

'Isn't Chico Buarque Brazil's Julio Iglesias?' she asked me. Catching my eye, Martin realised before I did that it'd be better if I kept my mouth shut.

The Palladium was as packed as the RFH had been for Caetano, again mainly with Brazilians. Martin and I had seats in the fifth row. A few rows behind us was the editor who'd commissioned the piece for the *Standard*. We'd never met before. He'd got his comp, and now greeted me, lifting his hand in a drinking motion – presumably to suggest we have a jar after the show.

Wrong: he meant during the *interval* – the first time I've ever known anyone to hope for an interval during a pop concert. Press people working behind desks, especially 'features' people, never cease to astonish me. Each and every one inhabits a delightful fantasy world, which after all is what they are creating for their readers. I remain envious of such a job, but wouldn't last a day.

The reception Chico received stepping on stage was more dignified than that which had greeted Caetano. There was a roar of welcome, but also respect in the air – partly because of the formal surroundings of the theatre, and partly because the Brazilians were I think more astonished than specifically *glad*, at this point, to see Chico. They quickly fell silent. For most of them, he was a hero of three decades' standing but had never played in London. The question in the air was, How on earth had he ended up here?

Perhaps more tangibly, we were, all of us, concerned for him. Chico was nervous. It showed all over his face. Wearing a yellow linen suit and maroon polo-neck, he began his first songs – recent ones – tentatively; his band – two drummers, guitarist, wind-player, pianist and bassist – was tight, and kept the atmosphere sparkling, but Chico was ill at ease. He looked stiff. He seemed to need the light electric guitar slung around his shoulder as a kind of defence against his own shyness: without it he wouldn't have known where to look.

But he sang some great songs: 'Ela desatinou' ('She Went Mad'), 'Vai trabalhar vagabundo' ('Go to Work, You Tramp'), 'Eu te amo' ('I Love You'). He relaxed more with 'O futebol' ('Football'), a rhythmic, jazzy number from his 1989 album: the song tells of a wish to compose as well and as accurately as Pelé once scored goals. He introduced it by reciting the names of Brazil's footballing greats, and adding George Best – 'and perhaps Gazza'.

It was the first time in the show he had spoken. The Brits were now, more or less, on his side too. From here on, he looked and sounded better. The main set lasted about an hour and a half. And then came the numbers we were waiting for: 'Apesar de você', and, as the first encore, 'Vai passar'. He set down his guitar, took off his jacket, and started to move – a slight, sightly, teasing samba. It was electric. On cue, the stalls erupted, and the audience ran forward, just as they had with Caetano.

Right in front of us in the aisle, a woman spent at least five minutes getting herself aligned with the stage for a photo, and then handed Martin her camera: she *had* to be in a shot with Chico. Behind us, another woman was screeching his name, and another 'A banda! A banda!' (No chance.) The whole place had suddenly gone mad, all the more startling because of the earlier decorum. And Chico was really enjoying himself.

Martin and I were on our feet along with everyone else. Three encores came and went, and Chico eventually, gracefully, understatedly, bowed out stage right.

We headed backstage, or at least I did. Martin wasn't sure if he should come: I said, Don't be an idiot, Chico is cool.

There was a scrum round the artist's entrance, inevitably of women. I sweet-talked the security guard, and we got through. The scrum wasn't much better inside. The Brazilian Ambassador had heaved into sight with his entire family, so we let him go first. And women, everywhere.

Chico was changing his shirt. Liz was standing behind him, as if she were about to hand him a towel – though I think her cigarettes were more in demand. Chico himself was alight, smiling, radiant. I took his hand, congratulated him, he embraced me, I introduced him to Martin, and what I really wanted to do was kiss him.

He was relieved that he'd got through his London baptism by fire, and more than delighted at his reception – as well he might be. The last two hours had been quite an achievement for a forty-nine-year-old singer previously unknown in Britain.

I told him I'd be in South America in the autumn. I said I would like to visit Brazil.

'You're coming to Rio?' he asked. I said I'd like to. 'You come to Rio, I'll show you Rio.' I said, 'OK, I'll be there.' He smiled, we shook hands, and the audience was over.

With those words ringing in my ears, Martin and I exited through a pullulation of fans, and went to a pub at the edge of Carnaby Street. I needed a huge drink. It was a hot night, so we sat outside.

I had never been so high. Martin had enjoyed the concert, but was still a little mystified at my growing euphoria. So I didn't really explain. I babbled. Martin laughed. He was right. I wasn't all there. I was altogether elsewhere. In Rio already.

'O futebol' (1989)

Para estufar esse filó
Como eu sonhei
Só
Se eu fosse o Rei

Para tirar efeito igual
Ao jugador
Qual
Compositor
Para aplicar uma firula exata
Que pintor
Para emplacar em que pinacoteca, nega
Pintura mais fundamental
Que um chute a gol
Com precisão
De flecha e folha seca

Parafusar algum joão
Na lateral
Não
Quando é fatal
Para avisar a finta enfim
Quando não é
Sim
No contrapé
Para avançar na vaga geometria
O corredor
Na paralela-do impossível, minha nega
No sentimento diagonal
Do homem-gol
Rasgando o chão
E costurando a linha

Parábola do homem comum
Roçando o céu
Um

Senhor chapéu
Para delírio das gerais
No coliseu
Mas
Que rei sou eu
Para anular a natural catimba
Do cantor
Paralisando esta canção capenga, nega
Para captar o visual
De um chute a gol
E a emoção
Da idéia quando ginga

(Para Mané para Didi para Mané
Mané para Didi para Mané
para Didi para Pagão
para Pelé Canhoteiro)

'Football'

Hitting the net
With a dream of a goal
If only
I were Pelé the King
Striking my songs home
The player as composer
A painter
Measuring exactly
To hang in a gallery, darling
No brushstroke's more perfect

Than a goal shot
With the precision
Of an arrow or a dry leaf

To foul some jock
On the sideline
No, when it's fatal
To feint finally
When it isn't
Yes, in the counterbalance
To advance in the free geometry
Of the runner
In the parallel of the impossible, my darling
In the diagonal feeling
Of the man-goal
Tearing the ground
And sewing up the line

In the stadium
A great flick–over–the–head
Clears the sky
For the delirium of the crowds
Parabola of the common man
But what a king am I
To cancel the natural time-gaining
Of the singer
Bringing to a standstill this limping song, darling
So as to catch the line
Of a shot at goal
And the emotion
Of the idea when it sways

(For Mané for Didi for Mané
Mané for Didi for Mané
for Didi for Pagão
for Pelé and Canhoteiro)

*   *   *

Copacabana beach came into view under brilliant flood-lights. The Atlantic was black, the sand phosphorus-blue. The high-rises banked down four kilometres of sickle-shaped coastline were almost invisible behind the lights' glare. Over the noise of the traffic on the Avenida Atlântica, the crashing of waves on to the sand was vivid ocean music. Ahead stood a yellow-floodlit muscle of rock, towering over Copacabana like a protective god: the Pão de Açúcar – the Sugar Loaf.

And here was Copacabana. Named after a saint. Containing 25,000 people per square mile. Crime-infested. Traditionally home to Brazil's great musicians, and its great clubs – home of the bossa nova. Where Chico Buarque was born. There was music in its very name. People play football on its beach under the floodlights in the early hours of the morning. Said to be the sexiest strip of sand in the world – people display themselves on it whatever their shape or colour.

Except there were neither football nor nakedness on show as I arrived, at night, driven from the airport in my friend João's car. It was raining. This didn't matter much; the mere thrill of seeing Copacabana drove any worries about weather from my mind. I trusted it wouldn't last. Rio de Janeiro was supposed to be eternally drenched in sun, no?

João, a friend of those old family friends whose daughter had been one of my first girlfriends, said it was pretty normal for it to rain around this time. The other good news he had for me as we drove to a seafront Italian restaurant was that inflation was running at thirty-five per cent a month. With $300 cash on me for four days, I had no clear idea how this would transfer into purchasing power in the city of my dreams, but when I heard these figures I confess I was worried.

I was staying in Ipanema, a smartish residential district to the west of Copacabana, and much safer than its bigger and more famous sister district; west of Ipanema is the more village-like district of Leblon. Together, Copacabana, Ipanema and Leblon comprise the best of Rio's urban beach zones. My hotel, the Ipanema Inn, where João dropped me off after dinner, was two minutes' walk from the sea.

It was grey and drizzly when I woke up, and warm. Sun was, I was convinced, on its way; I had left it behind, surely, a thousand kilometres to the south in Buenos Aires, where after a month of rain it had turned hot for a couple of days. Flying north, I seemed to have brought the last of the spring rains with me. I settled, more hurriedly than the weather strictly allowed, down to business.

Copious supplies of both T-shirts and patience were the order of the day – the former for dealing with the violent humidity, the latter with banks: three crisp $100 bills bought me half a dozen thick wodges of cruzeiros, the most useless currency I have ever held. There was a very long wait to change them.

My business was threefold: purchase of a book on the

bossa nova I knew I could only get in Brazil, dinner with Chico Buarque, and a visit to a samba school.

Samba schools are responsible for the great spectacle of Carnival in mid-February. The most famous ones, such as Mangueira, emanate from the *favelas*, the notorious hillside shanty towns of Rio, source of so much of the city's strife: drugs killings, street-children, pollution, thousands of deaths and tens of thousands of displaced people – all of them poor – in mudslides after rain.

All the schools are in competition for the honour of being adjudged the best of the year: best display, best costume, best samba-story – a narrative told to the rhythms of Brazil's indigenous black beat, known as *samba de enredo* – and best *bateria*: drums. They start rehearsing for the event in October.

Chico's own drummer, Wilson das Neves, I was to discover, is a big cheese in one such school: Império Serrano. Chico himself now doesn't particularly care for Carnival, and often leaves Rio for Paris when Carnival threatens to engulf the city in a tidal wave of samba lunacy. But his music is shot through with samba. 'Vai passar' is basically an unstoppable samba-hymn.

After money, the book. I hate shopping, anywhere in the world, so I thought I'd get it done before really starting. Reading a little about the bossa nova in Rio while I was there also seemed apt.

To my surprise, it didn't take long to find the book, in a store on Avenida Visconde de Pirajá, the main street running through Ipanema: *Chega de saudade*, by Ruy Castro – named after the first bossa, 'Chega de saudade' ('No More

Blues', roughly), composed by Antonio Carlos ('Tom') Jobim, with words by Vinícius de Moraes, and played and sung by João Gilberto in 1958: 'one minute and fifty-nine seconds which changed Brazilian popular music forever', as the book jacket says.

Next, orientation. Notwithstanding clouds and drizzle, which began to ease off mid-morning, I felt I had to check out the beach.

Ipanema beach is a good deal smaller than Copacabana, more European in scale. It's also a tad more exclusive: not so many tourists. The high-rises are slightly less high, and there are no bars or restaurants under them – except one, which is actually in Leblon (undiscovered on this visit). But as with Copacabana, there are plenty of beach-side stalls amidst the (not abundant) palm-trees, selling beer and coconuts.

The beach itself, as I walked along the pavement separated from the sand by a small wall, was more or less empty, the sky growly-grey. Far out in the bay white lumps of rock push out of the sea like giant shells – one a palm-stubbled island. To the west, where Leblon ends, the double-fingered mountain of Dois Irmãos (Two Brothers) towers above the high-rises, a luscious, rocky freak rebuking the cement and glass below. Crawling up its flank are the ragged contours of a *favela*.

The only seaside activity I was aware of was body-building. Men, in the briefest of briefs, slowly and ostentatiously curled themselves up and down over bars cemented into the sand, stretching limbs, flexing biceps, hoisting themselves into arm- and leg-wrenching positions which I suppose did some good. I suddenly had the idea I wasn't on a beach at all but visiting a menagerie of humanoid sloths and lemurs.

I followed a bottom. A girl with a tiny rucksack, her head plugged into a Walkman, had appeared from nowhere. She was marching just ahead of me, towards a spit of land that separates Ipanema and Copacabana. Scantily clad and with the tightest of hip-hugging shorts, auburn hair tied in a ponytail down her back, I thought, Yes, this is more like Ipanema. Her fast, sexy walk was about the same as my non-hiking stride. Very nice. Rather to my astonishment, I found myself following her on the way back too. I hadn't seen her turn round, and never saw her face.

Lunch was chicken risotto in a fake-tropical place opposite the hotel called Porto do Mare, all palm roofing and stuffed swordfish on the walls; there was a parrot too, a live one. Eric Clapton was droning through the speakers. I stared blankly at the list of drinks on the *cardápio* (menu), and asked spontaneously for a *caipirinha* – a drink I'd vaguely heard of but had never had before.

It came in a tumbler, stuffed with crushed ice and lime slices, and was transparent. It looked innocuous, and I was thirsty. I took a long draught through the straw provided, and was punched in the back of the mouth; the taste was sweet on my tongue, the ice soothing – soothing, because the liquid it was cooling was pure fire.

Made from the distilled juice of sugar cane, or *cachaça* – sugar rum, in essence – a *caipirinha*'s strength is modified in the glass by the packed ice and lime, and by additional sugar.

I eventually learnt that a *caipirinha* tastes far better without sugar, and now always ask for one *sem açúcar*. I say 'always' because that's what I drink in Brazil. Always. If I have any propensity towards alcoholism, *cachaça* will tip me over the brink. Luckily it's far too dear in Europe. Occasionally in Brazil, I plump for a *chopp* – European-tasting beer on tap. But a *caipirinha* is what tells you you're thousands of miles from Europe; like bossa nova, the *caipirinha* is a wild child unique to Brazil. One of its gifts to the world. On this first sampling, I had three in a row. And the chicken wasn't half bad.

'You'll be treated like an emperor,' Chico told me.

He had picked me up from the hotel at nine that evening after a very long siesta. On the phone as we fixed our date, he asked whether I wanted French, Italian, Portuguese ... I said Portuguese, as I had never eaten Portuguese before. So he drove us to a place called Antiquarius.

I was obviously intrigued to see the reactions of people in the restaurant. I'd boasted openly in Buenos Aires about who I was going to see in Rio. Back in London, I'd advertised my planned visit as 'seeing Rio with Brazil's most famous man'.

As luck would have it, Antiquarius was almost empty. The attentions of the *maître d'* were immediate, and we had about six waiters during the course of a not very complicated meal. At the odd table where there were diners, it was the women whose faces dropped. One not far from us simply gave up eating altogether, and stared at Chico from the moment we arrived till the moment we left.

Over our *bacalhau* (Portuguese-style cod), we were

talking about a visit he was proposing I should make on Saturday night to Império Serrano. If I wanted to see a samba school in rehearsal, this was one he could help me to get into. He would talk to Wilson das Neves. 'Wilson speaks no English, but you're a friend of mine, you'll have no problems.'

People do pay to see rehearsals, they pay to join in, but with an introduction like this I didn't even to have contemplate dollars. (Or so, then, I thought.)

Money is the life force behind Rio's Carnival. The spectacle has changed dramatically in as little as ten years; once, it was local, open, free, a giant street-fair. Now, it's tightly controlled, an international tourist attraction, televised – by the monopoly state channel, TV Globo – and enclosed in a 'Sambadrome', a processions arena designed in the early 1980s by Oscar Niemeyer, the architect responsible for Brazil's modern jungle capital, Brasília. As with the rehearsals, you can, as an outsider, pay to take part in Carnival; it'll probably set you back the price of your air fare again to do so.

This was all months off as Chico and I chatted. He'd just finished writing the songs for his new album *Paratodos* (*For Everyone*), which was under contract, and had been exhausted by the effort: three songs until the autumn of 1993, then seven between September and October.

'I've been taking medication to sleep at night,' he said, his eyes widening. 'There've been too many ideas rolling around my head.' In fact, he looked as well as he had earlier in the summer, and naturally was smoking nineteen to the dozen.

The red wine flowed, as did reminiscences about the

London concerts, his and Caetano's. I told him about Caetano's muddle over John Lennon. Chico laughed.

'That's Caetano,' he said. 'It's his style. He's always doing that sort of thing.'

We were joined for dessert by Chico's sister, Miúcha.

She doesn't look much like Chico, but has a friendly, even homely face, and is about five years older. What I did not know then – and it came as an immense surprise when I did find out – is that she was once married to the great João Gilberto.

This is really where Chico's story begins: he is even closer to the heart, the family heart, of Brazil's musical revolution than I thought. Once João Gilberto's brother-in-law! That truly is like being related to Elvis Presley.

'Besides being the brother-in-law of João Gilberto,' writes Ruy Castro in *Chega de saudade*, 'Chico was almost the nephew of bossa nova, because his father, Sérgio Buarque, was "an intimate friend" of Vinícius de Moraes for thirty years. And, before even "A banda", when Vinícius was asked casually who had something new to offer, he replied: "Chico Buarque de Hollanda".'

Three geniuses were behind bossa nova: Tom Jobim, Vinícius de Moraes and João Gilberto ('Jiouw Ji'beto'). Vinícius we've already met (and will meet again), and Jobim was a treat in store for me in February 1994. Both are dead. João Gilberto, now sixty-six, was the singer and guitarist from Bahia, in north-east Brazil, who performed their compositions. He had a high, light, tremor-free voice, and a precise, lyrical guitar technique.

The first bossa, 'Chega de saudade', was called at the time

a '*samba-canção*', 'samba-song' – because samba breaks down into all sorts of styles and forms: dance, carnival refrain, instrumental and so on. The new name, 'bossa nova', came along when quite a number of these *samba-canções*, sung by João Gilberto, had been released in the late 1950s and it became clear that this was in fact something quite other than samba. It means, more or less, 'new way'. No one has ever translated it satisfactorily: it's best as it is.

Samba is the traditional Brazilian black idiom. Bossa nova was invented and performed by whites, from Rio, taking the essential ingredients of samba, its native melody and poetry, and – put crudely – jazzing it up. This is what Chico had meant by 'white samba'.

The friendship between the US West Coast cool and Brazilian styles was in its very early stages in the late 1950s; jazz was not big in Brazil, and never really would be, but people like Tom Jobim were more than aware of what was going on in the States. His particular genius was to invent music which had a taste of jazz – syncopation, cross-rhythms, an improvisatory feel – but which pulsed at its centre with the lifeblood, the beat, the language, the soul of Brazil. To young men like Chico Buarque and Caetano Veloso when they heard the first bossas, this pulse was irresistible.

João Gilberto, meanwhile, has had an odd career. Undoubtedly the star of the first bossa-nova generation, he shone brightly throughout the 1960s, when for North Americans, in particular, he was the embodiment of Brazil's new music. He lived in New York from 1962, and recorded and performed there.

He also got married to Miúcha there (they'd met in Paris

earlier in 1962), after his first marriage to Astrud Weinert ('The Girl from Ipanema') ended in 1964. In the 1970s, by which time his marriage to Miúcha was over, he dipped from view; and after his return to Brazil became a recluse in a Leblon apartment. He got a reputation for chronic unreliability – cancelling a few hours before concerts, or just not showing up – and these days, as rumour has it, spends much of his life in Rio fending off bailiffs.

Chico and Miúcha told me about *bicho*, the gambling ruse that lies behind much of the financing of the samba schools.

It's an arcane, and sometimes murderous, business. Because gambling has been banned in Brazil since the war, a replacement game, played over animals – a kind of zoological lottery – took root some forty years ago. In Rio, you see people trying their luck with *bicho* lists on most street corners. It's as common as *pétanque* in the parks of French towns, or tennis in the gyms of Sweden.

The men in charge are the *bicheros*, the 'animal-bankers', bookies who, with top ranking in drugs circles and a finger in most samba-school pies, call the shots in the running of the schools. They operate like mafiosi, often get shot, and are not to be messed with. I was told that at Império Serrano, these would be the guys in the president's box with gold round their necks and wrists, and women on every limb.

It would also, Chico said as we moved on to our third brandy, be very loud. Império Serrano has a famous *bateria*.

★   ★   ★

In the breakfast area of the Ipanema Inn, two young American women were admiring the large hunks of melon placed before them. One of the girls was tall, slim, pretty, with long brown hair. The other was shorter, with a fuller figure, peachy skin and a gentle smile. She had a sharp New York accent; the other – I wasn't sure. It sounded a bit country.

As they got up to leave, I asked them where they were from. New York, was the unsurprising answer. Did they know the best way to the Sugar Loaf? Go by bus, they said. Could I join them? Sure, they said. We have to go change money, and we'll be right back.

They disappeared, and I spent the next fifteen minutes deliberating in my room: do I take my camera, and *look* like a tourist and therefore (still believing the horror stories about Rio's petty thieving) get it stolen as soon as I step on to the street? More to the point, what would these sassy-looking New Yorkers like to be seen with?

I tried threading the strap through the epaulette on my T-shirt. I looked like a boy scout. A man who has dinner with Chico Buarque in Rio does *not* pace the streets the next day looking like a boy scout. I abandoned the camera and waited downstairs for the girls.

They didn't show up. After half an hour, I guessed they'd been very fast at the bank – strange, that – got bored waiting for me, and pushed off by themselves. Perhaps I'd find them at the top of the Pão.

I took a three-quarter-hour bus ride through Copa-cabana. The main street through the middle of it is undis-tinguished. The occasional squat colonial façade is wedged between banks, shops and multi-storeys. All apartment blocks are behind bars, and have a security man standing outside. The hilltops, lower slopes glinting green through the side streets, were still covered, on this my third day, by a layer of baggy grey cloud. Pavement stalls spilt out on to the main thoroughfare, coconuts on sale everywhere. The ocean, a short walk away, is invisible behind the high-rises.

The Pão is a must in Rio, because it puts you on top. In a city you don't know, a city that's dangerous, a city stuffed with possible and impossible sex, it's best to be on top: right away, no dilly-dallying, get it *out* of the way . . .

The two Americans were waiting at the bottom of the funicular.

'Hi,' they chimed. 'We were ages at the bank, so took a taxi. You're James, aren't you?' (They'd dug my name out at hotel reception.) 'I'm Suzy,' said the shorter one.

'I'm Jenny,' said the willowy one. She really had very pretty brown eyes.

We shook hands. 'And this,' said Suzy, 'is Sérgio.' She introduced a dark, well-fed young man in Bermuda shorts. I shook his hand.

'He's been showing us around,' said Jenny. Oh yes? Sérgio looked about as smug as a young man could . . .

'He's wonderful,' gushed Suzy. (Did Sérgio rub his nails on his T-shirt, wink, smirk . . . ? Maybe not.)

From the Pão you see, inland, a tessellation of high-rises and highways slung out, like huge blocks of washing, between hills of velvet greenness. Climbing up each are *favelas*; a shock, if with the word 'Brazil' it's parrots you think of, are the black vultures circling menacingly above all these hills, like stray omens from an Edgar Allan Poe story.

Beyond, everything gets swallowed by nature: the real heights of Rio are the mountain forests of the Tijuca Park, which fills at least a third of the city, spilling down to the roads and condominiums like green lava. On the coastal side is the giant white sickle-blade of Copacabana (Ipanema beach can't be seen from this angle), brushed turquoise by the tides of the Gulf Stream. Swivel further round to the left and across the bay is Niterói, a sort of mini-Rio tucked into a white-beached bay of its own, and reached either by ferry or by a fourteen-kilometre bridge across the sea, one of the world's longest.

Directly below the Pão are beaches and inlets, and a yacht club; beyond, following the coast north, the beaches of Botafogo and Flamengo, Guanabara Bay, the office blocks of Rio's commercial district (the old Centro), and beyond that the endless, faceless environs of Rio's Zona Norte, or North Zone. Here, they say, seven murders a day take place.

On 1 January 1502, a Portuguese captain, André Gonçalves, arrived in the bay seen to the north of the Pão, and thought it was a river. So he called it Rio de Janeiro: January River.

Brazil had been accidentally discovered two years before, and it was Salvador da Bahia, in the north-east, that was to become the most important city in Brazil, a great colonial capital. That status passed to Rio only in 1763, by which time it had a population of 50,000 and many fine churches: the discovery of gold in the interior state of Minas Gerais helped underpin a rash of building, much of it elegant and of which isolated traces are visible today.

When the Portuguese court fled Napoleon's armies in 1808 and took up residence in Rio, Brazil's mountain city by the sea became the country's commercial, political and administrative centre, and the focal point of an empire. Dom João VI liked his new home so much that he refused to return to Lisbon.

Rio also began to boom on the coffee trade. It was opulent, but also overcrowded and disease-ridden; in fact the mainstay of the nineteenth-century economy was slavery. Blacks had dominated Rio's population for two centuries.

Modernisation came in the form of a much-needed sewage system in 1864. Trams and trains soon became the main form of transport; and as the middle classes sought less airless living space, a tunnel was dug under the mountain range that divides the north and south halves of the city. Copacabana became a desired part of suburban Rio.

Second Empire Paris was the model for urban planning for all cities which weren't New York and London at the end of the nineteenth century. This was when Rio lost its colonial character, and turned itself into a metropolis of wide avenues and mounumental façades. The rebuilder was President Rodrigues Alves (in power from 1902–6), a relatively enlightened post-imperial leader who also introduced a public health system. Today, it's not this Rio which either most visitors head for or most inhabitants enjoy: it's the beaches. They are where the money is, and where paradise might have been.

Copacabana became an image in the middle decades of this century of the ultimate urban leisure zone. Ipanema in the 1950s was barely populated. When Rio lost its status as capital in 1960 to Brasília, leisure, tourism and mass migration from the impoverished north-east swamped the city. Too much happened to a community that had suddenly lost an important slice of its political and economic infrastructure. Too many people wanted to live in Rio. Copacabana, then Ipanema and Leblon, were quickly overrun, and grew upwards, as that was all they could do. Today, in the physical Rio of beaches, high-rises, avenues and hills you see from the Pão, you are also looking at seven million souls: probably about four million too many.

When I first saw it from this high point, Rio looked threatening – or at least the clouds hanging over it did, like grey drapes smothering gleaming furniture. On the far side of the city, the Corcovado – the famous Christ with outstretched arms – was lost in a swirl of mist as if ready to be swept operatically into the skies. To the east, the ocean horizon was at least a promising blue.

I'd longed for this moment: to be standing above a city which for months had lodged itself in my mind like a throbbing chant. Rio had rung a new sound in my head, a new source of inspiration. Here, at last, the city lay spread beneath me, like the start of a day in which you know you will meet a lover, or receive an enormous cheque for a piece of tenderly created work. As yet, Rio didn't look as *tropical* as I'd hoped; there was too much cloud, and after weeks of gloom and rain in Buenos Aires, I was desperate for big heat. *Would* the sun come? Under it, what did this vividly imagined city hold in store? Was it playground or danger zone?

I had to get back to the hotel to take a call from Chico about Império Serrano. 'Suze' and 'Jen' – so Sérgio called them – had been enticed into a gemstone centre near the funicular terminus; Sérgio was by their side. I left the girls with their protector.

I missed the call. I caught the wrong bus, a '*circular*', one that goes right round the Lagoon beneath the Corcovado in the Zona Sur, the South Zone, and back up eastwards through Leblon. It took an hour and a half. I should have asked Sérgio.

As I came into reception, I was handed a note. 'Chico Buarque de Hollanda called . . .' Damn. Chico is not easy to reach on the line, and he was leaving the city the next day.

'You know this man?' the young male receptionist, called Osvi, asked. Well, yes. 'Congratulations,' he added, smiling.

'I had dinner with him last night. He came here to pick me up.'

Osvi's eyes widened. 'Chico Buarque came here?' He turned to his colleague, who was manning the phones. 'He says Chico Buarque came here last night.'

'Chico Buarque came here? *Here?* You mean to say . . .'

This could go on for a long time.

'When did he call?' I asked.

'Oh, a few minutes ago . . .'

Damn, and damn – that sucker of a bus . . .

A couple of hours later, I got through – and told him I'd taken a stupid bus. 'Adventurous, trying to use Rio buses,' Chico said drily.

He had fixed Império Serrano for me.

'But you'll have to organise your lift carefully,' he warned. 'Find a friend, or a taxi – and there's no point in going before midnight. It's a long way out, in the North Zone. You'll need an escort. Wilson will be waiting for you.'

Escort? That sounded a little ominous. And then I thought of Sérgio. Nice guy, good English, has a car . . .

That evening, we all met up again, me, the girls, Sérgio. I invited myself, with a little help from Suzy, who said they were giving Sérgio dinner because he was so kind. I was welcome to join them (meaning I was a handy extra male). The restaurant they'd chosen was Porto do Mare. Fish, Sérgio had assured them, was a speciality. I hadn't noticed that the day before. Amazingly, the girls paid for me too.

After dinner, Sérgio took us to a nearby bar − where I bought the *chopp*s. He knew the owners and wanted to organise a *feijoada* − Brazil's national bean dish − for the next day. We then moved on to a place, called the Cave, where what the girls called 'Brazilian jazz' was played.

It was terrible. The location was offputting, just an open bar area with dance floor under a supermarket in an aseptic Ipanema shopping mall. The five-piece band − pianist, trumpeter, guitarist, vibes-player and drummer − looked as if they *knew* they'd been hired for a blue-rinse tea-party. A drunk kept trying to stuff his hand up the trumpet. A couple in their sixties danced perfect steps, rigid looks on their faces suggesting they'd forgotten each other's names. That was it.

The idea was you ordered a drink and a song. I had a coke and rum, and asked the band leader, the vibes-player, for 'Chega de saudade'. They played it crashingly.

Suzy was well tanked and explaining something elaborate to Sérgio. I talked to Jenny, dressed in tight black leggings and a little, neat red jacket, and wearing tremendously high heels.

She was from Wisconsin, a farm girl. She lived in New York, and was unemployed right now. Her boyfriend ran a bar where she did the odd shift. If I was in New York, I should come visit – she'd make me a *caipirinha*. I said I'd be there, of course.

Suzy was persuaded by Vibes to sing. Sérgio grinned and played drums on the table with his hand and a cocktail stirrer. Suzy had already observed that Brazilians had a well-known urge to hit things with rhythm; in Sérgio's case, it was all hit and no rhythm. Suzy got in front of the microphone and lurched into a James Taylor number.

Her voice was as sweet as her smile, her key changes as unexpected as they were impressive. The band had no idea what she was singing, but followed obligingly. When she ran out of words, she threw her hands in the air. Vibes gave her a big kiss and a hug.

A plan was soon mooted to go with Vibes to a high-class jazz nightdive. As this was discussed round our table, the pianist, a mulatto, was called over. He was carrying a *cavaquinho*, a tiny guitar.

'Listen to him playing this,' said Vibes.

The sad-faced mulatto played a few tunes. He made a refined, doleful sound on the short strings, which also trilled. I asked him if he'd play 'Mano a mano' ('Hand to Hand'), a tango I'd first heard Caetano Veloso sing at the RFH, in Spanish. The tune chimed, clarion-like, through the drunken chatter. I thanked the pianist. He nodded and put down his instrument.

'He used to be a *great* musician,' Vibes whispered.

A definitive move was made to go clubbing. We trooped outside into the warm night. Vibes, as inebriated as Suzy and clearly delighted with her, would drive. That I didn't fancy. At night (and for most of the day) *cariocas* ignore traffic lights when they're red.

Was Jenny going with them? I shot a look at her, then at Sérgio. Sérgio grinned. Jenny turned to me, with her big brown Wisconsin eyes . . .

'Are you coming?' she asked. I thought. I was tempted. I was here for the music . . . I took both her hands.

'I shall love you and leave you.' (I hate that expression. I don't know why I used it.) 'I have a serious night tomorrow . . .' I kissed her on each cheek. 'See you in the morning.' I waved to the others.

'See you on the beach,' said Jenny, as she walked off with Sérgio.

On the beach?

The weather had turned. The day was going to be a scorcher – my first in tropical heat! Straight after breakfast, I hit Ipanema beach.

My first mistake was to think that, at ten in the morning, the sun would be averagely hot; I've sunbathed in the Mediterranean before, after all. But the sun wasn't just politely deceptive. It was atomic.

The second was to go so early. Ideally, I should have slept more, spent five minutes on the sand and ten in the sea – *and* in the evening.

Still, the spectacle was worth the effort. Beaching *cariocas* are a breed apart. They spread out across their elongated coral-white shorelines in a frivolous demonstration of urban luxuriance. Men play football, netball, any kind of ball, stretch and jump and do all that zoo-like muscle toning I'd seen on my first morning. They surf well, and, I noticed with some of the younger blades, in the briefest of briefs, when necking with girlfriends in the waves, or on deckchairs, don't try to hide their erections.

Women amble up and down, in pairs, in groups, alone and with their children, in those remarkable, *de rigueur* G-strings: an item known as '*fio dental*' in Portuguese – 'dental floss'. Bikini tops invariably in place (bare breasts not being considered an element of fashionable beach display in Brazil – during Carnival, it's quite different of course), what brings eyes out on stalks is the bottom half: a slight, pretty little triangle of fabric just where it should be, and nothing else.

Brazilians are into bottoms. I don't know why, but when it comes to the body, the buttock is supreme. Everywhere you walk, and not just on beaches, whole butts are on display, an entire, usually imagined (in less bottomy cultures) area of anatomy that Rio's female population parades like an *objet d'art*, a sort of sexualising insignia that has less sex than the collective, physical abandon of Carnival behind it – behind it, so to speak.

I could get carried away. After a while, butts are boring. The current of the ocean on Rio's beaches is strong, the waves big enough to cavort childishly around in. Little black boys on their surfboards need to be watched; they tumble over each other and innocent bathers like shrimps in a net. In the distance, Dois Irmãos is a tropical-green lighthouse, reassuring as you float on and are buffeted, like a melon, by implausibly warm sea.

I did this for an hour. Back at the hotel, I rested and slept. A call woke me. It was Jenny.

'Hi. We're going to the beach. You coming?'

Was I coming? I had no idea. Hadn't I just spent the morning on the beach? Wasn't I going to a samba school at midnight? I looked at my watch. It was noon. This was the girls' last day.

'Sure. I'll meet you . . .'

'Suzy will be down there, straight opposite the road. I've got to mail some cards. See you there.'

Suzy's bikini was a panther-dot job, fetching, not risqué – whatever, she looked less high-school, if a little hungover, today. Her skin was even whiter than mine.

When she arrived, Jenny revealed herself to be of bolder mettle. Whipping off her shorts, she'd gone native: the dental-floss treatment. She had the body for it, undeniably – little round breasts, pear-shaped hips, long arms, long legs, smooth, silky, shapely white buttocks . . .

The sun was getting to me. I *was* getting carried away. Good God, an erection . . . Surely not. I'd been on beaches with scantily dressed women before, with topless women, for God's sake, plenty of them!

Actually, when I thought about it, I hadn't. I mean, not with two nubile Americans, complete strangers, whose extremely ripe figures were now all but exposed in their entirety to me – their protector for today . . .

My girls from Ipanema . . .

*　　*　　*

By five o'clock, the fire in my skin was of Joan of Arc intensity. Water would turn to steam if thrown at it.

I'd used no cream, and had no emollient. I was looking at a chronic case of melanoma within days. As we ate our *feijoada* for four, the jokes made at my expense – 'You'll be hanging your back in the wardrobe with your shirts tonight' – were mild rebuke. I deserved jail, medical confinement. As far as my flesh was concerned, I was already there.

The real worry was my left foot. It had swollen to the size of a hedgehog, and my suede shoes weren't as supple as they might be. I was finding it hard to walk.

This was the girls' final treat in Rio. They were flying back to New York that night. Sérgio was holding their hands, drying their eyes, telling them Rio would wait from them, making terrible jokes – and not just about me. The girls were in full flood, particularly over their imminent, melancholy-making departure from the city they 'loved most in the world'. I confess I'd lost interest. Apart from my foot, my other worry now was how to get to Império Serrano.

Sérgio had made some enquiries. Some of his friends at the bar knew a guy who was a taxi-driver who knew how to get there, and who *might* be free at midnight. I'd put a desperate face on.

'OK,' said Sérgio, 'if you're really in trouble, call me. I'll try and help out. But I have to be up early for work tomorrow.' (He had a stall at Ipanema's bric-à-brac 'hippie market' which happens every Sunday.) 'Império Serrano . . .' He shook his head. 'I know you're a friend of Chico Buarque's, but this crazy plan . . .'

We had a third *caipirinha* each and demolished some more *feijoada*. Sérgio was driving the girls to the airport.

We said our goodbyes at the hotel. I kissed Jenny. She was nice. I promised to come and see her in her boyfriend's bar one day soon. On my way back to London. One day.

I hobbled to my room to try and sleep. I tried for three hours. My skin wouldn't let me drop off. My skin didn't want me to. It didn't want me, full stop. After I'd taken a cold shower, I've never shivered so much in my life. I was supposed to be in the tropics. I felt as if I were in the Arctic.

Sérgio wasn't in when I rang him, so I had no choice but to go and see Osvi.

He had a friend who could help out, a taxi-driver: the one option I'd been hoping to avoid. He rang Antonio.

'Antonio, I've got this guy who wants to go to Império Serrano, out in the North Zone. You know where it is? Yeah, well he's a friend of Chico Buarque's. Apparently he's going to be met there by his drummer. He also thinks he can get a lift back here with someone – maybe the drummer – early in the morning. No, doesn't sound likely to me either, but that's what he thinks.'

Osvi listened for a while, then looked up. 'It'll cost $40.' One way? 'Yeah.' I groaned. Could he do it for $30? He asked, then listened. 'Well, it's late at night, strange part of town . . .' I agreed: $40.

Half an hour later, I was speeding northwards through one of the tunnels that connect the two halves of the city. Antonio, young, with a pleasant face and a terrible cold, spoke no English, so I spoke to him in Spanish. He understood me. He was concerned about how I was going to get back, but I got little of the detail of what he was telling me. He spat a lot out of the window.

It took three-quarters of an hour to find the *quadra* of Império Serrano, a warehouse in a suburb in the North Zone called Madureira. The noise as we walked towards the *quadra* was terrific – amplified voices wailing above what sounded like an army of jungle-beat drummers. I gave Antonio his $40.

At the turnstile, Antonio spoke to the bouncer, explaining who I was. We were waved in.

Ahead lay a huge open floor: the samba space. People were milling about – clearly a lull in proceedings had been called. Nobody (thank God) looked at me *especially* closely, though had the lights been turned out the place could have been amply illuminated by my sunburn.

I followed Antonio towards the stage, raised about seven feet above the floor at the far end of the hall. Whoever and wherever Wilson was, I wasn't going to recognise him; I confess I didn't remember him from Chico's London concert. I let Antonio ask for me.

Minutes later, we'd been ushered to the president's box, part of a long balcony above the dance floor. There I was greeted by Wilson, a smiling but serious-faced black man, in his fifties, who asked me how I was. Then followed a line of Portuguese, which I could only nod and smile politely back at. The tone was: make yourself at home. I did, and helped myself to a beer – someone else's.

Antonio meanwhile was conducting conversations with various people, and reported back: no way was I going to get out of here without him. He would stay. However long it took, he would stay. I patted him on the back, gave him some of my beer, and pictured an ever-diminishing supply of dollars.

Below, the dancers were taking their places. On stage, a couple of black guys approached the microphones, introduced by someone called the *locutor*, the compère; a teenage boy stood behind them, starting up a slow beat on a big drum hanging from his shoulder. On each side of the stage was a mountain of speakers, sixteen in all. Opposite the box was the pride of Império Serrano: the *bateria*.

This was composed of three rows of about twenty men in each, of every age, colour and shape, either beating something – big drums, small drums, boxes, tins – or shaking something – rattles, devices of wood and wire. At either end of the front row were what looked like conductors, standing with their backs to the hall. As the big drum on stage began to rumble, they raised their arms to catch the attention of their talkative *bateria*.

The singers' voices thundered through the speakers, less a tune than a chant at a volume I'd never heard before. At a stroke, the *bateria* slammed into action. It sounded like a storm of birds with metal wings taking to the skies, in perfect synchronicity. The movement of the drummers' arms alone would have powered a national electricity grid.

Then the floor below began to move.

What happened was this: a procession, led by a large, openly smiling black woman in her thirties, wound in a figure-of-eight across the floor. The woman gyrated to the rhythm, swung her wide hips, and threw her bare arms in the air at regular intervals. She was followed by a crew of women, including a few grannies, as well as children. Some in the procession tried to dance as well as their leader, some barely danced at all. Many just thrust their arms in the air at the right moment.

'*Cordão*' came into my head: 'chain', a word used for a formation of dancers in a Carnival procession. It's the title of one of Chico's songs – in which he links the idea of a Carnival *cordão* with an image of being 'chained' up, held back, censored. In the song, he sets himself free.

Alongside this *cordão* marched a majordomo, a white-haired seventy-year-old black man, dressed all in white, carrying a whistle round his neck. He blew it to get people in line, shouted orders, waved his arms and gave directions.

A young black boy came up to him and asked him to watch: he executed thirty seconds of intricate footwork, legs seeming to fold in on each other, feet whirring over a small patch of floor, arms outstretched as if balancing the body on a tightrope. At the end of the display, the majordomo patted the boy's head, and they bowed to each other.

A wilder-looking figure jumped into the space they'd left: a stocky man in a white blouson and jeans, waving a fan. He danced by himself, looking up occasionally at the box, a camp grin on his face. His fan fluttered by his cheek like a tropical butterfly; in his finnicky solo dance, he was perhaps trying to be one. Throughout the night, he was drawn to the floor like a moth to light.

The heaving scene was kept in check by two sets of couples, dressed more elaborately than any of the other revellers, carrying between them swirling banners on poles. They swooped up and down the floor, and when they'd completed a turn bowed deeply before the box, gesturing to each other and the banner – the insignia of Império Serrano. The fat ladies in the box, the tall black men in their fabulous shirts, the beer-drinkers and the girlfriends all clapped – no sign of anything resembling an animal-banker, though.

Over on stage, the singers were indefatigable. Wilson paced up and down behind them, deep in thought. He would sometimes disappear altogether, then emerge as if from nowhere in the box, and chat with one of the spectators. Back on stage, he would consult with the *locutor*, presumably about the goings-on down on the floor, up in the *bateria*, in front of them on stage, perhaps in the box . . . At least I hope this was what Wilson was concerned about. Some years ago, an Império Serrano bigwig – the then president, I think – was shot dead.

The rehearsal continued long into the night. I'd seen what I'd come to see. I'd heard what I'd never heard before – and by about 3.30 was aware of a numbness in my right ear. It was time to go.

I told Antonio (who I don't think had seen anything quite like this either) that we should make a move. We nodded farewells to those left in the box, and walked round to the stage. I thanked Wilson fulsomely, in Spanish, and asked him how often he'd be doing this – surveying all the samba he was master of. The answer was clear: 'Every Saturday till Carnival.' I said I'd be back. He smiled broadly.

*   *   *

The next day, my right ear was blocked with sixteen speakers and sixty drummers. My left buzzed with shouts, whistling and the roar of the ocean. My left foot remained hugely swollen, crippling me for twenty-four hours. I was also $80 poorer: Antonio, who to give him his due had stayed the course with me for my entire samba outing, insisted on another $40 for the return journey. I was too tired to argue, and swore I'd start learning Portuguese.

In New York four days later I called Jenny, but got her boyfriend's answerphone. I left a message, telling her to make me that *caipirinha* anyway. Two weeks later in London, skin was still peeling from my back and chest.

'Cordão' (1971)

Ninguém
Ninguém vai me segurar
Ninguém há de me fechar
As portas do coração
Ninguém
Ninguém vai me sujeitar
A trancar no peito a minha paixão

Eu não
Eu não vou desesperar
Eu não vou renunciar
Fugir
Ninguém

Ninguém vai me acorrentar
Enquanto eu puder cantar
Enquanto eu poder sorrir

Ninguém
Ninguém vai me ver sofrer
Ninguém vai me surpreender
Na noite da solidão
Pois quem
Tiver nada pra perder
Vai formar comigo o imenso cordão

E então
Quero ver o vendaval
Quero ver o carnaval
Sair
Ninguém
Ninguém vai me acorrentar
Enquanto eu puder cantar
Enquanto eu puder sorrir
Enquanto eu puder cantar
Alguém vai ter que me ouvir
Enquanto eu puder cantar
Enquanto eu puder seguir
Enquanto eu puder cantar
Enquanto eu puder sorrir

'Chain'

No one
No one is going to hold me down
No one has to shut me off
From the doors of the heart
No one
No one is going to force my passion
To be locked inside my chest

I'm not
I'm not going to despair
I'm not going to give up
Nor flee
No one
No one is going to chain me up
As long as I can sing
As long as I can smile

No one
No one is going to see me suffer
No one is going to surprise me
In the solitude of the night
So who he
Has nothing to lose
Is going to make with me an immense chain

And then
I want to see the gale
I want to see the carnival
And go out

No one
No one is going to chain me up
As long as I can sing
As long as I can smile
As long as I can sing
Someone is going to have to listen to me
As long as I can sing
As long as I can carry on
As long as I can sing
As long as I can smile

Four

Carnaval!

Chico was more relaxed than I'd ever seen him. Up in his spacious house in Gávea, a rich residential area of Rio nestling under the shadow of Dois Irmãos, he was giving an interview for German radio to my companion for Carnival 1994, Krimhilde.

A month of concerts at Rio's main concert-nightclub, the Canecão, had been a triumph. Krimhilde and I had gone two nights before. Tickets had been provided for a table right under the stage, a little to the right. The place was packed. More than half the audience was under thirty.

The occasion was of course quite different to the London concert. Sleek, sportily dressed, openly and noisily adored by everyone in the club, Chico hadn't once looked nervous. This was his patch, these were his people. Nor, of course, had the stage been hastily adapted from another show – as the London Palladium back in July 1993 had been (from *Joseph's Amazing Technicolour Dreamcoat*). Chico was master of his space, moving across the stage in brisk strides. He'd jogged on at the start, and then sang a wide range of songs from his seemingly bottomless fund of hits.

Many new ones were there, as were 'Apesar de você' and 'Vai passar', presented together in a medley: but the one that got the place rocking after two hours was 'Quem te viu, quem te vê' ('Who Saw You, Who Sees You' – the Portuguese is a popular expression for someone who's changed a lot), a ballad from 1966 (the same year as 'A banda', which of course he didn't sing). He sang 'Quem te viu' three times, a blonde woman going berserk under his feet as he did so, waving her arms and blowing kisses.

I took Krimhilde to meet him backstage, having greeted Marieta, who'd been sitting – perhaps to her embarrassment – at the same table as the blonde. Chico had changed into a green silk shirt, and looked hot, utterly magnificent, and was being utterly mobbed. He embraced me, shook Krimhilde's hand, and confirmed our meeting for Krimhilde's interview the following Monday. I felt proud as punch to be introducing her to him – and in *Rio* too: her idea, I should add, not mine.

On top of the success of the concerts, Chico's new album, *Paratodos*, was also selling like hot cakes. Always worried about his public and whether he could still attract the crowds he has done for the last thirty years, Chico could be sure: his star was shining bright.

Francisco Buarque de Hollanda was born in Rio de Janeiro on 19 June 1944. He was the fourth in a family of seven children, and the third son.

Heloísa, the eldest daughter, nicknamed Miúcha, had always been musical. Chico remembers her playing the guitar in her teens, and bringing home musical friends, such as the curiously named Baden Powell. Chico's three younger sisters, Piii, Ana and Cristina, all sing (the latter two have recorded), and Chico sang his first songs to Ana's guitar-playing. One trick he liked to perform was to sing unseen from behind a door, and pretend it was the radio. Television, to have such a monumental impact on Chico's later career, was still some years off.

The family moved to São Paulo in 1946: to a house in rua Henrique Schaumann in the district of Pinheiros, near the city's university. Sérgio Buarque, Chico's father, a *paulista*, and a teacher and journalist, had been asked to be director of a historical and political museum, the Museu do Ipiranga. Chico's grandparents stayed in Rio, and during the school holidays he'd go and stay with them, bringing back the Rio suntan and accent to São Paulo. There, he was nicknamed 'Carioca'.

Chico's mother, Maria Amélia Cesário Alvim, is a *carioca*. Both parents were musical. Sérgio had tinkled on the piano since boyhood, was fond of old-fashioned sambas and Italian music, and sang 'Adiós muchachos' in German. Maria Amélia played classical piano. One of Sérgio's uncles, meanwhile, his father's brother, was a composer of some repute: a man called Luiz Moreira.

The Buarques then moved to Italy in 1953. Sérgio had been appointed to a professorship of Brazilian studies at Rome University. They stayed for two years. Chico attended an American school, where naturally he was taught in English. At home, he spoke Portuguese; in the street, Italian.

Vinícius de Moraes was an old friend of Sérgio's. At this time, Vinícius was Brazilian consul in Rome, and often visited the Buarques. He came with a guitar. There was an out-of-tune piano in the house, and music was constantly in the air. When Vinícius came, Chico would stay at the top of the stairs when sent to bed, so as to miss nothing of the illustrious visitor's conversation.

Back in São Paulo in 1954, Chico wanted only to play football, and to be a footballer. Attending the Colégio Santa Cruz, he would take the bus at 6.30 in the morning in order to have time before classes started at 7.20 to kick a ball around with a friend at the school gates. In 1957, his delight was total when the family moved from the rua Henrique Schaumann to a Norman-style house in São Paulo's Pacaembu district: the city's finest stadium, built by the dictator Getúlio Vargas in the 1930s and named after the district, was four blocks from his front door. From this date, Chico's idol was Paulo César de Araújo, or 'Pagão', centre forward of a São Paulo state team, Santos – later Pelé's team.

Chico was an avid reader. His father was an admirer of French writers, and had done much to disseminate their work in Brazil through his journalism and other writings. Sérgio encouraged Chico to read, in French, the great novelists of the nineteenth century – Stendhal, Balzac, Flaubert – as well as the more contemporary Sartre and Camus. Chico also lapped up Tolstoy and Dostoevsky. When a friend observed that he read only foreign literature, Chico immediately turned to Brazilian writers, including Mário de Andrade – a first edition of whose comic novel *Macunaíma*, borrowed from his father's library, Chico proudly showed off at school.

Football, music, reading – and eventually writing: at college, in May 1961, Chico started his own magazine, called *O Verbâmidas*, and published stories in it. One day, he thought, he would have his own page in the respected São Paulo journal *Manchete* (*Headlines*). Like his father, he too would be a writer.

Before creativity, however, came religion: for a brief period from the age of fourteen, Chico caught it very badly. Without knowing what it might lead to, he became involved at the Colégio Santa Cruz with a religious movement, the Ultramontanos. Ironically, given Chico's political battles against dictatorship in the 1970s, the Ultramontanos were in embryo what later became the fascist TFP: standing for 'Tradição, Família e Propriedade' ('Tradition, Family and Property').

The Ultramontanos were harmless enough, but when in the summer holidays of 1959 Chico gave up football and began walking eight kilometres each day to mass from a friend's country ranch, his parents became alarmed. They sent him for six months to a boarding school in Cataguases, Minas Gerais, to study alone, separating him from this friend, Joaquim de Alcântara Machado, as well as from priests and religion. By the following college term, reunited, the two boys had been cured of their zeal.

Yet this wasn't the end of Chico's interest in causes. A charitable body he also joined while at Santa Cruz organised nocturnal expeditions to central São Paulo to help down-and-outs – squalor and poverty being as much features of São Paulo and Rio de Janeiro in the late 1950s as they are today, though not on such an overwhelming scale.

Chico was struck by how the urban dispossessed would disappear when they saw help approaching.

'So we left blankets,' he remembered many years later, 'rather like people leaving a piece of meat for a cat, knowing it will come back for it later ... It's very important for a guy of sixteen, from an élite school, to have contact with poverty.'

Chico was by no means as good as gold. At the age of seventeen, he stole a car – with another friend, his neighbour Olivier Jolles: joy-riding, no less, early 1960s-São Paulo style. It was December 1961. They got caught by the police, and spent a night in the cells, sharing theirs with a horse-thief. The next day, the story hit a São Paulo paper, *Última Hora* (*Final Hour*), where the two teenagers were featured in a photograph with their eyes blocked out by black oblongs, and identified only by their initials.

Chico's parents were travelling. It was left to Miúcha to discover what had happened to her brother – from the paper – and get him out of jail. It was, Chico wryly observed later, the first time he'd got into a newspaper. Punishment, once Sérgio and Maria Amélia had returned, was severe. Until his eighteenth birthday, on 19 June 1962, he was not allowed to go out unaccompanied at night. Missing that year's Carnival, in February, was purgatory.

Thirty-one years later, Chico had no hesitation over what picture to use for the cover of *Paratodos*, his most autobiographical album to date: the mugshot taken of him at São Paulo's rua Brigadeiro police station, aged seventeen, and known to the public the day after the theft only as 'F.B.H.'

Little did F.B.H. know then that it was to be the first of many, many visits to police stations, in another city – Rio – and in a less tolerant era.

★   ★   ★

Chico had welcomed Krimhilde and me just before flying
to Paris – escaping Carnival, as he often does. He was light
of step, smiling, loose-limbed. He'd been playing football
all afternoon, and had a month's holiday ahead.

Halfway through the interview, which I wasn't sitting in
on (I was reading on a balcony overlooking the semi-jungle
that surrounds the house), a noise like chainsaws started up.
At first I thought it might be birds. But no flock of birds
makes so steady and electrical a din. Crickets, obviously –
but what crickets . . .

Chico had to take a phone call. Krimhilde came out on
to the balcony.

'I could kill those bastards!' she hissed at the insects
hidden in the trees. I smiled.

'I don't know: bit of tropical flavour for your broadcast?'
Krimhilde was unamused.

'The technicians in Cologne will murder me . . .'

I'd met Krim (so I called her) in London shortly after
returning from my first South American trip. She was
doing a couple of radio interviews with British authors
being published in Germany. We met at a fearful books
do in the West End, and had escaped to have a more
relaxing drink nearby. We liked each other – she found
me splendidly 'British' (Germans have a clear idea about
what they mean by 'British': the British on the whole,
I think, don't), while I found her frankness refreshing. I
was whirling after my first blast of Rio, and planning –
somehow – to make a return trip to see Carnival.

I told Krim about Brazil. She hearkened to my connection with Chico, and back in Cologne – Germany's
media city – managed to persuade various stations to run

features about him, in tandem with the appearance of the German edition of *Estorvo*. She was also spoiling for some adventure. She rang me one day in December to say she was coming to Rio with me. I said OK. I don't know why I said OK, but I did.

And now here we were: and with a little help from Roger and Rachel Preston, preparing to join a samba school for 1994's Carnival parade.

When Krim's interview was over, we had a beer with Chico.

'So, you're going out with Mangueira?' For a second, even Chico looked envious. 'You're going to have a great time, a *great* time. It's the best school. I went out with them a few years ago, it was in honour of our great poet, Carlos Drummond de Andrade, and I sang, and . . .' He ran out of words in English, and grinned. 'You'll love it.'

Krim and I looked at each other. We were quite happy to believe Chico, but had no real notion what was in store for us. Carnival was just an idea, an event with a seductive name in a seductive city to which we'd committed ourselves — to the tune of £100 each, the cost of our still unseen costumes — but which could, for all we knew, just be embarrassing. Neither of us actually knew how to samba.

I asked Chico if this mattered. He shook his head. 'Lots of people don't. But it's such an atmosphere, you'll just get carried away. Are you fit?' My turn to shake the head. Krim looked more positive (she hadn't a spare ounce on her . . .). 'You will be by the time you've finished.'

I then asked him, before I forgot, where I could find Tom Jobim.

'He's at the Plataforma every day for lunch – same table.' (The Plataforma is a famous *churrascaria* (steak- and barbecue-house) in Leblon.) 'He's been going there for years. Say you're a friend of mine.'

As he led us towards the front porch, he explained a rather obscure bit of wordplay he'd used in one of the songs on *Paratodos*. The song, 'Piano na Mangueira', was composed with Jobim, with Jobim singing, badly, in alternation with Chico.

'There's a line about waiting at the Plataforma' – and he sang the line – 'which is all about the first railway station out of Rio, in Mangueira . . . Tom's restaurant.' He grinned once more. I took his hand to shake it, thinking I'd have to consult the words again.★

He kissed Krim, and embraced me, and I nearly got into the wrong taxi – Chico's, waiting to take him to the airport. Once in the right car, we waved goodbye, and descended the Gávea hillside, the huge, automatic portcullis that shields Chico Buarque's condominium from the threats of the Rio streets slowly closing behind us, like a safe door locking away a hoard of precious stones.

In 1963, Chico matriculated at São Paulo University's Faculty of Architecture and Urbanism.

He did not attend to his official studies with quite the same zeal he did his music. He loved the old *sambistas* –

★ The full name of the district, and of the samba school, is Estação Primeira de Mangueira, First Station of Mangueira, which is – indeed – the first stop for the train leaving Rio's central railway station.

Noel Rosa and Ismael Silva amongst them – but was also taken with Elvis Presley and Jacques Brel. Above all, it was João Gilberto's 'Chega de saudade' which had stuck, like a limpet.

Bossa nova now hummed as a background noise to nationwide experimentation: the daring films of Brazilian *cinema novo* and the unfolding adventure of Oscar Niemeyer's Brasília were emblems of aspiration for any young artist at the time.

Under the influence of Gilberto and with his mate Olivier Jolles, Chico began to learn how to play the guitar. He was pretty bad at it. He has endured throughout his career more or less constant carping about his shortcomings on the instrument over which his future brother-in-law had such mastery, and of which his exact bossa contemporary, Gilberto Gil, is such a versatile practitioner (Gil's greatest acoustic song, 'Oriente', from 1972, is the evidence).

No matter: the guitar is what Chico has always composed on, from his earliest songwriting days. He had intimate relationships with those he owned at the time, and he gave them names: 'Nelson', 'Joaquim' and 'Julieta' were all early six-stringed friends. One, from Spain, was called 'El Cordobés' (after the famous 1960s bullfighter); he left it in a taxi. A few years later, he left a prestigious song-contest trophy in the back of an impresario's Oldsmobile. There is a careless side to Chico: the vagueness of a dreamer.

Dreamers don't always succeed. When Chico moved to Rio de Janeiro, to Copacabana, in 1966, he did so with three aims (which amount to one) in mind: to compose, sing and perform.

He'd been writing songs throughout 1965. São Paulo had its own bohemian student circuit, centred on various bars, including one called Juão Sebastião, where *caipirinhas* were drunk and songs hammered out. Its coterie, which included the singer Toquinho, was nicknamed 'Sambafo' – probably by Chico, who had a thing about inventing names. (Cars, like guitars, had them: his parents' was 'Nelson', his first car 'Clovis'.) Most of the songs were skits on the contemporary rock 'n' roll numbers that were creeping into Brazil; some were protest songs; one was a prototype of a song that made its way into *Roda viva*.

Nineteen sixty-four had in fact been the year of Chico's first public appearances. A bossa show in May was followed by a television performance with his three sisters, Piii, Ana and Cristina, in October: the company transmitting the show was called TV Record.

Then in November, he and Toquinho were part of the line-up in a show called *Mens sana in corpore samba* (*Healthy in Mind, Samba in Body* – wordplay that naturally appealed to Chico), star billing being taken by a beautiful singer called Sylvinha Telles. In 1952, ten years before Miúcha Buarque met him, she had been João Gilberto's lover. On this occasion, Chico sang one of his own early songs called 'Alvorada' ('Dawn'), though it seems he didn't think much of it: it was never recorded. He also met Marieta Severo.

Chico's first professional engagement was just before Christmas 1964, at a cinema called Ouro Verde in Campinas, a town a hundred kilometres to the north of São Paulo. He was paid 50,000 cruzeiros, then roughly the equivalent of $30. Chico's mother, Maria Amélia, was horrified that her son was now *making* money from singing.

In January 1965, Chico met Gilberto Gil for the first time, in the Juão Sebastião bar. Gil was starting to work in the area he'd studied in (business administration) in Salvador. A few months later, employed in an office there, he came off duty to find a group of mendicant singers playing in front of the city's municipal library.

The group was passing around a hat to buy drinks. Gil was astonished to discover that one of the singers was Chico Buarque, 'disguised' in a blind man's dark glasses. Chico was on a trip to Bahia with some university friends. Rumbled by Gil, who quickly joined in the music-making, Chico gave the hat money to a tramp parked outside the library door.

In São Paulo, word had spread that Chico Buarque had the makings of a serious musician. His first major commission was to write the music for a dramatisation of a poem by the Brazilian João Cabral de Mello Neto, *Morte e vida severina* (*Death and Life of a Stone*, in one translation⋆). It was premièred in São Paulo in September 1965, and went down well at a student festival of theatre in Nancy, France, the following spring; thereafter it toured to Paris and Portugal.

The benchmark event of Chico's budding musical career was the appearance in the spring of 1965 of his first record: a single called 'Pedro Pedreira', a sweetly melodic ballad sixty lines long, about a man waiting for a train. Chico was asked to sing it wherever he went, particularly in front of São Paulo students. It became a campus anthem.

⋆ By Thomas Colchie (1973). *Severino* is a word used for the north-east of Brazil.

In 1966, he played it for Tom Jobim, partly to see if he could get the bossa maestro to land him a contract with a producer, Aloysio de Oliveira, who'd been behind a seminal Jobim record, *Caymmi visita Tom*, which Chico admired profoundly. In the event, Chico wasn't signed up, but he did earn the lasting respect – and friendship – of Tom Jobim, worth far more than a record deal.

'Pedro Pedreira' was the first song he presented at a competition for the year's 'best song', in April 1965, shortly before the general release of the single. The song remained unclassified, the winner being Edu Lobo and Vinícius de Moraes's 'Arrastão' ('Trawling'), sung by one of the great Brazilian female voices of the century, Elis Regina.

The following year, however, there was no escaping Chico Buarque de Hollanda. Now married to Marieta, he dropped his studies and settled in Rio de Janeiro – keeping a *pied à terre* in São Paulo, which he still visited once a week.

The timing of his move, from a professional point of view, was perfect. The international profile of *Morte e vida severina* had given the young musician considerable clout in this musically most competitive of cities.

A show of his songs was compiled, called *Meu refrão* (*My Refrain*), and was put on at a nightclub, Arpège, in the Leme district of Rio. It went down a storm, even if there was the slightly troublesome business of having to leave out one song, 'Tamandaré' – apparently 'offensive' to the patron of Brazil's navy, Admiral Tamandaré, whose bust illustrated one side of the one-cruzeiro note. Little did Chico know then that this was to be, for him, the merest embryonic tick foreshadowing his future viral enemy, censorship.

'A banda' was already written when *Meu refrão* opened. The song was first heard in public on the night of 10 October 1966, at the 'II Festival de Música Popular Brasileira', and broadcast by the now increasingly powerful TV Record.

Chico played the guitar, shyly, to one side of the singer Nara Leão. (She would star alongside Chico in a 1972 film, *Quando o carnaval chegar*, *When Carnival Comes*.) The song's quiet melancholy, vivid small-town setting and easily singable chorus gave it universal appeal and instant hit status. Oddly, given the immense fame of the song in the years ahead, it wasn't the clear winner of the competition: 'A banda' ran neck and neck in the final round with Geraldo Vandré's 'Disparada' ('Shoot Ahead'). Even if the jury had, in a preliminary vote, put 'A banda' in front, Chico was quite happy that the prize be divided. And it was. Each musician received the equivalent of $6,500.

In the singles stakes, however, 'A banda' was the one to shoot ahead. Nara Leão's version sold 55,000 copies in four days, and 100,000 before the week was out. Chico's first album appeared, with *his* version, later the same month.

The months following were a whirlwind. Chico never stopped travelling, performing shows all over Brazil and Latin America. He saw 'A banda' translated into different languages across the globe (with the notable exception of English). By July 1967 he had released a second album. His store of songs from pre-'A banda' days seemed endless, though Chico now rates very few of them. Of the twenty-four songs recorded on these two albums, probably only two, 'A Rita' and 'Quem te viu, quem te vê', please him enough for him to consider performing them today.

As a result largely of the televising of the 1966 and succeeding annual song festivals, Chico's face – to say nothing of his voice – became one of the most famous in Brazil in the late 1960s: this in spite of his being far from natural TV material. Retiring, nervous in front of big audiences and uncomfortable in glamorous surroundings or studios, he was in fact considered a bit of a production liability. It mattered little: audiences adored him, partly *because* he made no effort to act the star. He was a star without trying.

The songs flowed – 'Carolina' was his big hit of 1967, appearing on his third, 1968 album – though 1967's 'III Festival de Música Popular Brasileria' was won by Edu Lobo with 'Ponteio' ('Strumming'). Perhaps the most significant aspect of that year's festival was the arrival of two songs from Salvador da Bahia, competing side by side: 'Domingo no parque' ('Sunday in the Park'), by Gilberto Gil, and 'Alegria, alegria', by Caetano Veloso. Chico competed with 'Roda viva'.

Caetano had become a fan of Chico's in 1965, on hearing a song of his, 'Olê, olá', at one of São Paulo's student shows. He copied out the words and sent them to a girlfriend. He loved Chico's naturally fluid rhymes. They became fast friends, and went on enormous nocturnal walks through São Paulo together. In 1967, however, as the musical atmosphere became more febrile, and as Caetano began nurturing his own compositional ambitions, their ways parted: Caetano and Gil's 'Tropicalismo', a radical departure from the accepted Brazilian idiom, was not at all Chico's cup of tea.

'We wanted to do something that was, in a way, ugly,'

recalled Caetano, 'while Chico carried on doing only what was nice.'

By mid-1968, Chico was probably the most popular man in Brazil. Only Pelé, in the wake of Brazil's 1970 World Cup victory, would exceed the musician's renown. In Rio, Chico moved from flat to flat, and rarely took time off.

One person he now began to spend a lot of time with was Tom Jobim.

This is how Chico explained it to me in 1996:

Tom never had a paternal air, and soon we were friends. In 1967, I began visiting his house, in rua Nascimento, in Ipanema. At the the time I was living in rua Dias Ferreira, in Leblon.

In 1968, we had our first partnership: 'Retrato em branco e preto' ['Portrait in Black and White']. I really learnt with him how to put words and music together. Even Vinícius favoured this pairing-up of me and Tom. Various records of ours then followed.

I always kept in touch with him, and when he came back from New York, where he spent so much time in the 1960s, we used to meet and have lots of beers together, mainly in a restaurant called Antonio's in Leblon. At the end of the 1960s, Tom, Vinícius and I always met there.

From this time, Tom greatly influenced me. I began to learn the piano, and one day we went to Lapa together to buy a piano for me [it still stands in Chico's study and work-room] . . .

Caetano's 'Tropicalismo' coincided exactly with the time when I was beginning to work with Tom, when I was learning the piano. I was very interested in recuperating . . . in learning the music that I knew existed already, both to form and *in*form myself as a musician.

Fame in itself was always unimportant to Chico. What mattered to him at the age of twenty-four was to learn, and to communicate: hence the hours of informal lessons he took from Tom Jobim – 'a teacher without showing it', said Chico, 'a disguised teacher'.

Together they composed a song called 'Sabiá' ('Thrush'). It did well in the Brazilian phase of Rio's 1968 'III Festival Internacional de Canção' ('3rd International Song Festival' – these annual events in Brazil in the late 1960s had and have no equivalent in Europe or North America so far as I know). 'Sabiá' was adjudged the winner, ahead of Geraldo Vandré's 'Pra não dizer que não falei de flores' ('Don't Say I Haven't Spoken about Flowers'). Vandré's song was overtly anti-regime, and the audience loved it. 'Sabiá' was a gentle romance. The judges, buckling under pressure from the military not to reward Vandré, ignored its clear popularity: 'Sabiá' had won, and Vandré had not – and the audience, in the smaller stadium next to the great football stadium Maracanã, was furious.

Chico was with Marieta in Venice, enjoying a late honeymoon. Tom Jobim was left facing the Rio crowds – who took these song competitions very seriously indeed: having opinions about music is a Brazilian's proof of his freedom. In a political climate proving less free day by day, the public call for favouring a song criticising Brazil's rulers had an inflammatory edge to it.

'*Chico, volte, pelo amor de Deus,*' Jobim telegraphed Chico in Italy, 'Chico, come back, for the love of God.' Chico thought it was a joke, and phoned Jobim. Jobim was serious. Chico returned. The situation was defused: in the competition's final, international phase, Vandré's fans − 'Sabiá''s enemies − had gone, and Chico triumphed. 'Sabiá' was the winner of one of the last of the great song-fests in Rio.

Within three months, Chico, and the two rising stars from Bahia with whom − more by circumstance than precise artistic compatibility − he became closely associated, Caetano Veloso and Gilberto Gil, had been chased out of the country that had made them heroes.

Krim and I were staying with João, the friend who'd met me at Galeão airport the previous October. He lived in the top apartment of a high-rise in Leblon. It had plenty of room, and two patios swamped in exotic greenery and orchids.

João is a handsome, grizzled, gentle giant of a man. He runs a theatre in a shopping mall in Ipanema. In its early days, it had been involved in the first staging of Chico's post-*Roda viva* play, *Opera do Malandro*.

At the apartment, Krim was discussing Chico's smile with João.

'He's got perfect teeth, when you see them,' said Krim. 'But it's a defensive smile. He hides behind it.'

'No,' said João firmly. 'This is a real smile. Chico is very, *very* happy about the success of his concerts. He knows he's still popular, and this is very, *very* important for him.'

During her interview, Krim had tossed a couple of

questions at Chico about his attitude towards women in *Estorvo* – a strange and dark attitude, she thought. Apparently, Chico had just shone his teeth at her, and said nothing.

I'd already asked her whether she found him attractive – whether 'women in general' might – and her affirmative surprised me. Krim was not easily pleased. After the concert, I'd teased her with a speculation about Chico's surely having had dozens of women in his time, any woman he wanted – you know, usual macho pop-star stuff. Having met him, Krim was absolutely certain that I was wrong.

'He's far too complicated for that,' she said decisively.

I observed to João that Chico was probably now on his way to Paris.

'Quite right to get away for Carnival.' João stroked his full, grey-white beard. 'It isn't what it was. It's all money and Hollywood now. It's been taken off the street. I used to go, used to love it, but not any more. I watch a bit on TV, that's all.'

Krim looked perplexed. Coming from Cologne, where one of Europe's great carnivals takes place every February and into which she throws herself (so she'd intimated) with determined abandon, she wasn't prepared for a *carioca* knocking what she'd been led to believe was the greatest carnival in the world – greater, if possible, than her own.

'Why don't you like it?' she asked. João's answer was dispiriting. The drums were now fake – instead of the old leather, as on African drums, they were stretched with modern plastic. The money was ridiculous – it was the rich who now paid for the poor to be in their (the poor's) own

Carnival, so it was no longer theirs. TV Globo really owned Carnival. As for the *bicheros*, the animal-bankers, well, most of them were in jail, but that wouldn't stop one second or ounce of corruption from seeping through into the whole fiasco . . .

'Still, it's a great spectacle,' João concluded. 'You won't have seen anything like it.' That was nice to know. We'd only crossed an ocean to be in it. 'But can you samba?'

That embarrassing question again, containing a possible torpedoing of the most frivolous plan either of us had ever had, to disport ourselves in front of hundreds of thousands . . . I couldn't speak for Krim, but I *was* a touch jittery. 'Well, don't worry,' said João. 'You'll pick it up as you go along.' And he laughed.

The next day, we had our first look at proto-Carnival. The *banda* of Carmen Miranda, a famous transvestite troupe, was supposed to be parading through Ipanema.

Subsequent to dinner with Chico and Marieta in Vauxhall in July 1993, I'd seen nothing of Roger and Rachel Preston throughout the rest of the summer. However, on my return from Rio in November, I'd got in touch with them when I knew I was aiming to return for Carnival to talk about where to stay, what to do once in Rio and so on. I knew they had a flat there and were thinking of going themselves; what I didn't know was that they had not only *gone* to Carnival every year since 1987, but gone *out*, with Mangueira, every year too. They were Carnival-mad.

My other reason for talking to Roger was that he was preparing a rather remarkable show at the Royal Albert

Hall for June 1994: getting the four great musicians from Salvador da Bahia – Caetano Veloso, Gilberto Gil, Maria Bethânia and Gal Costa – to perform together for the first time ever outside Brazil.

When I first heard about this, I thought it quixotic. Who on earth in London would go? And to the *Albert Hall*? Who in London had really heard of any of these people? Well, there was Gilberto Gil. He was and is known outside Brazil, and not just in London. Then I remembered Caetano's RFH concert, Chico at the Palladium . . . and Liz Calder's fan club.

The 'Four Baianos', as they were known, were to be the climax of a month-long festival celebrating Bahia. With around 100,000 Brazilians in the city, maybe it wasn't such a daft idea after all. There had to be some journalism in it. And that was what Roger and I were chatting about one Sunday morning before Christmas.

I confirmed, too, that I would be going to Carnival. Somehow.

'So, James,' said Roger, puffing on a pipe, 'if you come, you will take part, won't you?' I had no idea. I hadn't thought of it. 'Well,' he continued, 'we're going out with Mangueira, and I think you should come too. We can fix it.'

I said OK. Again, I don't know why I said OK, but I couldn't think of any reason not to go out with Mangueira. I didn't know what it entailed, but if the Prestons could fix it . . .

Their passion for Brazil and Carnival was growing more extraordinary each time I met them.

* * *

The Prestons, picking us up for the Carmen Miranda parade, first drove Krim and me to the Ipanema house of an artist friend of theirs, Darcy.

When we came into Darcy's front room, full of his twirling, carnivalesque papier-mâché sculptures, the first thing to greet us were stomachs, men's stomachs, a whole gang of them, round, tanned, recumbent, not a shirt in sight – apart from our own. It was hot, and getting hotter.

One of the rounder stomachs was Darcy's, who bounced up and offered us *caipirinhas*. He was tall, ebullient, full of nervous energy, a bit like a bear who's just come out of the woods. This was offset by an equally tall, unflappable Dutchman called Kees, an old friend of Darcy's who spends the European winter months in Rio and is inclined to say things like: 'It is very important that people know how to live here. It is good for us to come here and live like them. This is good.'

In a corner of the room a couple of the bellies were putting the final touches to the make-up and costume of a guy they'd met on the beach, who was desperate to take part in the *banda*. His face was blue, his wig yellow, his backside bursting out of a sequinned mini-skirt: no fake breasts, just a fetching open blouse. When he moved, he tottered on sparkly high heels.

We piled out on to the sweltering Ipanema street, cups of *caipirinha* in hand, and headed for where the *banda* was due to start. As we walked, Krim made her first observation about a physiological oddity of mine.

'You sweat a lot, don't you?'

I was pouring, it was true, and there was nothing I could do about it. I told her of the first time I'd ever gone down into the New York subway, in late August in 1985 – the experience had seemed more than just a warm-up for Hell. Thereafter I'd taken a towel with me, to mop up when necessary.

'Is this a particularly English difficulty?' Krim asked. I said it was probably a genetic fault, and she agreed – an awkward one, she thought. What was I going to do on Carnival night? 'If you take a towel on parade with you, Mangueira will lose.' Perhaps the easiest thing would be for me to go without my costume, naked. 'In which case you'll get arrested,' said Krim. I wasn't so sure.

The nakedness that awaited us in the *banda* of Carmen Miranda was of a special kind. The participants were men, mostly, all wearing the most sumptuous, extravagant dresses; feathers, plastic fruit, popcorn, black leather, sequins, hair-rollers, a wild assortment of props to make up a mad rash of colour and eccentric fittings. Under them, arms were sinuous, legs juicy. Hips swung, eyes rolled, tongues flicked in and out at spectators. It was as if the Ugly Sisters had escaped from their panto, mated, multiplied by the dozen, and gone on a mad bender in the louchest nightclub imaginable.

Floats began to idle by. Again, the occupants were men, but men with a difference. They had breasts, fabulous, perfectly shaped mammaries, and very few were covered. Most of these manufactured appendages were of sculptural smoothness, and dark – there were virtually no white-skinned transsexuals on show. Many were black; most were mulatto.

Roger, puffing on his pipe, was agog. 'There *are* some fine tits here today,' he observed. Rachel agreed, and was almost dancing. Darcy was giggling with Krim, who, as a float piled high with *grandes dames* went by, had asked which one was Carmen Miranda. I was still sweating; Kees had found a cardboard Skol fan to keep me cool. 'This is good for you,' he said. We had lost our blue-faced friend amidst the breasty heaving.

Conspicuously absent that afternoon was an essential ingredient of a Carnival parade, a band. It had failed to show up. The parade was desultory. Nothing actually *happened* for over an hour. We looked, enjoyed it, but couldn't feel part of much. This was really a show for crazily dressed participants to primp and preen in front of each other. But it wasn't going anywhere.

We had more pressing matters ahead: a visit to Mangueira. Real Carnival was a week away, and it was important for us to get to know the people involved in our *ala* – 'wing', the group we'd be with during Mangueira's parade – and some idea of our costumes.

These had a pre-history. Over the New Year, Krim and I had measured ourselves. She'd faxed me her centimetres from Cologne, and I'd faxed hers and mine to the Prestons in Portugal (where they have a holiday house). All they knew about the costumes was that they were white and gold. They'd then sent the information to the 'lady in Mangueira' who was being paid for stitching miles of white and gold together, and in January was anxious to know the size of these two 'European journalists' (as we'd come to describe ourselves) who were joining Mangueira so late in the day. Time had been short.

On the plane to Rio, Krim was worried. She'd seen pictures of the practically naked women who dance on the floats, and suspected that a dental-floss number awaited her. She looked at me with her most piercing expression of ironic concern.

'I'm warning you. If you laugh at the thing that's been made for me, I shall lock myself in my room. I'll take the next plane home, I promise. *Ich warne dich.*'

After Carmen Miranda, the Prestons drove us to Mangueira, in the North Zone.

Mangueira has one of the best-known samba schools. Since the 1930s, it has had a consistently high profile, and in the 1980s won the Carnival parade competition three times. In the intervening years, Carnival changed, moving from Rio's streets to Oscar Niemeyer's Sambadrome. The concomitant problems of drugs and the dirty dealings of *bicheros* grew as Carnival burgeoned into a multimillion-dollar media show. Mangueira, almost uniquely, remained free of *bicheros*, though not of drugs and everyday violence, as we were, fleetingly, to see.

The reason for our going with Mangueira and not Império Serrano, whom I'd been with in the autumn, was simple: the Prestons had friends and connections in the *favela*. (In fact when I'd told Roger about my visit to Império Serrano, he'd tuttutted, and said he'd 'have words' with Chico . . . 'Eighty dollars for a taxi-ride?') Through them, everything, from costumes and rehearsals to drinks – and one major interview – was organised. And without their fluent Portuguese, we'd have been mere spectators, and lost.

At the foot of the Mangueira hill, the Buraco Quente, cars were piling in: tonight, there was to be a sort of rehearsal, a lining-up of all the *alas* in the correct order

at the bottom of the *favela* – Roger and Rachel were keen
to give us a taste of what lay ahead.

The previous night, they'd been in Mangueira's *quadra*,
the gym–cum–warehouse where the samba schools rehearse,
crushed in with three thousand other revellers until the
early hours trying to enjoy themselves in what sounded
like Black Hole of Calcutta conditions. I began to think
they were a little crazy. Not only were they going out
with Mangueira, they were joining a smaller school, the
Caprichosos, on the night *after* Mangueira. In their fifties,
they made Krim and me feel like pensioners.

Roger parked the car and we walked towards an entrance
to the *favela*. Kids were thick on the ground, touting for a
tip when a car found a space. The people milling around
were mainly black, though those whites who – like us
– had connections mingled happily, greeting, and being
greeted by, the *favelados* with easy familiarity.

Roger and Rachel took us to Lia's house. They embraced
her affectionately, a big, black woman with a radiantly
smiling face, but a body that had seen too much work
and produced we weren't quite sure how many of the
children that teemed around the house's doorway.

'House' is a misnomer. It was more a workshop, or a
series of them, barely roofed, trees growing through the
middle of rooms, the tattered drapes separating sections of
the complex shaking in the hot breeze.

Lia took us to a back room. It was stashed with great
wodges of white and gold material. The costumes weren't
ready yet – 'quite normal', said Rachel – but from the
patter of Roger's Portuguese, and Lia's smiling responses,
we guessed that completion wasn't far off. The headgear

looked good: gold helmets with white feathers and little shells, like pale coffee beans, glued on to the struts.

Krim caught my eye. Somewhere in all this glittering viscose was our £200-worth; judging by the stacks of trousers and skirts, and Lia's gestures as to what covered a girl's torso – a kind of bikini top – Krim's fears about indecent exposure could now be allayed. She was in the clear. I smiled. So did she, just.

Back at the front door, a granny had appeared, and volubly greeted Roger and Rachel. She embraced us too, and introduced us to one of her granddaughters, a gorgeous little black girl with white ribbons in her hair, and who'd been born two years previously – much longed-for, we gathered – just as Carnival was beginning: a Carnival baby brings with her special possibilities. Granny was tiny but spry, and did a few samba steps to get us in the mood. Krim responded with elegant footwork, while I bowed, for want of a better gesture.

What had actually distracted my attention was a guy behind me standing with a machine-gun slung from his shoulder. It was dark, and in the shadows of a doorway a young boy was handing a wad of notes to an older boy, perhaps in his late teens, who counted the bills quickly. The man with the machine-gun stood a few feet away, relaxed, apparently unconcerned, attracting a few admiring ragamuffins, one of whom brought him a beer.

Lia's house seemed happy enough, but from her doorway upwards, into the heart of Mangueira, it was no-go, even for the police. I asked Roger if there was any way one could get up the hill.

'Not on your own,' he said, puffing coolly on his pipe.

Could someone take me? 'Probably, if we find the right person.' The subject was dropped. I asked Krim whether she'd be interested in going into the *favela*. Her 'no' was emphatic. (So, a *favela* adventure was clearly going to be no pushover.)

The rehearsal, like the Carmen Miranda parade, was a non-event – or rather, a hugely delayed one. By ten o'clock, nothing was happening; the idea had been for the *alas* to gather round their signs, poles stretched along the roadway indicating each section of the planned parade, but there seemed to be many more poles than paraders. A man was issuing directives over a tannoy, a few drums had started up, but midnight looked like being the earliest kick-off. We decided to conserve already heat-worn energies.

The Prestons dropped us off at a bus stop, or what looked like one. (These things are arbitrary in Rio; co-equal with contempt for red traffic lights, catching a bus simply involves standing where it seems others might be waiting for one, and waving your arm should one approach.)

Krim preferred a taxi. I convinced her to try a bus, though having already told her about taking the *circular* last time and missing Chico's call, I was on shaky terrain. We took one that threatened to go the long way round, but luckily it slammed straight into a Sunday-night traffic jam, did an about-turn, right in the middle of the road, and headed for Leblon on the shorter route directly westwards. The journey, I proclaimed, was cut by at least half – probably not true, but in the taxi–bus debate thereafter, I tended to win.

*   *   *

We conserved our energies all week. February 1994 was to be the hottest of the century.

We got hooked on *sucos* – fresh fruit juices – and did a little shopping each morning. We made it to Ipanema beach a couple of times, but it was mostly too hot. We decided to stay just this side of being European, knowing we'd have our work cut out for Carnival.

On the beach, the bodies, young, middle-aged and old, were of course very beautiful. Krim – who'd never crossed the Atlantic before – found Brazilian children irresistible. At the same time she found my observations about shameless shoreside male priapism extremely dubious, convinced that I'd made it up. I told her she just wasn't looking hard enough. She told me I was a fantasist.

On Carnival Friday, we had lunch with Tom Jobim at the Plataforma, the famous Leblon barbecue joint Chico had told us about.

I borrowed Krim's tape-recorder, with a microphone far superior to the one inbuilt into my dilapidated plastic box – the same machine I'd interviewed Chico on a year and a half earlier. I also thought I'd have to borrow her credit card, as I didn't have one and wasn't sure whether lunch was to be my shout. She said she didn't have it with her, and asked me whether I always planned my interviews so badly.

'You have a strange way of trusting everything to fate, don't you?' Another genetic fault, apparently.

We were arguing about this inadequacy just as Tom Jobim's agent, Gilda Mattoso, arrived. She was joined soon after by Jobim's wife. Then Chico's manager Vinícius turned up. It was going be one hell of an expensive lunch.

Jobim, a national institution, lunched every day at the Plataforma, as Chico had told us. For our meeting, he had to be rung twice to be reminded to come. His problem, we gathered, was that he'd been called out by a friend to help with a hosepipe in the garden. He arrived an hour late, a droll, shambolic figure, satchel hanging round his waist like a recusant schoolboy, wearing exactly the same clothes, we noticed, as he had been when Krim and I had seen him – astonishingly but auspiciously enough – at Rio airport the week before on our arrival. Then, he'd been meeting his family from New York.

When he joined us at the table, Jobim's first action was to order up a large bottle of whisky, one that was brought to him every day, with notches on it to mark his tab. He then told us he drank very little.

'I don't need it,' he said, as he poured a slug into a large glass. 'I used to drink a lot, but not now.' He lifted his glass, toasted Krim and me, and quaffed the Scotch as if it were wine.

One of my first questions was whether the bossa nova still meant anything, whether it was still valid – who played it now? His answer was oddly disinterested.

'I don't know what you'd call it, whether you'd now call bossa nova jazz. Categories are always a problem, and jazz never dies. Bossa nova actually means "new way", but now it's really been around too long. It probably should go away.'

Antonio Carlos Brasileiro de Almeida Jobim was born in Barra da Tijuca, a suburb of Rio de Janeiro, in 1927. His family soon moved to Ipanema. His father was a diplomat who died when Tom (as he became known to all his friends – pronounced as in the French *ton*) was five. His mother remarried, and his stepfather encouraged him to study architecture.

But music, particularly the music of Brazil's multifarious birds, was what fascinated him. Inside the house, his step-sister Helena's piano was the main object of his attentions as a boy; his stepfather therefore put Tom in the hands of one Hans Joachim Koellreuter, a musicologist trained in the Second Viennese School's twelve-tone system, and a refugee from Nazi Germany. From 1937, Koellreuter had a significant influence on a broad range of musicians, including João Gilberto.

'He taught a bunch of us,' remembered Jobim. 'I wasn't especially influenced by his way of thinking, but I understood it. In a young country like Brazil, you didn't need to be an atonalist!'

Jobim's other major influence was Heitor Villa-Lobos, the Brazilian lyric composer of the inimitable *Bachianas brasileiras* and other folk-based works. Jobim studied theory and harmony hard, and by his early twenties was fully versed in the classical repertoire.

'I had an erudite education up to a point, but I also had the streets of Rio, the guitar players under the lamps at night. So on the one hand, there were Bach, Mozart, Beethoven, Brahms, Debussy. On the other, there were the samba, the blacks, the African beat. The two things met easily, just as in jazz – the European thing with the African thing.' (Jobim's garrulousness, I noticed, was pronounced.) 'The countries where the blacks didn't go have no samba, no swing – and that's with all the due respect I have, say, for Russia, with its incredible people, Stravinsky, Prokofiev . . .

'But what swings? The US of A, the Caribbean and Brazil. That's it. The mainstream for me is the Caribbean. The rest of the world plays different music. Beethoven is beautiful, but the black thing is so strong that everyone's becoming black.'

He took another draught of Scotch, and intoned: 'Black, black, black is the colour of my true love's hair . . .'

Jobim wrote a symphony in 1954, called *Sinfonía do Rio de Janeiro*, with a friend of his, Billy Blanco. It has been said that one of its movements, 'Hino ao Sol' ('Hymn to the Sun'), was the first bossa nova.

Bossa nova *per se* was a few years off. But as Jobim – then slim, finely groomed and extremely good-looking – worked his way around the clubs of Copacabana and Ipanema, playing the piano for a crust by night and composing by day, something obviously clicked inside him: white poetry, black rhythms, mulatto textures . . . The music available in Brazil, and in this particular corner of it – two stretches of unspoilt Atlantic beach packed with clubs, bars and places where *cariocas* thought, ate and drank music – was unique, and endless.

Jobim had a composer's ambitions and a natural musician's feeling for improvisation: what could *he* add to his country's bulging bag of sound worlds?

He needed a catalyst. It came in the form of Vinícius de Moraes, specifically Vinícius's play, *Orfeu da conceição* (*Orpheus of the Conception*).

Vinícius had brought *Orfeu* to Rio in 1956 to have it premièred. He was looking for someone to write a score for it. It was to be a play with songs. He was introduced to Jobim in a Copacabana bar, and asked him whether he'd be interested in doing the music. 'Do I get paid?' asked Jobim. The answer being yes – though not much – he was hired.

Here is how Jobim described Vinícius to Krim and me:

I had a very good relationship with him. He was like an elder brother to me. Actually, he was a cousin of mine, a distant one. He'd studied English at Oxford, and knew all the French poets – he was a published poet himself, of course, long before he was involved in music. But not only did he know languages, he was very musical, with a good ear.

I'd always known about him, because he was already famous. He'd composed with many guys before me. Back from England, he'd been Brazilian consul in Los Angeles. He was very well informed – a mix of Portuguese and Swede: very universal.

He had in fact invited another guy to do the music for *Orfeu da conceição*, but he was sick and refused, so he came to me. In the beginning, we were kind of ceremonial together. Then, after two or three bad songs, we started to write good ones . . .

The result was a collaboration at least as significant as Bertolt Brecht and Kurt Weill's. The impact on the first *Orfeu* audience of Vinícius and Jobim's first song together, 'Se todos fossem iguais a você' ('If Everyone Were Like You'), was immense. Other songs heard for the first time that September night at Rio's Teatro Municipal – with sets designed by Oscar Niemeyer – such as 'Mulher, sempre mulher' ('Woman, Always Woman') and 'Lamento no morro' ('Hillside Lament') were just as durable.

Orfeu da conceição became Marcel Camus's famous 1959 film, *Orfeu negro* (*Black Orfeus*). It took the Palme d'Or at Cannes and won an Oscar for best foreign film. The film was a stylised, humanised, not to say romanticised, reworking of the Orpheus myth, with a picturesque Rio *favela* at its heart. For years the film served as one of the mediums through which a certain kind of Rio – sensual, paradisaical – was purveyed the world over.

The appearance of the film was, finally, the harbinger of the bossa nova's ascendancy. The twenty-eight-year-old João Gilberto from Salvador da Bahia had already arrived on the scene with a completely novel guitar style – smooth, syncopated, sensuous – and been immediately welcomed by Jobim and Vinícius as 'one of them': white artists forging a distinct musical culture within a predominantly black context.

Together, the three men produced 'Chega de saudade', recorded as the first side of a 78rpm disc on 10 July 1958, with 'Bim-bom', also sung by Gilberto, on the other. The record's release, followed by Gilberto's first album, *Chega de saudade*, in February 1959, launched a new epoch and a new way of making music in Brazil.

Most significant for the *second* stage of this epoch – the mid-1960s – is that the three men who shaped it all heard 'Chega de saudade' at the same time at different ends of the country, and decided there and then to become musicians: Chico Buarque in São Paulo, and Caetano Veloso and Gilberto Gil in Salvador.

Not all Jobim's bossas were written with Vinícius. Famous

songs, 'Foi a noite' ('It Was Last Night'), 'Desafinado' ('Out of Tune') and 'Samba de uma nota só' ('One-Note Samba'), were composed collaboratively with another musician of this South Zone circle, Newton Mendonça. But great bossas now flowed from Jobim's pen, 'Insensatez' ('Folly'), 'Corcovado', 'A primeira vez' ('The First Time'), 'A felicidade' ('Happiness') – *Orfeu negro*'s theme tune; and all were sung by João Gilberto. The songs in turn flooded the airwaves, both at home and abroad. By the early 1960s foreign musicians, mainly North American jazz artists, were picking up on this deliciously exotic rhythm, and trying it out themselves.

The story of the bossa nova very quickly becomes the story of the 'Garota de Ipanema', 'The Girl from Ipanema', which, when released in North America in 1964, put the sound on the world map. That story is a supplement to this one and can be read elsewhere.★

The consequences of the success of 'The Girl', however, were not good for indigenous bossa nova; North American recording companies moved in on the artists and, in a material sense, the art itself, which led to João Gilberto moving to New York for the rest of the 1960s, and Tom Jobim spending a good part of the rest of his professional life there.

Back in Brazil, in very different cultural and political circumstances to those which obtained during the bossa's first wave, this remarkable invention passed into the hands

★ The main reason for the meeting with Jobim was to talk about the making of the song, 'The Girl from Ipanema' (1964), composed by Jobim, with lyrics by Vinícius, and sung by João Gilberto (who also plays the guitar) and his then wife, Astrud. The result was the first history of the song in English, which can be found in *Lives of the Great Songs* (Penguin, 1995), pp.190–6.

of singer-songwriters who began to speak for more than just the musically educated: Chico Buarque, *primus inter pares*, would come to speak for an entire people.

Ipanema, an Indian word which means 'bad water' (supposedly because the fishing was bad), was once as clean and bright as *Orfeu negro* and 'The Girl' suggested it was.

'Then,' said Jobim, who remembered it as if it were yesterday, 'the atmosphere was very different to that of Copacabana. It was a young suburb, attractive, because the sea was clean, there were fewer people and new buildings, with sand dunes and wonderful surfing. Because it was so much further from the centre, it was actually for paupers.'

I had one final question for him. Did he feel proud to be the inventor of bossa nova?

After quarter of a bottle of Scotch, the answer was as oblique as it was well lubricated.

'What's the point in becoming a fashion? How boring to stay a modernist. I'd rather be an eternalist.'

Thus ended one of the last interviews Tom Jobim gave. He died of a heart attack in New York in November 1994, just eight months after Krim and I had met him. It was alleged that the New York doctors made an error when operating on Jobim after his collapse, that he might have survived. This may be true; it may be wishful thinking. Jobim did not look in good health when I met him. Yet national heroes become even more expansively mythologised in death than they are when alive.

In Rio de Janeiro, Brazil's outgoing president, Itamar Franco, called for three days' mourning.

★   ★   ★

That same Friday night, Krim and I went back to Mangueira. This was for a rehearsal proper.

With the sort of connections they have, the Prestons had reserved a box in the *quadra*, like the one I'd been in at Império Serrano. We got there at ten, and not much was going on. At the far end was a stage, where the *bateria* was taking shape – a few guys wandered about bringing their drums on, the odd beat sounded. Up on the left-hand side, opposite the boxes, was a space for the singers.

Slowly people filed in. Some went to tables, some to ground-level boxes. Many came in in groups, and many were white – that's to say, like us, not from the *favela* – who had obviously paid their way into Mangueira's parade; and it was easy to believe that Mangueira's samba school was not made up of Mangueira at all, but a host of well-to-do, middle-class *cariocas* grafting themselves on to Carnival for one night of the year, squeezing the *favelados* out of their pride of place and snatching the glory that actually belonged to people like Lia.

If that was the 'politically correct' view – held, for example, by João – it was not entirely factually correct. True, during this rehearsal we saw hundreds of white people enjoying themselves, like us. But there was no resentment in the air on the part of Mangueirenses also rehearsing, and also enjoying themselves. Racial tension – race – was not an issue; the people who ran the show were black, every last man and woman of them, and more to the point the best dancers were, well, absolutely not white.

The only liquor on sale in the *quadra* was beer. Entry into the *quadra* was tightly controlled, so drugs were kept out. There was only one reason to be there, and that was to samba – or, in our case, wiggle in some kind of imitation of samba.

Another was to learn the song. This year it had been composed to honour Caetano Veloso, Gilberto Gil, Maria Bethânia and Gal Costa: the 'Four Baianos' due to appear at the Royal Albert Hall in July. The first verse of the song was a paean to the beauties of Bahia itself, the second a play on the titles of various of the musicians' own songs. It was already popular on the airwaves, and I had the tune more or less sorted out, in my head at least.

The words would take a little longer. It was important to try and get them right, as part of the point of dancing down a kilometre and a half of sambadrome was to yell out the song. You'd look pretty stupid if you couldn't, as not only would the rest of the parade be singing for all they were worth, so would the audience – thousands of them.

'Atrás da verde e rosa . . .'

Me leva que eu vou
Sonho meu
Atrás da verde e rosa
Só não vai quem já morreu

Bahia é luz
De poetas ao luar
Misticismo de um povo
Salve todos os orixás

Quem me mandou
Estrelas de lá
Foi São Salvador
Prá noite brilhar
Mangueira!
Jogando flores pelo mar
Se encantou com a musa
Que a Bahia dá
Obá berimbau ganzá
Ô capoeira
Joga um verso prá laiá

Caetano e Gil ô
Com a tropicália no olhar
Doces Bárbaros ensinando
A brisa a bailar
A meiguice de uma voz
Uma canção
No teatro Opinião
Bethânia explode coração
Domingo no Parque amor
Alegria, alegria, eu vou
A flor na Festa do Interior
Seu nome é Gal
Aplausos ao cancioneiro
É carnaval é Rio de Janeiro

Me leva que eu vou
Sonho meu
Atrás da verde e rosa
Só não vai quem já morreu

'Behind the Pink and Green . . .'

My dream, take me,
I will follow you
Behind the pink and green
Where only those who aren't dead stand

Bahia is light
Of the poets in the moonlight
A people's mysticism
Hail to all the gods
Who sent me
Stars from there
It was the Saint Salvador
Lighting up the night
Mangueira!
Throwing flowers into the sea
Delighted with the inspiration
Which only Bahia can give
Oh harp and rattle
Oh *capoeira*
Playing a verse just like that

Oh Caetano and Gil
With Tropicália in your eyes
Sweet Barbarians who teach
The winds
To dance
The sweetness of a voice
In the Opinião Theatre
Bethânia bursts the heart

A Sunday in the Park, with love,
I want Happiness, Happiness,
A flower at the Party in the Countryside
Its name is Gal
Applause for the singer
It is Carnival, it is Rio de Janeiro

My dream, take me,
I will follow you
Behind the pink and green
Where only those who aren't dead stand

*   *   *

Things were moving by eleven. A circle of dancers had formed, the *bateria* struck up, a couple of singers appeared opposite our box. 'Me leva que eu vou/Sonho meu . . .' With these words, a familiar refrain floating into the hot, beery air, the drums burst into action: a crisp, relentless, sexy rhythm.

For the first half-hour we watched from the Prestons' box. Krim was restless; she felt rebellious about being in a 'superior' position, and wanted to join the crowd. She was right; the time of watching was over. Carnival could no longer be just a vicarious pleasure; now was the moment to take the first real steps, however faltering, however ungainly – however sweat-soaked. The following Monday, that kilometre and a half awaited us. The Europeans had now to become just a little African.

We plunged in. At first it was just a matter of miming, attempting a few tentative steps, then stamping the feet; arms would come later. My suede shoes, which had been so painful last autumn, came into their own: the soles cushioned my heavier stomps, while the soft leather caused no pinching. They were a little chunky; with my longish shorts, I probably looked as though I'd fallen out of a safari tour. Krim, dressed in jeans and bikini top, kept her distance from this sore thumb. No matter: a samba rehearsal is not a fashion parade.

We pranced round in circles for an hour. Krim closed her eyes, and followed the beat with pretty, rolling movements, particularly with her arms. Rachel bounced around with a disco eagerness twenty years younger than her age. Roger, who clutched either his pipe or a beer can, or sometimes both, jigged up and down with an incoherence that could only be English; his nose got redder as the night wore on, his smile larger. Like me, he was keen to lose weight, though he had a little further to go, especially round the belly. His task was made no easier by a tremendous capacity for *caipirinhas*.

The *quadra* was packed. Some of the dancers were in teams, in uniform T-shirts of white and gold, or pink and green, Mangueira's colours – more fashion-conscious, therefore, than the average participant. During pauses in the music, they huddled together, practised handclaps in unison – the words too – and generally behaved like cheerleaders. Others, black, not in teams but often in family groups, sauntered off towards a table at the side, sat down and urged other members of their party to join in the mêlée. Children were everywhere.

From the box, I'd been watching two women. One was black, dressed in a green top and jean-shorts. She'd been dancing from the start, sometimes by herself, sometimes with a male partner, sometimes with a girlfriend.

Hers was raw samba, a convulsion that began at the hips and radiated through her legs, like two forks of electrical shock from the same source. Her concentration was intense, and shone through her smile. She was wickedly fast.

From this shameless burst of danced energy in the middle of a woman's body, simple aesthetic pleasure is to be had; pleasure becomes hypnotic when the legs, and then the arms, move in concert, and never seem to stop. And neither elegance nor symmetry, nor rhythm, is lost. I do not know how it is done.

Which is why I was watching. The other woman was a mulatta, dressed in a light red trouser suit. She had long curly hair, and wore arm bangles. Her samba was a kind of shudder, from head to foot. Raising her hands from her waist to her face, an effortless wave ran through her body, each section of it responding to the previous sway to left or right: knees, hips, chest, shoulders, head, and back again.

Hers was a gentler samba. She was surrounded by a group of kids, maybe brothers and sisters, or nephews and nieces, entranced. They pleaded with her to show them how to do it, again and again. Only a sense of gringo self-consciousness prevented my asking if I could join the class.

I watched for minutes on end. The *bateria* was at full throttle. Krim came up behind me:

'I know why you like this one.'

'Why?' I asked, surprised.

'Because she's like a flamenco dancer.'

Another of Krim's devastating observations; I couldn't argue, not least because of the noise.

We carried on dancing. The Prestons were back up in

the box, mingling with friends, embracing old acquaint-ances. I'd noticed how much embracing they did in Brazil. We stayed down on the floor.

At about one a.m., a girl appeared on a podium just in front of the jumpsuited guy who was 'conducting' the *bateria*. She began to samba with a ferocity at first startling, then jaw-dropping.

Like the black girl, she wore jean-shorts, and a skimpy red top, tasselled and sequinned. She had slightly oriental features, and long, straight black hair. She swung from side to side for a few minutes, positioning her feet forwards, then back, with the precision of a ballet dancer. Then, that shock again: her body seemed to jump out of its skin, her hair flail, her arms dislocate from her shoulders. Her legs would execute a high-octane cross-hatch of steps and jumps, she would turn her back to the *quadra*, and her hips for a few seconds did something that can only be described as pure sex.

I had stopped dancing and was, clearly, ogling. In the ruck behind me, Krim was intrigued, ostensibly by the girl, more in fact – as she caught my eye, and smiled briefly – by the look of bare hunger on my face. I smiled back, just as briefly, and indicated to her a scene unfolding under the samba dancer's podium.

A *favela* family was dancing in a circle. Into its centre little girls in white, aged between seven and eleven, jumped and sambaed like perfectly calibrated rubber puppets; there was no position their limbs seemed incapable of twisting themselves into.

They were soon joined by a filthy old man in torn espadrilles, tattered trousers and with broken teeth. His samba was a slide, a jerk and a wink. The girls took turns to jig in front of him, while an older girl stood at the edge of the circle keeping watch. I'd never seen children having such a sophisticatedly enjoyable time.

Krim sidled over to me. I came clean with her.

'OK, I admit. This is better than flamenco.' Her face expressed 'I-told-you-so', but she wasn't going to mention it.

It was time to go. A lift in the Prestons' car was our safest route to the South Zone. But there was still one duty left: costumes.

Lia greeted us rapturously. Granny was delighted we'd been rehearsing, and insisted we did some turns with her. Krim moved expertly on her feet. I improved on my bow. Children were everywhere, including the little Carnival girl with white ribbons in her hair, and her serious, adult countenance.

The costumes were ready and brought to us in plastic binbags. Paper tags with strange writing – 'Jaine', 'Qurimil' – were attached with pins; a white feather peeked through the bags' knots, evidence of the hat. The rest was layered invisibly beneath.

We couldn't wait to try them on. Back at João's flat, Krim didn't need much persuading. After ten minutes she emerged from upstairs, in shimmering white and gold. She descended to João's front room like an African princess. Every inch of the costume was made for her: skirt, trousers (underneath), top (everything between the shoulders and midriff covered), even the hat with the feather. Her colouring – red-brown hair, brown eyes and fair skin

– was an exotic complement to the white and gold. A triumph.

Best of all was a big golden sash tied in a bow at the back, an exclusively feminine feature of the outfit. In the fashion stakes, this was to put the ladies way ahead of the men: the men, in the same garb, frankly looked a bit daft – I'd certainly *never* worn a skirt before, and instantly got tangled up in my beads.

'You're a *candomblé* priest,' said João, smiling through his beard as I displayed myself a few minutes after Krim's catwalk. As he fiddled with our arm sashes and other paraphernalia, João was enjoying himself. I wasn't so sure. What the hell was a *candomblé* priest anyway?

Carnival night came and went in a flash of inspired energy.

Krim and I were to be driven to the Sambadrome by Roger's former chauffeur, Paulo. We had arranged to meet the Prestons inside the processions area, before the actual physical entrance to the Sambadrome.

They had told us that Paulo had sometimes gone on strike for days on end because he was convinced someone had put the evil eye on him. This kind of superstitious belief was still very common in Brazil, they said. We prayed, *please*, that the spirits would stay calm on Carnival Sunday.

Paulo arrived on the dot, at ten p.m. He was a charming man who spoke no English. He was very excited about our going out with Mangueira. Once inside the Sambadrome he would take us as far as he could. Beyond a certain point, however, only those in legitimate costume could proceed.

(Thank God we'd paid our £100.) It was important to get there on time – i.e. at eleven – because if we didn't, we would miss Roger and Rachel, never find our *ala*, and lose out on the parade altogether. Unthinkable.

The only hitch in an otherwise straightforward journey from the South Zone was Paulo's insistence that he pick up his girlfriend Isabel in Botafogo, halfway between Ipanema and the Sambadrome. She was to keep him company for the night, which would be spent (rather shamingly, we felt) in the car, driving first us, then the Prestons, all over Rio. It took him half an hour to dig her out of her flat, but this in truth was preferable to any encounter with the evil eye. A complicated series of negotiations with the road police, conducted with aplomb by Paulo, who repeatedly pointed to the two costumed characters in the back of his car and said 'Mangueira' a lot, led us to the back of the Sambadrome. We got out, and followed Paulo and Isabel.

Costumes and floats assailed us on all sides. There were psychedelic feathers, sumptuous head-dresses, diamantine sequins, bare breasts, serpentine cloaks, angels' wings, pop-star boots, gilded loincloths, stuffed animals, plastic animals, miniature jungles, chariots, cars, huge tea-pots and aeroplanes everywhere we looked. The noise from the Sambadrome itself was muffled, but constant: the samba school before Mangueira was halfway through its parade. We had forty minutes.

As we approached the final gate, beyond which Paulo could not go, a float apparently lifted by a series of coloured airsocks, perhaps to rise at some later stage, balloon-like, into the sky, came menacingly into view: giant multicoloured condoms.

On the other side of the gate, left to our own devices, Krim repeated something she'd said the week before, at the Carmen Miranda parade:

'I tell you, I'm getting a *lot* of ideas for next year's carnival in Cologne.'

This was a nice observation, but untimely in what I was convinced was impending disaster: we would never find Roger and Rachel, we would join the wrong *ala*, or even the wrong school, and stumble like idiots into the Sambadrome; our costumes would get torn, we would get robbed or kidnapped or raped or all three. Everything was about to go wrong, I could *feel* it. I took Krim's hand and, tight-lipped, led her through a jumble of backstage props that not even Fellini – Nero, even – could in their wildest fantasies have dreamt up.

In the event, we moonwalked. The Prestons, a fraction worried about Paulo's reliability, were happy to see us, and instantly introduced us to others in the *ala*. Roger marvelled at Krim's Carnival beauty; Rachel betted I'd never worn a skirt before. I was still struggling with my beads.

Pink and green silk bracelets were produced, the colours of Mangueira. These are talismanic wristbands, associated with Salvador's great church honouring many Bahians' version of Christ – Senhor do Bonfim. They are supposed to be worn until they rot from your arms.

All around was a sea of white and gold. Some people huddled in circles, singing the song to each other and clapping. Some adjusted their helmets, while others jumped up and down as if in warm-up for a race. Behind us, Granny from the *favela* was whirling on her feet, her beaming smile the best encouragement for us to sprout wings. I felt we would need them.

Soon, it was Mangueira's turn. We moved forward, held in check and in line by one of the many *ala* sergeant-majors who'd keep the paraders together in their appropriate groups for the entire eighty minutes. (Eighty minutes is the designated time for a samba school to get through its parade; take too long, or be too quick, and you lose points.)

Roger and Rachel were convinced that Mangueira was going to win this year, the first time since 1987. This, amongst other technical details, was the subject of their febrile conversation as we moved closer to the entrance. Krim and I simply held our breath.

The moment came. The first bars of the song, then the *bateria*, tolling, cracking, rumbling, as if heralding entrance into Rome's Colosseum, had us all joining hands and the *ala* of three hundred dividing into lines. Ahead were the *baianas*, the ladies dressed in extravagant, flying-saucer costumes mandatory to every samba school, and beyond them the first float of the parade. Behind was the rest of the school, some five thousand dancers, and somewhere amongst them the floats carrying Caetano, Gil, Bethânia and Gal.

We never saw them, except on TV later. Before we knew it, fireworks had burst into the night sky, and the song was in full flood: 'Me leva que eu vou/Sonho meu . . .' As we rounded the corner into the Sambadrome proper, the roar of thousands singing those words smashed into us. Flags waved, streamers shot across our heads, the drums seemed to get louder with every step we took. The public wanted Mangueria. They'd been waiting all year for Mangueira.

This wasn't being thrown to the lions; this was the greatest high on earth. Where else, apart from in Rio de Janeiro's Sambadrome, could you wear white and gold fancy dress, sing a song fifty times, dance like a dervish for an hour and ten minutes, and have tens of thousands singing your praises?

Our *ala* was exemplary. The straight lines disappeared soon after we started processing, but it held its own inner equilibrium. Granny behind us lost her helmet at one point, but seemed undeterred. Roger and Rachel threw their chests out at the wailing, photo-snapping spectators in the front-row boxes with an exhibitionist gaiety I'd never have suspected of them. Krim and I whirled and twirled, jumped, stamped and shouted, and did more than passably good impressions of singers at home in their song:

> Aplausos ao cancioneiro
> É carnaval é Rio de Janeiro . . .

At the end, I felt shattered. Krim immediately said it had gone too quickly, and wanted to do it all over again. I couldn't have agreed with her less. Roger helped us find Paulo, and went back to the box he'd hired for two nights, and to which we were invited the next night – the last night of Carnival. Back at João's, I fell asleep with my skirt on. Krim watched the parades for what remained of the night on TV.

Mangueira came eleventh. Everyone who expected the

school to win said this was typical: Mangueira was so good, and had such an advantage with its homage to the Bahians, that the judges were bound to mark it down. Suspicions were bolstered when a story about sabotage to Gilberto Gil's float started to circulate.

From Roger's box the next night, Krim and I were treated to the sight of the Prestons, Darcy and a friend of his parading with the Caprichosos: a minor samba school, scheduled for the early evening. Our friends were dressed like footballers, and had painted faces. It had started to rain by the time they went out, and they didn't notice. I did, and looking at the darkening sky wondered how many hours we'd have to endure it. I was exhausted, and getting wet makes exhaustion worse. Krim was beside herself with enthusiasm throughout the entire night, and commandeered my camera, later claiming that all the best photos, you know, the properly composed ones, were taken by her. I tried to snapshot as much nakedness as possible, and am convinced that the high-street film-developers back in Islington censored the most revealing ones.

As the parades went by, and seemed to get longer and more and more elaborate, my head began to spin and my eyelids drop. Eventually I fell asleep on a plastic mac, my elbow resting on my knee. Roger has a snap to prove it. At four in the morning, as we all left the Sambadrome – and how reluctant the Prestons were to leave! – Roger handed me a little packet he'd found on offer, from a whole bag of similar packets, at one of the inner exits: a Carnival condom.

'Here,' he said, with a chuckle, 'you may need this.' The innuendo was quite uncalled-for. He hadn't seen me lay a finger on Krim. Frankly, I had no idea what he meant.

The other big Carnival event was President Itamar Franco's unfortunate association with a girl wearing no knickers – and in a *bichero*'s box, to make matters worse. Clearly set up by a cartel of press photographers, she'd lifted one arm at an opportune moment to wave at a parade, her other arm draped round the president's shoulder. The next day, her pubic hair was on the front page of every Brazilian newspaper. The president somehow survived the embarrassment.

Only in Brazil.

'Vai passar' (1984)

Vai passar
Nessa avenida um samba popular
Cada paralelepípedo
Da velha cidade
Essa noite vai
Se arrepiar
Ao lembrar
Que aqui passaram sambas imortais
Que aqui sangaram pelos nossos pés
Que aqui sambaram nossos ancestrais

Num tempo
Página infeliz da nossa história
Passagem desbotada na memória

Das nossas novas gerações
Dormia
A nossa pátria mãe tão distraída
Sem perceber que era subtraída
Em tenebrosas transações

Seus filhos
Erravam cegos pelo continente
Levavam pedras feito penitentes
Erguendo estranhas catedrais
E um dia, afinal
Tinham direito a uma alegria fugaz
Uma ofegante epidemia
Que se chamava carnaval
O carnaval, o carnaval (vai passar)
Palmas pra ala dos barões famintos
O bloco dos napoleões retintos
E os pigmeus do bulevar
Meu Deus, vem olhar
Vem ver de perto uma cidade a cantar
A evolução da liberdade
Até o dia clarear

Ai, que vida boa, olerê
Ai, que vida boa, olará,
O estandarte do sanatório geral vai passar
Ai, que vida boa, olerê
Ai, que vida boa, olará
O estandarte do sanitório geral
Vai passar

'On Its Way'

On its way
A samba's coming down the street
All the cobblestones
Of the old city
Tonight will
Be shivering
Remembering
That immortal sambas passed by here
That here they bled about our feet
That our ancestors danced here

There was a time
Unhappy page of our history
A faded passage in the memory
Of our younger generations
When our fatherland
Slept, a distracted mother
Didn't see she was diminished
By shady transactions

Her sons
Wandered the continent blindly
Carrying stones as if in penitence
Erecting strange cathedrals
Until one day, finally,
They had the right to a fleeting joy
A panting epidemic
That was called Carnival
On Carnival, oh Carnival

(On its way)
So a hand for the famished–barons block
The black-Napoleons block
And the pygmies in the boulevard
My God, come and see,
Come and watch, close up, the city singing
The evolution of freedom
Until the day dawns

Oh, what a good life, *olerê*
Oh, what a good life, *olará*
The banner of the lunatic asylum on its way
Oh, what a good life, *olerê*
Oh, what a good life, *olará*
The banner of the lunatic asylum
On its way

Five

A Visit to Caetano Veloso, and Other Conversations

On the Thursday after Carnival, Krim left for Cologne with Chico Buarque in her pocket. I spent the following weekend in the inland colonial town of Ouro Preto in Minas Gerais, doing nothing except cooling off in a little swimming pool and looking at jewel-like eighteenth-century churches. Then I travelled to Salvador da Bahia.

Salvador da Bahia, Brazil's first capital, could be one of those cities that serves as a last refuge for cracked European minds. You might expect to find a Malcolm Lowry here, frying his brains on a cocktail of tropical sun and *caipirinhas*.

In fact, on my first day, I did find just such a figure: an old codger in shorts and T-shirt sitting at a bar near my beach hotel, drinking beer, talking and laughing merrily to himself. The bar had a speciality: '*Man spricht Deutsch*', announced a sign amidst the palms. My Lowry, who looked

European, was clearly polyglot – the trouble was, nothing he said made any sense, neither his amalgam of Portuguese, German and French, nor his laughter. He was laughing at nothing.

Further up the road, I waited for a bus to take me into Salvador's historic city centre. Two pretty teenage girls stood nearby, clutching school files. Below them, two filthy black boys ragged about on the pavement. They eyed the girls, and asked them for money. The girls smiled back, and did nothing, evidently used to such overtures from street-children. Then one of the boys let out a screech of laughter, and extracted his little erect penis. His friend tried to punch it down. The girls, looking fractionally shocked, moved away.

Much of the Terreiro de Jesus, the bit of the historic city centre I'd come to see, and the streets around it were in a state of apparent disinterment: in one of those daft decisions which belong more to South American literature than fact, the local government had ordered not just one or two or three 'historic' buildings to be restored, but every edifice within roughly a quarter-mile radius.

Was I in a place which – despite its name – God had forsaken?

Sightseeing was out of the question. The streets were ditches, the dust was choking. Gangs of military police on each street corner and cohorts of blue-boilersuited builders on the disembowelled pavements made the prospect of exploration about as appetising as queuing for a Prince concert at Wembley. Gasping for breath and sanity, I plunged towards a church, the Igreja da Terceira Ordem de São Francisco . . .

★   ★   ★

Salvador (meaning 'Saviour', as in Christ) first sprouted on a clifftop looking over a huge bay shaped like a mouth: Baía de Todos os Santos (Bay of All the Saints), as it was called apparently after Amerigo Vespucci sailed into it on 1 November 1501 – All Saints' Day.

The city was colonised half a century later. For the remainder of the 1500s, Salvador became a fecund trading centre – first in sugar cane, then tobacco, then gold and diamonds. By the early seventeenth century the city was second in opulence only to Lisbon in a then fabulously wealthy empire.

Bahia was also fabulously licentious, the scene of things that could be barely imagined in the Catholic austerity of Portuguese court life back across the Atlantic: 'a hell for blacks, a purgatory for whites and a paradise for mulattos', wrote one historian at the time.

'Renowned for its tropical exuberance and volatile inhabitants,' wrote a more circumspect Giovanni Pontiero,★ 'the *Bay of All Saints and every conceivable sin* [Salvador's nickname] became a bustling metropolis where fortunes were quickly made and lost, where white settlers consorted freely with blacks and mulattos on the plantations and in the brothels.' Salvador became not only a second imperial capital for the colonisers, but also a sexual playground for them, an image it has never quite lost, though today's colonisers are

---

★ Giovanni Pontiero was a gifted translator from Portuguese who died in 1996. He was the great Portuguese novelist José Saramago's translator, as well as that of Brazilian feminist novelist Clarice Lispector. This passage is taken from his foreword to Brazilian novelist Ana Miranda's *Bay of All Saints and Every Conceivable Sin* (1992).

a pinker, loucher breed of North American and European gringo supporting Bahia's open sex-tourism industry.

Salvador was first port of call for Brazil's slaves. The trade between Portugal, Angola and Brazil was on a spectacular scale. In 1587 there were four thousand blacks to the city's twelve thousand whites, along with eight thousand Christianised Indians. Within a century, blacks constituted half Salvador's population, and today make up most of its 2.1 million – though as in Rio, this is probably a million too many. The bulk of the city's blacks live in chronic poverty. The *favelas* are, if anything, worse than Rio's.

The slave trade terminated in Brazil – with a bit of help from British abolitionist fervour and Royal Navy gunboats – in 1854, though slavery itself survived another thirty-five years. The emancipation of Brazil's slaves in a law of 13 May 1888 gave the country the unenviable distinction of being the last American country to abolish slavery. The statistics are overwhelming: through the 1700s and 1800s, *ten million* slaves were transported to Brazil – ten times the number shipped to the United States. By 1860 they numbered only half their North American cousins, due to an appallingly high death rate.

Yet for all this, Brazil is racially better tempered than the United States. It is a much blacker country. Only a fool would pretend that racial prejudice does not exist there – and of course the reins of power and most of the country's wealth lie in the hands of non-blacks. But there seems to be less vestigial resentment on both sides, less demarcation and self-consciousness at large than exist in most multiracial societies. John Updike, who published a novel about the country in 1994 – called *Brazil* – put it nicely:

> Of all the world's melting pots, Brazil is the most melted. It's the brownest. In the US, we had to fight a civil war to end slavery, and racial tensions have persisted. The Portuguese had little dread of the African races, and the mestizo-mulatto society they made could be a model of how to behave.*

This might be accused of bending over backwards in the direction of political correctness and ignoring the reason (endemic, grinding poverty) why Brazil could *not* ever be such a model. But the observation's generosity helps one forgive Updike for writing one of the worst books of his career.

In Bahia, the outstanding feature of black culture is its Africanness. Unlike anywhere else in Brazil, or indeed most of the Caribbean further to the north, the African gods familiar to those first wretched sixteenth-century transportees are still worshipped by thousands of their descendants today. This is *candomblé*, a celebratory from of religion with its host of *orixás* – gods – and system of priests and initiates.

Somewhat improbably, the Catholic Church never bothered to expunge this tendency from the black population in Bahia, mainly because of the sheer numbers of slaves who ended up there, and also because the Church's efforts were more fully absorbed in taming and converting the interior. If the races were allowed to intermarry, moreover – which they did – then the Church had more souls to save.

Technically, *candomblé* cults were forbidden by law until

---

* Interview with the author, *The Guardian*, 4.4.94.

1970. However, after Salvador lost its status as capital to Rio de Janeiro in 1763, and the city went into a long administrative and economic decline, obscure rituals honouring untroublesome gods, invariably in secret, were considered harmless. Worshippers were left in peace.

Less peaceful were the *quilombos*, all over the country, communities of slave militants who tried to set themselves up as independent political entities. One, Palmares, lasted most of the seventeenth century. Most *quilombos* (including, eventually, Palmares) were suppressed with predictably efficient imperial brutality.

With Brazilian democracy in the ascendant today and a degree of political autonomy granted to all states, it is easy in Bahia – particularly if you swallow wholesale the glossy literature churned out by the state tourist agency, Bahiatursa – to believe that everyone's happy in the land of Brazilianised Africa. Where there are blacks, there is music; where there is music, there is Carnival (Salvador's is certainly one of the world's best); where there is Carnival, everyone's welcome. Something like that.

On my third day, well looked after by Bahiatursa but beginning to suffocate under the happy-happy-land propaganda, I sought out Juana Elbein dos Santos.

She is a *gemütlich*-looking Austrian lady in her sixties who studied anthropology in Paris. She lived in Buenos Aires for ten years before coming to Brazil in the early 1960s. In Salvador, she met and married a Bahian writer and sculptor, Deos Coretes dos Santos, who today has elevated status in a *candomblé* group – a close-knit organisation whose focal point is a *terreiro*, or cult house.

Juana has an office in a converted schoolhouse in the middle of modern Salvador. Her driver picked me up near my hotel on a hot, sultry, grey afternoon, and I was whisked away for a chat first in the back of her car, then in her office. Her main interest is in what she calls 'human diversity'. This, she said, finds one of its liveliest repositories in Bahia. She much prefers her phrase to the more usual, and faintly patronising, 'Afro-Brazilian culture'.

In 1974, she founded the Society for Studies in Black Culture in Brazil – a non-political body, she quickly pointed out. Its aims are to monitor the black experience of Brazil, and the way in which blacks may best articulate that experience, and their needs, in a society which all too readily blurs the distinctions of race and type in the interest of promoting a pretty picture of miscegenation – not, I have to add, a word Juana likes. She doesn't like the word 'black' either.

'I prefer New African, or New Brazilian. I don't know how to call them really. They are very conscious of their strengths.'

She speaks fluent English, with just a hint of Vienna.

'The black people of Brazil have always organised themselves into institutions. In these groups, there is no ambiguity: you may be white or yellow or black. You simply belong to a group – not in a religious way, more just as a way of life. Me, I'm white, European. If you ask who is *black* in Brazil, the answer is: Those who belong to an institution. When you put three blacks together, you have an institution. Some North American anthropologists call these groups "defensive", which is true up to a point: but what makes them so strong is that they believe in themselves.'

Juana was really talking about *terreiros* and their sense of otherness, or cultural uniqueness. She is not a defender of syncretism – the combining of religions, in this case Catholicism and the *orixás* – and, interestingly (because not a lot of whites in Brazil would say it, though I wondered whether her being a non-Brazilian white helped), is adamant that these black groupings should maintain their communal separateness:

'Black institutions have long experience of disguising themselves. Since they came to Brazil, these people have had to become Catholic. They've had to go to church. They've had to be baptised. They've had to disguise their own beliefs. So the tension between authentic black religion and what's put on for local colour is not difficult for them to deal with here.

'There's no discontinuity,' she went on, 'between life and religion in these communities, between their way of looking at family life, their way of eating, dressing, hating and loving – religion is the connective tissue of the community. I've been in trouble for calling *terreiros* "communities", but I see them as more than examples of religious togetherness. The Africanness of these communities is innate.'

Juana was talkative and jolly. I wanted to hear more, but she was due at another meeting where her fellow society members would be discussing how to lure J.K. Galbraith to Salvador to talk about 'human diversity from an economic point of view'.

I remembered I had once seen a besuited Galbraith – very tall, patrician, like a US senator – sipping tea in a London publisher's office. It was mid-winter. Somehow, the idea of the great man lecturing in tropical Salvador da Bahia was about as plausible as my having a beer with Pelé, or Chico Buarque, in my Islington local.

Juana called for her driver and said she'd take me to the old city centre, where I was due to meet Billy from Olodum.

Olodum are known the world over. They're Bahia's top drumming outfit, or one of them. In Salvador, one thriving black institution, the kind Juana is so keen on, is the 'Afro-Block', not dissimilar from a Rio samba school, only smaller, and based on drumming and rhythms drawn directly from the members' African roots (and as far as I know they are drugs-free). Olodum is one such Afro-Block. They made it big in 1991 when they were invited by Paul Simon to play in New York's Central Park.

After the South African *Graceland* album of 1985, Simon moved on to Brazil. He'd been told some interesting things were happening in Bahia, and was introduced to Olodum in 1989. He said he'd like to record a samba rhythm of theirs. He did just that, and it cropped up on his 1990 album, *The Rhythm of the Saints*. Contrary to sniffy reports about Simon's apparently plundering music that wasn't his, he paid Olodum handsomely. He also made them famous.

Billy is a fantastic-looking man: he has very black skin, of a type you see quite often in Brazil, and stacks of thick, wiry hair. He is really Olodum's PR man, one of the group's few members who speaks English. With me, he was gracious, and patient – because until I got to Bahia, I'd never heard of Olodum. (I'd not progressed beyond *Graceland* in the Paul Simon world-music tour; David Byrne's descent on Brazil – he produced three Brazilian compilations in the late 1980s – had also completely passed me by.) As we talked, Billy dropped (to me) surprising references to Olodum's recent appearances in places like St-Martin-in-the-Fields and Battersea Park.

'We've also participated in Notting Hill's carnival,' he said, 'which for us is the second best carnival in the world.' What, after Rio's? I asked tactlessly. 'No, no, Salvador's of course!' Of course. I had Rio on the brain. But *Notting Hill*? Wrong time of year *really* to be Carnival, racially a divisive spectacle, track record opposite to everything I now felt Carnival stood for. Billy was being polite, surely.

Olodum, like most Afro-Blocks, has a social function: educational programmes – 'English, French and cooking classes,' said Billy – and a remit to get street-children *off* the street and into classes (even if they're just drumming classes) and some kind of care. State welfare is, catastrophi-cally, non-existent in Brazil.

'It's very hard to get anything from the government, to get them to take any responsibility for a community like this, so we started our social project in 1982.' (Olodum was founded in 1979.)

The upshot is that Olodum, situated in the heart of Pelourinho, Salvador's former slave-auction zone,* has become a quasi-welfare centre, with boutique, job- and health-advisory clinics, disco and bar, and its famous Tues-day nights, when as many as five thousand people come to hear the drums.

After all this upbeat stuff, Billy, at the end of our talk, had some pretty brisk things to say about the life of Brazil's blacks.

* *Pelourinho* means 'whipping post' – a wooden post at which slaves were legally whipped as punishment until the 1830s.

'The big problem in our society is racism. Black people are not well treated here. Black people do not participate in a society trying to get things better for us. But we don't want apartheid. We don't want to see one half favoured and the other not. That's why Olodum is so active in getting things done – schooling, for instance. If you don't study, you'll be nothing in the future. We need, all the time, to look forward to the future.

'We follow the examples of Nelson Mandela, Martin Luther King, Malcolm X, Marcus Garvey, Bob Marley – the black leaders of the world. And it's very important we work within human rights, which is why Olodum is not a racist group.'

The Igreja da Terceira Ordem (Third Order) de São Francisco, built in 1703 and situated in the Terreiro de Jesus in the city's old quarter, is part of a kind of Salvadoran holy of holies.

The church's façade is an abundant display of colonial rococo, Portuguese devotional carving at its most zealous and confident. It's like a frieze of hundreds of stone ice-cream cones, all knobs and whirls and loops and curls. For 150 years, it was hidden from view: then, in 1936, a workman installing wiring chipped off some of the plaster that had, for some reason, been laid over the façade. It took another nine years before it could be seen again in its original splendour.

Next to this church is the Igreja de São Francisco, not as stunning on the outside as the Third Order. Inside, it's a grotto of colonial baroque. Gold leaf adorns every inch of available wall. Statues and carvings drip down on all sides. Some of the angels have disproportionately large breasts. The carvers were black slaves, who cheekily imbued these Christian icons with the more openly sexual symbolism of their own god-system. Today, São Francisco is a centre for *candomblé* devotions alongside more conventional Catholic worship: syncretism at its most blatant, I'd say.

I wasn't here to pray. I was killing time on my first Bahia afternoon. I was due to meet Caetano Veloso that same evening: an interview with Salvador's native singing god.

From the RFH to Caetano's front door in seven months. Not bad going, though I said it myself. Professional pride had in fact been completely overtaken by something far wilder: I was, as I looked at central Salvador's historic edifices, really that fifteen-year-old pop fan again, off to meet his number-one hero. Quite ridiculous.

Caetano lives in an oceanside house out of the city centre. Like Chico in Rio, Caetano had his house built for him; and some house, when I eventually found it, tucked away on a small hill above the main coast road, it is: a whitewashed modern structure, perched on a cliff looking over the sea and a beach. On the patio, with the Atlantic roaring beneath, is a swimming pool. I hadn't thought of Caetano and swimming pools. The scene was positively Hockneyesque.

I wasn't invited in to the house. Wearing shorts and a red T-shirt, Caetano greeted me once the doorman had accepted I wasn't *just* a fan (two real ones at the gate were begging him to take messages). Caetano ushered me to a loggia near the pool. This was to be an alfresco interview.

Caetano, soft-spoken, charm itself – that much I had imagined – was sun-tanned, although he is also naturally dark, darker than I remembered him from the RFH. His father, a post-master, was mulatto. His musical mother, Dona Canô, is white.

We didn't start talking about his family. Instead, Caetano told me about an honorary visit he'd made to Olodum during the previous year's Carnival.

'They had a festival in Pelourinho, and I was invited to become an "Olodum Citizen",' he said. 'At the concert, with a packed audience, people generally were not behaving in an acceptable manner, and fighting broke out. Some dark guys were there just for the fighting, and that's boring, sad. It shows that we're socially in a bad situation. But then the police, who were mostly dark too, intervened and behaved even worse. Everything's going towards degradation.

'Most people are black in Bahia. Many are mulattos, some of them look white. But we're all mulattos, we're all shades in Brazil, above all in Bahia. It's not true that we live in a racial democracy, as is often said, that it's a racial paradise and that we don't have racial conflicts. We have our difficulties, though our racial situation is different from most. It's full of suggestions.'

Caetano, with Gilberto Gil, had written a samba-rap about the Pelourinho incident, called 'Haiti'. It opens their collaborative 1992–3 *Tropicália 2* album, celebrating the twenty-fifth anniversary of their musical 'movement' in the late 1960s, Tropicalismo – and the fact that both men were fifty:

Quando você for convidado pro subir no adro
Da Fundação Casa de Jorge Amado
Pra ver do alto a fila de soldados, quase todos pretos
Dando porrada na nuca de malandros pretos
De ladrões mulatos e outros quase brancos
Tratados como pretos
Só pra mostrar aos outros quase pretos
(E são quase todos pretos)
E aos quase brancos pobres como pretos
Como é que pretos, pobres e mulatos
E quase brancos quase pretos de tão pobres são tratados
E não importa se olhos do mundo inteiro
Possam estar por um momento voltados para o largo
Onde os escravos eram castigados
E hoje um batuque um batuque
Com a pureza de meninos uniformizados de escola
    secundária em dia de parada
E a grandeza épica de um povo em formação
Nos atrai, nos deslumbra e estimula
Não importa nada: nem o traço do sobrado
Nem a lente do Fantástico, nem o disco de Paul
    Simon
Ninguém, ninguém é cidadão
Se você for ver a festa do Pelo, e se você não for
Pense no Haiti, reze pelo Haiti
O Haiti é aqui, o Haiti não é aqui

E na TV se você vir um deputado em pânico mal
    dissimulado
Diante de qualquer, mas qualquer mesmo, qualquer
    qualquer

Plano de educação que pareça fácil
Que pareça fácil e rápido
E vá representar uma ameaça de democratização
Do ensino de primeiro grau
E se esse mesmo deputado defender a adoção da pena
  capital
E o venerável cardeal disser que vé tanto espírito no
  feto
E nenhum no marginal
E se, ao furar o sinal, a velho sinal
Vermelho habitual,
Notar um homem mijando na esquina da rua sobre
  um
Saco brilhante de lixo do Leblon
E quando ouvir o silêncio sorridente de São Paulo
Diante da chacina
111 presos indefesos, mas presos são quase todos pretos
Ou quase pretos, ou quase brancos quase pretos de
  tão pobres
E pobres são como podres e todos sabem como se
  tratam os pretos
E quando você for dar uma volta no Caribe
E quando for trepar sem camisinha
E apresentar sua participação inteligente no bloqueia a
  Cuba
Pense no Haiti, reze pelo Haiti
O Haiti é aqui, o Haiti não é aqui

When you're invited up on the terrace
Of the Casa de Jorge Amado Foundation
To watch from above the row of soldiers, almost all
  black,
Beating on the necks of black good-for-nothings
Of mulatto thieves and other almost-whites
Treated just like the blacks
Just to show the other almost-blacks
(And they're almost all black)
And the almost-whites poor like the blacks
How it is that blacks, poor men and mulattos
And almost-whites, so poor they're almost black,
  are treated
And it doesn't matter if the eyes of the whole world
Might for a moment be turned to the square
Where the slaves were punished
And today a pounding of drums a pounding of drums
With the purity of boys in secondary-school uniforms
  on parade day
And the epic grandeur of a people in formation
Attracts us, astonishes us and stimulates us
Nothing matters: not the trace of the house's
  architecture
Nor the camera lens from Fantástico, nor Paul Simon's
  record
No one, no one's a citizen
If you go to the party there at Pelo, and if you
  don't go
Think about Haiti, pray for Haiti
Haiti is here, Haiti is not here

And on TV, if you see a congressman in badly
  concealed panic
When faced by any, absolutely any, any any
Plan for education that seems easy
That seems fast and easy
And will represent a threat to the democratisation
Of primary-school education
And if this same congressman should defend the
  adoption of capital punishment
And the venerable cardinal should declare that he sees
  so much soul in the foetus
And none in the criminal
And if, when you skip a red light, the old familiar
Red light,
You should notice on a street corner a man pissing
On a shiny bag of garbage from Leblon
And when you hear the smiling silence of São Paulo
In response to the massacre of
111 defenceless prisoners, but prisoners are almost all
  blacks
Or almost-blacks or almost-whites so poor they're
  almost black
And poor men are rotten and everyone knows
How blacks are treated
And when you go on holiday in the Caribbean
And when you screw without a condom
And participate intelligently in the blockade of Cuba
Think about Haiti, pray for Haiti
Haiti is here, Haiti is not here

*   *   *

Caetano Emmanuel Viana Telles Veloso was born in 1942 in a small town to the north of Salvador, Santo Amaro da Purificação. It's a colonial gem in the Recôncavo, uncommonly lush terrain spanning out from Salvador's concave bay (hence the name) towards mangrove swamps. The Portuguese made a great success of the area, growing first sugar, and then tobacco and spices. Unlike many agricultural centres in colonial Brazil, the Recôncavo prospered throughout the eighteenth and nineteenth centuries, and helped furnish Salvador with some of its more lavish building.

Santo Amaro boasts a seventeenth-century church, some churches from the eighteenth, and a clutch of other fine Portuguese edifices, including a whitewashed Convento dos Humildes. The town, which straddles a small river, has a charmed ambience for a suggestible young poet to grow up in.

Caetano's father died in 1983. He calls his mother, now eighty-eight, 'very joyful'. She has (he says) a wonderful voice, and still sings at home. She taught Caetano old Brazilian folk-songs, though it was his younger sister, Maria – Caetano helped his parents name her Maria Bethânia – who caught the professional singing bug first; Caetano only went south with her to look after her. She wasn't out of her teens when she had her first engagement in Rio de Janeiro.

The Veloso children were eight in number, along with two more who were adopted. They were all Catholic, and musical; Veloso Senior's sister sang in the church choir, and the religious zeal permeating the whole area was a unifying force for this large Santo Amaro family.

Caetano sang Brazilian and Spanish-American and Portuguese and American songs from an early age. There was a piano at home, which he started on before taking lessons with a local woman teacher. Then, when he moved to Salvador to study, he became aware of 'Bahian sounds' on the radio.

'I asked my mother to buy me a cheap guitar, and tried to learn how to play it. I'm still trying.'

In 1959, Caetano was seventeen. He was studying philosophy. He was interested in film. He might become a writer. But he had one overriding obsession: the music of João Gilberto.

The year before, 'Chega de saudade' had attacked him, just as it had Chico and – unbeknownst to Caetano at the time – fellow Bahian Gilberto Gil. João Gilberto's sound simply made Caetano 'fall more in love' (as he put it to me) with Brazilian popular music. He wasn't yet at all sure he wanted to be a professional musician; if none of his first plans worked – film, writing – he'd become a teacher. But now music, in 1959, began to take up an even larger slice of his life.

This period in Salvador was culturally alight and artistically ambitious. Caetano remembers David Tudor playing works by John Cage at the university in 1960, the year he and Gil met. Classical music concerts were a weekly event. Theatre and dance were everywhere, on stage and in the street. American culture – the movies, rock 'n' roll – had been around in Brazil for a while. Bill Haley and Elvis were known, but they didn't dominate the Brazilians. Far from it: Dorival Caymmi and João Gilberto from Bahia, Luiz Gonzaga from the *sertão* (the desert lands of the north-east's interior) and Jobim in Rio were the heroes of the hour, Caetano's not least of all.

Then, in the early to mid-1960s, something really new and foreign did reach Brazil: certain British bands, it seemed, were taking North American rock 'n' roll into uncharted waters. The pop sound from across the Atlantic was fresh, alive, progressive. Caetano found himself tuning in attentively to the Beatles and the Rolling Stones: 'an intellectual excitement', he calls them, 'much more aware than rock 'n' roll. This music was second thoughts about rock 'n' roll.'

By 1964, Bethânia's talents and ambitions were to the fore. Before she went professional as a soloist, she joined a group of musicians, young Bahians who'd all discovered each other – her brother, Gilberto Gil, and a nineteen-year-old girl with a big voice called Gal Costa – in various shows that year at Salvador's Vila Velha theatre. Together they performed bossa novas and sambas. The last show Bethânia had to herself, which propelled her to Rio in early 1965 and into the lead rôle of a show called *Opinião* (*Opinion*). She came in as a substitute for Nara Leão (the singer who'd make Chico's 'A banda' famous the following year).

Bethânia, a small, striking woman with almost Indian features, was an immediate hit. A rabble-rousing song from the show, 'Carcará', was released in March 1965, and turned her into an overnight star throughout Brazil. The flip side of the single carried a song composed by her brother, 'E de manhã' ('It's Morning'). Veloso Senior had insisted that Caetano accompany her to Rio, as she was still only eighteen. The move south was, then, a potential break for Caetano too – and he abandoned his studies.

Bethânia, meanwhile, wanted all the Bahians to perform together in Rio, but *Opinião*'s director Augusto Boal wanted only her for his show. Bethânia was unimpressed, and slunk off to São Paulo. Boal pursued her, and finally agreed – in September 1965 – to give the Bahians their first show outside Salvador, in São Paulo. It was called 'Arena Canta Bahia'.

Yet around their heads as they came to prominence raged a fraught, even tortured debate: what *was* Brazilian music? Something called 'MPB' (Música Popular Brasileira), a term coined by critics and the press in the early 1960s, was applied to the new Brazilian sound, which at this stage was still really bossa nova. The young Bahians excelled at bossa. Soon, 'MPB' was being applied to this new generation of talents – Chico Buarque, and, imminently, Caetano and Gil. But did it, does it, mean anything?

Music, a yardstick of identity in Brazil, inevitably carries with it nationalistic connotations. So when the military took over in 1964 and conservative nationalism gripped the country, even 'MPB' became suspect. The bossa nova, claimed one critic in a book published at the time, was itself 'too Americanised' to be 'truly' Brazilian.

Caetano trashed this ridiculous notion in an article, one of his first, in 1965. He admits, however, that he wasn't then doing anything significantly different from other young musicians: he'd started composing songs, romantic bossas mainly, and didn't exhibit an overweening individualism (an abundant lyricism, certainly) in his first album,

Domingo (*Sunday*), released in July 1967, a collaboration with Gal Costa.

Nineteen sixty-five had been Bethânia's year; 1966 was Chico's; 1967, the latter part of it, was Caetano Veloso's. Apart from the album, his big noise in October was 'Alegria, alegria'. The song aroused fury at that year's São Paulo Brazilian song-fest, partly because, like Gil's 'Domingo no parque' at the same event, it used electric guitar.

This may seem a perfectly extraordinary reason for musical controversy in the 1960s. But we are in Brazil, not North America: Brazilian song-making was traditionally an acoustic art — bossa nova not least of all. The advent of electrification in music — amps, speakers, drum sets, flat guitars with wires and knobs — was a profound shock, a 'contamination'. It all looked and *sounded* too much like gringo 'pop' for comfort. Those defensive nationalistic sensitivities were, suddenly and unexpectedly, being given a real going-over.

What's more, Caetano's lyrics were distinctly peculiar:

The sun scatters into guerrillas, spaceships, crimes
Into lovely Claudia Cardinales, I'm on my way
Into president's faces, big loving kisses
Into teeth, legs, flags, bombs, and Brigitte Bardot . . .

Foreign sex symbols? Presidents? Bombs? And later in the song, he even drinks a Coca-Cola! What on earth was he on about?

Gringo pop. At least that was part of it. Caetano had absorbed the quick-fix urban imagery of Anglo-American pop like blotting paper. He adored the Beatles and the Stones. This didn't mean he loved João Gilberto or the great *sambistas*, such as Noel Rosa, any less, though he would soon be accused of as much.

He was also fascinated by literature. At around this time he and Gil encountered concrete poetry – verse that celebrates its own physical shape on the page, and of which there were some notable practitioners in São Paulo in the 1960s – as well as the work of an iconoclastic figure called Oswald de Andrade.

Andrade, who was born in 1890 and died in 1953 when Caetano was eleven, was a kind of Brazilian Ezra Pound. He issued manifestos, was belligerently anti-establishment, scorned *belles lettres*, and generally made an intellectual nuisance of himself. With a brilliant and radical turn of mind, he must have been an inspiring figure for a twenty-five-year-old musician beginning to feel suffocated by an intolerant aesthetic climate, itself exacerbated by the hardening political status quo.

Over forty years before, in a 1924 manifesto, Andrade had urged his readers to 'see with free eyes'. This could be a motto for the 1967–8 Caetano Veloso. Then, in 1928, Andrade had coined a terrible pun which finds echoes in much of Caetano's linguistically more self-conscious work. Playing on the name of an indigenous tribe, the Tupy, Andrade's parodic 'Tupy or not Tupy, that is the question' encapsulated a preoccupation that runs through much Brazilian art and thought, and, latterly, its best pop: what *is* Brazilian identity, in a country which (in Updike's phrase) finds itself racially so 'melted'? Caetano's answer, in 1967–8, was that there wasn't one – or to suggest that at least the country would be a lot healthier if there wasn't one. It was quite the wrong moment to say it.

Thus it was that 1968 saw the birth of Tropicalismo. Now, it would be easy to get bogged down in a long cultural discussion about this strange and today remote phenomenon. At the time, Tropicalismo did come as a great explosion in Brazil, and I'll try and present just the essentials here.

Basically, Caetano, with Gil, wanted to show that pop music, that which was now showcased annually at the song-fests in Rio and São Paulo, didn't have to be 'Brazilian' to be *echt*. Things were happening beyond Brazil's shores that could not be ignored – and not, of course, just in musical fields. A social revolution had taken place in North America and much of Europe; 1968 was the axiomatic year: student barricades in Paris, Soviet tanks in Prague, riots in Chicago, the RUC and Catholics clashing in Londonderry. And in Brazil?

Bossa nova had proved its staying power. Samba would never die. The bold film-makers of *cinema novo*, the unveiling of the bow-and-arrow-shaped new capital in 1960, the country's football success in both the 1958 and 1962 World Cups and the economic boom that accompanied all of these lent Brazil a veneer of emancipation and youthful vitality. Yet in most important aspects of national life, certainly after the 1964 coup, Brazil battened down its hatches: politically, socially, morally.

Fascism doesn't just involve a few military bigheads

kicking parliamentarians out of their ministries and stopping the vote. It also needs, and is fed by, popular support: Hitler, Mussolini and more to the point Franco (who lasted an incredible thirty-five years in Spain) each proved this. Brazil's generals similarly answered some deep need in the country's psyche for totalitarian rule – and this was something Caetano had referred to in his 1993 London concert when talking about his exile.

'Fascism was in our people, in our system, something deep inside us,' he'd said, 'and it had to be overcome.'

Tropicalismo was not, of course, the weapon to deal with so deep a political fault line. In 1968, Caetano Veloso was a relatively inexperienced poet excited by music everywhere, including that of his own country. He was no politician. His exuberant brand of social criticism was less ideological than anarchic. But he was bored by nationalism, and said so. Nationalists, he claimed, would have musicians like him and Gil and Chico stockpiled as tunesmiths churning out traditional fare for foreign consumption: a picture of Brazil as happy-happy-land (and now, recklessly, with an export economy imposed as a supposed cure for the country's ills).

Caetano Veloso wasn't going to pronounce on current affairs: his audience was Brazil's young, eager for the new. He would, also, resist straitjacketing.

'Tropicalismo,' read a statement by Caetano in the Rio *Jornal de música*, 'is an attempt to unite all possible combinations of elements. It is also called *som universal* [universal sound] because it unites the most recent national accomplishments (the Beatles, Jimi Hendrix, the second rock generation). But it also includes *choro*, Noel Rosa and *música caipira*.'★

Maybe so, though Caetano may have had a preference in these heady days for 'Purple Haze'. The conciliatory gesture towards the Brazilian spirit sounds slightly flippant. It was this that really annoyed his critics. Here was a gifted musician, a nice Bahian boy with a sweet voice and a lovely line in bossa nova, suddenly being insupportably satirical, and *North American* with it. Claus Schreiner records another response Caetano gave to a question as to whether Tropicalismo was a musical movement or a philosophy:

'Both. And even more than that, it's a fad. I think it's silly to assume that a person can use Tropicalismo to guide his actions. It's ridiculous to use the name and then go sauntering about with it. Tropicalismo is *neo-anthropophagism*.'

Well, yes – here, Caetano was cheekily recalling Oswald de Andrade. In 1928, Andrade had defined 'anthropophagism' as the manner in which Brazil absorbed stimuli from abroad and adapted them critically for home consumption: 'similar', observed one of Andrade's commentators, 'to the cannibalism of our savages'.

So now the new music embraced *cannibalism* too: Caetano couldn't have been more inflammatory if he'd tried.

His second album, called *Caetano Veloso* and featuring him on his own, was the first full-blown Tropicalista musical statement. Released in early 1968, it trumpeted

★ *Choro* is traditional Brazilian dance music, a bit like tango, which took root in Rio in the 1930s; *música caipira* is rural folk music.

the movement with the song 'Tropicália', really a montage swirling with lingustic disjunctions and Surrealist imagery: 'Long live the bossa-sa-sa! Long live the stra-stra-straw huts!' goes the first refrain line; in the background, a jingle of native drums, bird song and strange voices. Another song on the album, 'Superbacana' (*bacana* means 'cool' or 'great'), is a typical 1960s sugar pop song and, verging on nonsense, parodies the type of advert, even the very era, its music reflects.

The next record Caetano was involved in was a collective Tropicalista effort. *Tropicália ou Panis et Circensis* takes the second half of its title from the Roman satirist Juvenal; in his tenth *Satire* he heaps contempt on the masses who bray for nothing other than '*Panem et circenses*' – bread and entertainment.

To us, it may seem a touch high-faluting for a bunch of pop musicians to be fooling around with Latin poetry: but Portuguese is as close to Latin as a modern Romance language can get. Also, along with Gil, there were two poet-lyricists behind this album – Torquato Neto and José Carlos Capinan – a fellow Bahian songwriter Tom Zé, as well as singers Gal Costa and Nara Leão. The band was called Os Mutantes.

The record was a linear sequence of sounds and songs stitched together without track-breaks, featuring yet more Surrealism, parody, urban satire and not a lot of obvious pop. However, one excellent song was Caetano's 'Baby':

> You need to know about swimming pools, marga-
>   rine,
> Caroline, gasoline

You need to know about me, baby, baby, I know it's so
You need to have ice cream at the snack bar, to hang
   around with us
To see me up close, to hear that song by Roberto
   [Carlos] ...

Charles Perrone has an amazingly portentous gloss on this, but he's not wrong (take a deep breath): 'Unveiling youth's concern with being up-to-date, the importance of English in formulas for success [the word 'baby' is sung in English, while the second verse opens with 'You need to learn English to learn what I know . . .'], and the creation of false needs by consumerism, the casually toned text effectively presents questions of cultural penetration (imperialism) without making overt sociological statements.'

And Perrone doesn't say any more about Roberto Carlos! Roberto Carlos is an idol in Brazil, and has been since the 1960s: a classic crooner, a housewife's fantasy, a genuine Brazilian Julio Iglesias, unrepentantly kitsch, and actually not a bad songwriter. Caetano likes him for all these reasons.

'For us,' he told me in his Salvador loggia, 'to have accepted the Beatles and the Stones meant we must be against the "defensive" nationalistic position in Brazilian pop. Accepting Roberto Carlos too − in spite of the fact that we had a whole line of Brazilian imitators of international pop, which was at a low intellectual level (to match the audiences who liked them), he could come up with rock-like chart songs that were naïve but powerful and vital. He, therefore, was "international", like us.

'Anyhow, in 1967, we had new material to say things

against this position. That's why it was a scandal. The imitators of Anglo-American stuff were commercial and weren't respected. We were. We accepted everything, not only rock 'n' roll but Roberto Carlos, and Brazilian samba-ballads, mostly played in brothels, and tangos, anything that was kitsch and in bad taste – even Carmen Miranda . . .'

The continuous scandal of Caetano's 1968 now began to unfold. First, he was disqualified from a samba competition in the middle of the year for using electric guitar. Undeterred, he mounted, with Gil, a spectacular *mise en scène* at São Paulo's September song-fest. Caetano belted out a strident rock number, called 'É proibido proibir' ('Prohibiting Prohibited'), based on the slogan of a French student group prominent in the May riots in Paris.

The São Paulo audience hated it. They roared their disapproval. The boy from Bahia was actually being booed off stage. Caetano rose, in a now famous riposte, to the occasion.

So these are the young people who say they want to take power! . . . You're out of it! You don't get anything! You're the same as those thugs who beat up the actors of *Roda viva*! This is the problem: you all want to police Brazilian music! . . . Gilberto Gil and I are here to do away with the imbecility that rules in Brazil! If you're the same in politics as you are in music, we're done for . . . God is on the loose! . . . And I say no to no! I say prohibiting prohibited . . . Enough!

Recorded for posterity, this was a remarkably forthright assault not only on the audience but also on the whole established structure of a song competition. A participant does *not* insult the people he's supposed to be pleasing! A Brazilian punk, ten years *avant la lettre*?

There was also the question of Caetano's clothes:

'I was dressed in black and green plastic, with strange Indian things round my neck, and electric cords put together, with huge hair – it was very crazy.

'Gil's song ['Questão de ordem' ('Question of Order')] was even more experimental, very much influenced by Jimi Hendrix. He was really just speaking above basic chords. No one knew Hendrix in Brazil then. The audience thought it was just mad singing, wailing, above the guitars. So we were disqualified.'

The two musicians still weren't going to leave silently. The finals of the 1968 competition (eventually won by Chico and Jobim's 'Sabiá') moved to Rio. Caetano and Gil mounted their own show in a club there, with Os Mutantes, as a kind of alternative to the festival. This is when things took a sinister turn.

Caetano recalls the sequence of events, leading up and subsequent to his and Gil's detention by the federal police in São Paulo – on 27 December 1968 – as if they happened yesterday:

Our show was very avant-garde, very heavy politically. We also had a banner with a photo of one of the famous bandits from one of the *favelas*, who'd been killed by the police. At that time, the image of the *favela* bandit was a very romantic one. On the banner was written: 'Be a Criminal, Be a Hero!' Someone from the Church came to see it, and said it was unacceptable and he called the police, and they closed the nightclub – he managed to get a decree to close it down.

Then there was a right-winger, a fascist, in São Paulo, who worked for TV and radio, a horrible guy, who had heard something about it, and said over the air that we should be 'imprisoned'. He'd heard something about a flag, with the photo and the phrase. He said we'd used the 'Brazilian flag', which was enough to put us in prison. The authorities also wanted to know if what we were doing wasn't all a sophisticated plan to destroy Brazilian society, and to corrupt the power of the military – really far-fetched stuff. Then came the questioning sessions, which were very tough.

We spent two months in jail. I only saw Gil when we were transported from one place to another. For the first week, I was alone on the floor, in a solitary cell. There was just enough space for me to lie down – Gil too. Then they took us to another place, with a bigger cell, packed with people. Not everyone could sleep at the same time. We spent two more weeks there. Then we were transferred to another place, where we were each put in one enormous, clean cell to ourselves. That lasted a month.

Finally, we were taken in an air-force plane to Bahia. There, we could be at home, but we were guarded. We had to report every night to the colonel there, and couldn't leave the town. This went on for four months. Eventually, they took us back to Rio – and put us on a plane to Europe.

Salvador, Rio and Brasília had each been negotiating our exit papers. We were told, 'We want you to leave, and we'll put your papers in order.' But we'd been six months without working. We were both married. We had to earn some money. They said, 'OK, you have permission to give one show' – a farewell show, though it wasn't called that* – 'after which you'll have four days for your papers to be put in order, and then you go: you choose where.'

We didn't go straight to London, but to Portugal, where our manager was. But Portugal was of course under military dictatorship. So from there, we went to Paris, where things were still reeling from '68. So London was the best bet, particularly from the point of view of the music.

No official reason was ever provided for this bizarre episode of ejection. Most accounts have the two men going into 'self-imposed exile', which as Caetano's story makes plain is very far from the case. They were – putting it mildly – bullied into leaving. Had they stayed, further 'decrees' would no doubt have been issued to prevent their performing and indeed recording. At worst, those 'questioning sessions' might have turned into torture. As it was, their popularity made them, as far as the government

---

* It was called 'Barra 69', and took place at the Teatro Castro Alves in Salvador.

was concerned, so dangerous that not even four months' house arrest was thought sufficient to keep them from causing trouble.

Perhaps the strangest aspect of the story is that neither Caetano nor Gil was overtly political; unlike Chico, whose work in the years ahead would become sharply critical of the regime, none of Caetano's or Gil's songs, and no part of Tropicalismo, took a confrontational stance towards the generals. It seems, though this has never been stated or proven, that the pair were simply considered 'subversive': a threat to the Church, family values, the probity of youth and so on.

They touched down in London in September 1969. Creedence Clearwater Revival and Bob Dylan ('Lay Lady Lay') were in the Top Ten. So were Marvin Gaye ('Too Busy Thinking about My Baby') and the Gainsbourg–Birkin 'Je t'aime'.

Caetano felt completely disorientated:

I was in a very bad psychological state, depressed and afraid. It was terrible. We were convinced about London, but I was so afraid. For the whole of the first year I didn't enjoy it – though I was relieved. I was unhappy, it was dark, but at least it was peaceful. I loved all the walls made from brick. The sky was mostly grey too. For the first year, we lived in Chelsea, just off the King's Road, near the Picasso café. On the corner was a record shop where I bought *Abbey Road*, which came out my first week there.

The King's Road was colourful, with beautiful

people walking around, but I was depressed. We all lived together, me and my wife, Gil and his wife, in a three-storey house, with our manager too. We thought we were going to have to live there for years. We certainly didn't know when we would be allowed to go back to Brazil. Then we split, because we didn't want to live forever together. We had money from songs played in Brazil. Everything that could legally come to England we got.

We moved to separate apartments in Notting Hill Gate. I lived in Elgin Crescent, near Portobello Road. I'd never heard reggae before, and I remember walking down Portobello Road, asking people, 'What's this?' I was really impressed by it. It was then that I wrote a song in English, called 'Nine Out of Ten', which is about Portobello and talks about reggae – I and my Brazilian friends were all talking about it. 'Walking down Portobello to the sound of reggae/ I'm alive' was one of the lines. The song was my first English one that was not depressed!

Depression notwithstanding, Caetano composed busily while in England. One of his first English songs recalled the last days of 1968:

> They are chasing me
> In the hot sun of a Christmas Day
> Machine gun
> In the hot sun of a Christmas Day

He produced two LPs in London. One was called *Caetano*

Veloso, the other *Transa* (for which see below). He scored a big hit in Brazil in 1970 with 'London, London', sung for him by Gal Costa: she was one of Caetano's principal supporters back home, and her burgeoning solo career and big following amongst the young for the moment kept the spirit (if not the letter) of Tropicalismo alive.

'I've never been an artist engaged politically,' Gal told me in 1995. 'My political position was to defend in Brazil what Caetano and Gil stood for, while they were in exile, with all my force.'

Gal was one of the pretexts on which Caetano was able to return to Brazil for a brief visit in the New Year of 1971. He was to appear in a TV show with her and João Gilberto, on the understanding that no mention of his being 'in exile' were made.

The circumstances surrounding this visit were as bizarre as the humiliations of mid-1969:

My second London album, *Transa*, was due to be released in the UK. The visit in fact started because my parents were going to celebrate their fortieth anniversary. All the sons and daughters were going to be there except me. So everyone was sad. Maria Bethânia, famous as she was then, went to the authorities to ask if I could have special permission to come back for the celebration, and they said yes. So she called me and gave me a particular date – 1 January – when I'd be met at the airport, then taken to her house, from where we'd go to Bahia. There, I'd be put under the same restrictions as when I was under arrest. So I said OK.

When I arrived at the airport, my wife was allowed to pass, while they held me, put me in a VW and took me off alone, like a kidnapping. They weren't wearing uniforms, and it was frightening, as it would be anywhere. They were military and took me to a place where they sat me in front of a big tape recorder, and interrogated me for six hours. It was psychological torture.

Then they asked me to write a song, backing them! The regime was building a huge road across the Amazon.★ And of course I didn't want to do such a song. They were threatening me ... it was very painful. That's why it took six hours.

I was obliged to appear on TV as if everything were normal: no mention of my arrest, no mention of the fact that I was in exile, nor was anything allowed to be said in the press.

High points of Caetano's London stay included seeing the Rolling Stones playing live. 'They were the most beautiful thing on stage a human being could have seen,' Caetano rhapsodised a quarter of a century later. 'They were like gods. I saw them at the Lyceum and at the Round House.'

Caetano, who remains something of a teenybopper at

★ Caetano is referring to the 'Transamazonica', Highway BR-230, which was started in the 1960s and which leads across the region from the middle of the state of Piauí to the heart of the Brazilian Amazon about 2,500 kilometres to the west. His real answer to the military's blandishments came in early 1972, with the release of *Transa* not in London, but in Brazil.

heart, has never lost his enthusiasm for Mick Jagger. He even interviewed him on Brazilian TV in 1981, in French (which Mick, almost alone amongst English pop stars, speaks), as the programme's producer spoke no English. Caetano enjoyed the experience, though not the broadcast, as the producer hadn't bothered to find English subtitles. People I know who saw the show said it was excruciating.

Later that year, Mick and Caetano met again at a mutual friend's house in New York, just before Caetano's first concert there. The friend was 'in fashion', and was used to having celebrities round. At the dinner table were gathered: Jagger, Bianca *and* Jerry Hall (at least this was how Caetano remembered it), Calvin Klein and Andy Warhol. It must have been one hell of a dinner. I was particularly curious about Warhol.

'Andy Warhol was very talkative with me. I mean, you can't say he was a talkative person, but he was very open. I saw him many times in New York after that, and he always recognised me, saying, How's Brazil? How've you been? Here again? He was fantastic and very funny.'

This was all at the outset of what might be called Caetano's 'post-Brazil' career. In the late 1970s and 1980s, he made successful appearances in Europe, especially France and Italy, where he is well known today, and began to break through in the US at just the moment he went gold in Brazil (100,000 copies of a record sold) in 1981 – surprisingly, given his superstardom, for the first time. He adapted readily to rock, funk and soul, and has ever since manifested a muscial cosmopolitanism which has its roots in Tropicalismo.

Tropicalismo itself had died by the time Caetano and Gil left Brazil. Indeed, one of their last gestures within the remit of the 'movement' was to unfurl a banner on a short-lived TV show they had in 1968, which read: 'Here Lies Tropicalismo'.

When they returned to Brazil in early 1972, naturally one of the first things they did was give a concert – in March, in Rio. Caetano was well aware of the mythical status they had achieved while in England, mainly because nothing about them had been permitted to appear in the Brazilian press. It was assumed that the two Bahians would herald their return with lashings of rock 'n' roll picked up in London.

Fans were to be disappointed.

It was as if audiences were awaiting the second coming. Well, I just did a show, and the audience didn't actually know much about me. The left, who'd not supported us and who knew we'd been in jail and exile, now decided to love us, because we represented resistance. We were almost heroes. But we weren't, at least not the leftist heroes they wanted us to be. I came back singing Tropicalismo, not something which was identified with international rock 'n' roll.

Claus Schreiner was at the concert:

The numbers hadn't changed much, consisting mostly of pieces from the period before his exile. There were a few new songs by Lennon and McCartney, Jimi Hendrix and Steve Winwood, but the new instrumentation, which now tended much more heavily toward rock music, was especially striking. (I wasn't much impressed by the concert, as the voice was too often overlaid with a badly modulated band sound, a problem with which the Brazilians at that time had had little experience.)

Caetano, it has to be said, has never been one to do what might be professionally obvious. Delighted to be back in Brazil, he retreated to Bahia, where he stayed in seclusion for much of the 1970s, reorientating himself after the traumas of exile. He produced an LP in late 1972 called *Araçá azul* (Perrone translates it as *Blue Cattley Guava*), which was dottily offbeat. It was also one of the worst-selling albums of any star of his generation.

Salvador felt violently postcoital. A heaving, damp Carnival, which Caetano was determined to be present at after the Mangueira parade, had left the city centre looking sweaty and worn-out. The street excavations didn't help. The sun barely shone during my three days there. When it did, one afternoon, I took tentatively to a strip of beach in front of my hotel. The sea *felt* dirty. I had a fit of ocean-phobia; unaccountably, images of piss and blood floated into my head.

On my last night, I wandered around a dripping city centre. I'd tried a bit of the trumpeted local cuisine, a *casquinha de siri* – crab gratin, served by one of those Bahian black ladies swathed in white. I'm usually a lover of crab, but this thing was so disgusting I couldn't get through half of it. Below Pelourinho, I remember above all a doorway opening on to a well-lit workshop that made me think I was not in Jorge Amado's Bahia but in Thomas Mann's Venice; perhaps Carnival had taken its toll. The shop was full of coffins.

I had one more night in Rio before flying back to London. I spent it in a friend's house in the old district of Santa Teresa, above the Centro, looking over a *favela* which, on my last afternoon in the city, a Saturday, crackled with the sound of gunshot.

The house was almost troglodytic: built into rock, its front room had no window, just a large, glassless aperture, which had a magnificent view towards Guanabara Bay and the North Zone. A fierce, black-eyed storm brewing over the sea hours before I was due to leave – first signs of cooling after the century's hottest February in Rio – looked as though it would ground all aircraft.

At the airport, I saw a familiar face; Antonio, my $80 taxi-driver from the previous November's trip to Império Serrano, waiting, or perhaps looking, for a customer. He smiled.

'Need a lift?' his expression said. I told him I'd been out with Mangueira, visited Bahia, and was now on my way back to London. 'And Império Serrano?' he asked.

'*Talvez no ano próximo*,' I answered. Maybe next year.

'Branquinha' (1989)

Eu sou apenas um velho baiano
Um fulano, um caetano, um mano qualquer
Vou contra a via, canto contra a melodia,
Nada contra a maré
Que é que tu vê, que é que tu quer,
Tu que é tão rainha?
Branquinha
Carioca de luz própria, luz
Só minha
Quando todos os seus rosas nus
Todinha
Carnação da canção que compus
Qeum conduz
Vem, seduz
Este mulato franzino, menino,
Destino de nunca ser homem não
Este macaco complexo
Este sexo equívoco
Este mico-leão
Namorando a lua e repetindo:
A lua é minha
Branquinha
Pororoquinha, guerreiro é
Rainha
De janeiro, do rio, do ondo é
Sozinha
Mão no leme, pé no furacão
Meu irmão
Neste mundo vão

Mão no leme, pé no carnaval
Meu igual
Neste mundo mau

'Little White One'

I'm just an old Bahian
Anyone, a Caetano, anyone's brother
I go against the grain, sing against the melody,
Swim against the tide
What is it you see, what is it you want,
You who are so much the queen?
Little white one
Carioca with her own lighting, light
Just mine
When all that's pink is nude
All an
Incarnation of the song I composed
Who conducts
Come, seduce
This frail mulatto, boy,
Destined never to be a man
This complex monkey
This dubious sex
This monkey-lion
Courting the moon and repeating:
The moon is mine
Little white one
Little tidal wave, warrior

Queen
Of January, of Rio, of where it
Alone
Hand on the helm, foot in the hurricane
Is my brother
In this vain world

Hand on the helm, foot in the carnival
My equal
In this evil world

Six

All This Brazilian Music

I still see Krim from time to time. She phoned me in mid-1994 to enthuse over one of the songs on Chico's *Paratodos*, and said she found the voice on 'Piano na Mangueira' particularly sexy. Which one? I asked her. What do you mean, which one? Exactly what I said, I said. Chico's of course, she said, perplexed. One of the voices is Chico's, I told her. The other, the deeper one, in the second line, is Tom Jobim's. Oh, then it must be Jobim's, she said.

Her interests really lay elsewhere: fashion, clothes, things which I'm too stupid to understand. She's been working on a book about hairdressers since that phone call. At the heart of our association was the simple fact that she found my attachment to Brazilian pop irremediably childish. Still, February 1994 wouldn't have been the same without her.

The year 1994–5 was a good one for Brazil in London.

The four Bahians, Caetano, Gil, Gal and Bethânia, rocked the Albert Hall at the beginning of June 1994 (see Appendix One), and it was topped by a cumbersome parade of a bit of Mangueira, which frankly looked silly and took away valuable extra time from the singers (who did only *one* encore!). But it was uplifting, in such unlikely surroundings, to hear February's samba refrain again.

Apparently, certain members of Mangueira also made a killing on touted samba-school T-shirts and stage passes, which angered the Prestons, the show's producers. So intense was their displeasure that they refused, for the first time in nine years, to go out with Mangueira for 1995's Carnival.

In July, three weeks after the Bahia-fest, Milton Nascimento, from Minas Gerais and much better known outside Brazil than Chico or Caetano, played at the RFH, though it was hardly a rerun of Caetano's show the year before. Nascimento is a mood and ambience man, thoughtful, a bit static, with an international hard core of jazz and funk and 'world music' (dread phrase, in my view) fans, without the street appeal of Chico, and without the unconventional poetry of Caetano. But he is an original, versatile, full of the hymns and chimes of his native state, sung in an unmistakable falsetto voice. The critics call it 'soaring'. I find him quite dull.

Then, in August, Caetano returned to do a peculiar concert at the Queen Elizabeth Hall with a New York post-punk cult figure called Arto Lindsay.

Lindsay, who's been closely involved in producing some of Caetano's recent records, makes a speciality of 'guitar noise'. He can't actually play the instrument, and admits he can't. He was brought up in Brazil, and speaks Portuguese fluently. He's translated Caetano's words into English for album sleeve notes. Beyond that, it's hard to know what Caetano sees in him; musically, they're about as compatible as Kurt Cobain and Simon Rattle.

I took Martin to the QEH. Still no convert, he was none-theless prepared to indulge my obviously unquenchable wish to become a Brazilian pop star, like a fond uncle watching a small nephew learning to paint. At the end of the show's first half, which featured Lindsay 'playing' with his musicians, and 'singing' in a nasal, deadpan shriek, and no Caetano, Martin turned to me and said: 'James, if this goes on, I'm not staying a second longer. Not one. I'm off.'

'Wait for Caetano,' I hissed, slightly upset on Martin's behalf, and slightly annoyed at Caetano. I'd built this up as a unique London appearance of one of the greatest artists I knew on earth, and all Martin had got so far was caterwauling. We survived a grumpy interval, in which I naturally bought the drinks (and dinner later would of *course* be on me). What was Caetano playing at?

Much was forgiven in the second half when Caetano appeared and performed solo, with acoustic guitar, for about forty-five minutes. It was blissful, but too short. Then it was back to clanging and caterwauling. Still, this forty-five minutes *had* offered a glimpse of the genius I knew Caetano to be, and was enough – just enough – to reassure Martin I wasn't yet off my trolley, even if Mr Lindsay was.

(Actually, that's not quite fair. I'd interviewed Lindsay in New York earlier in the year, about his own life and his connection with Caetano, and he was charming and bright. It's just that he should, in my view, be kept away from the guitar, and from any concert stage on which Caetano is performing. The man has no music.)

July 1995 saw both Gil and Gal performing in separate concerts at the RFH, again, I suspect, on the basis of capacity crowds the producers knew or hoped could be drawn by these types of star after Caetano's 1993 sell-out.

Gil needed no special introduction. Ever since his exile in London, he'd kept his Anglo-Saxon musical contacts very warm. He'd bought his first electric guitar in Shaftesbury Avenue. He'd jammed with Pink Floyd's guitarist David Gilmour and drummer Bill Bruford in places such as the Revolution Club and the Marquee, and played with Weather Report at Ronnie Scott's. He'd lapped up Frank Zappa and B.B. King during their early-1970s visits to London. He'd listened to Traffic, the Moody Blues, Hawkwind. Gil was, is, a known superstar, and possibly, like Nascimento, even bigger outside Brazil than in.

He was born Gilberto Passos Gil Moreira in 1942 in Salvador. He was brought up in Ituaçu, in the backlands, and was exposed early on to the accordion music of Luiz Gonzaga and market-square guitarists. In 1960, he went to Salvador University, where he met Caetano. Their careers were closely linked thereafter; before the launch of Tropicalismo, Gil made a name for himself with songs such as 'Roda' ('Round'), 'Procissão' ('Procession') and

'Louvação' ('Praise'), and appeared on the all-important TV bossa shows of the mid-1960s.

His most fertile, purely Brazilian phase was from Tropicalismo in 1967 to participation in Nigeria's 1977 Festival of Black Art and Culture – the moment when Gil became much more self-conscious about his black roots, and more international. To this ten-year period, containing his exile in London (which saw the release of three LPs), belong such wondrous songs as 'Lunik 9', 'Aquele abraço' ('That Embrace', his farewell to Brazil in 1968), 'Oriente', and 'Expresso 2222'. All swing with Gil's rhythmic exuberance, conceptual inventiveness and a kind of cosmic imagery; in his best songs, Gil travels far and wide.

In the late 1970s, he explored more freely than Caetano would ever want to the broader highways of international pop, and toured the world – not unlike a conventional rock king. Being black and speaking good English, it was easy for him to cross cultural barriers within the Anglo-American industry, absorbing reggae, US jazz, Caribbean rhythms and, of increasing importance to him in the 1980s, the fresh pop sounds from black Africa. In 1985, he even had a UK hit, with 'Toda menina baiana' ('Every Bahian Girl'), a popular disco number.

Gil is also a great showman; he stole the limelight at the 1994 Albert Hall concert, and proved at the RFH a year later that his abilities to judge his audience, fire them up and run with them were as sharp as ever. He looks indecently fit, young – and smiles beatifically. His music smiles. His guitar technique is leagues ahead of his peers. Perhaps lacking the lyric originality of Chico and Caetano, he is still the more instinctive musician.

Significantly, Gal Costa arrived three weeks after Gil in London with a show comprising Chico's and Caetano's songs, and no one else's. She's been singing them for years (she doesn't compose), though she sings many others' too. She has a minimal profile outside Brazil (where she's loved) – this in spite of the fact that in 1985 *Time* magazine rated her as one of the grand 'divas' of contemporary pop, along with Kate Bush and Whitney Houston. She has a bigger voice than either.

A couple of weeks before her London appearance I met Gal in Portugal. She was giving a concert in a castle outside the old university city of Coimbra. On the afternoon of the show she spared me some time after a dreary press conference.

(Most of the Portuguese journalists barely concealed their boredom, which astonished me; this was a major star, after all, agreeing to field their uninspiring questions. Would English journos greet Whitney Houston in Manchester, say, with such world-weariness? Maybe it was something to do with temperament – the Portuguese, unlike Brazilians, are an old-fashioned and reserved lot. Maybe it was something about its being a Saturday, or Coimbra's being deeply provincial. I never got to the bottom of it, nor indeed of why Gal was performing there rather than Lisbon.)

She's now over fifty, but looks thirty-five. That day, she was dressed in a loose dark-blue silk suit. Her abundant, near-black hair was combed and frizzed up around delicious dark features. She is ridiculously soft-spoken for a singer of her vocal range. Still, I think she enjoyed having a proper conversation with someone who knew both Chico and Caetano, and something of their work, though she was unsure of her English; for that, her friend, a Brazilian lady of her age in tight jeans and a white T-shirt who lives in New York, chipped in fluently more often than was necessary.

I wanted to know about Gal and Chico and Caetano. Gal had, after all, known them and their music for three and a half decades longer than I had.

'Caetano is the Brazilian composer who knows exactly how I sing,' she replied. 'We have a very strong musical identification. Caetano knows my voice and feelings best. Chico is more classical, and I love him. Caetano's work is more open and diverse; he writes ballads, rap, experimental songs, because that's his personality. Chico, being more classical, writes sambas and ballads; he's a wonderful poet and that's basically the difference.'

Another one is that Caetano has written many songs for her, while Chico has written only a few. She sang many of Caetano's that night – 'Ciúme' ('Jealousy'), 'Lindeza' ('Beauty'), both pretty – though ironically the song that really got the audience going was Chico's 'Quem te viu, quem te vê'. So excited was one young man that he jumped up on stage and presented her with a rose, and then thought he'd have a dance with Gal – and was ushered off. Gal looked momentarily shocked, but smiled when she realised he meant no harm. I learnt later that he was the son of the Portuguese ambassador to Brazil.

In London, Gal performed the same set, though with an additional encore: 'London, London' – of course. What was odd about the rendition was her having to put specs on and read the words from a special wooden bookstand. The audience didn't mind one bit, but it gave the song an

inappropriately academic air. I hadn't realised her English
was *that* bad – and she'd made the song a hit in 1970!

Samba, bossa, *choro*, *forro*, *frevo*, *baião*, *afoxé*, *iêiêiê*: the list of
terms and forms of Brazilian styles goes on and on. These
things are beloved of musicologists and invite tome after
huge tome. This book is not one of them. It is enough
to restate that Brazil is the world's most musical nation,
and that if Brazilians live for and through anything, it is
their rhythms and melodies. Their music is as fantastically
variegated as the birds and beasts of their rain forest.

Whether Brazilian music is as much under threat as the
forest is more difficult to gauge. Bossa nova has seen its
heyday, and everyone complains about the trivialisation
of samba. Brazilian rock is the same as it is anywhere else.
The Afro-Blocks of Bahia are exhilarating but not terribly
original. Old folk forms, a few of which I have just listed,
tend to be performed by artists little known outside their
field or city and listened to by specialists. Chico, Caetano
and Gil have probably done their best work, though I
wouldn't put it past Caetano to do something musically
surprising and outstanding before he's sixty. Wait for the
year 2002.

All told, the Brazilian musician-making machine is not
infallible. The 1970s and 1980s have turned up no one of
the stature of the Bahians, Chico, Nascimento. There are
of course some individual talents who have shone through
– Rita Lee, Djavan and João Bosco, to name but three –
and legions of Brazilian groups and singers who've ridden
high on the rock, punk and post-punk waves of the last two
decades. To include them here would be to recite a tedious

catechism of names unknown outside Brazil (though I can't resist mentioning Secos & Molhados – Dry & Wet – a sort of São Paulo equivalent of Queen, who made it big in 1973, and whose singer, Ney Matogrosso, has been dubbed, in his solo career, 'Brazil's Alice Cooper').

Rita Lee was a member of Os Mutantes and appeared on the collaborative Tropicalismo album of 1968. She tried to go it alone as a rock singer in the 1970s, but failed: she was arrested for drug possession and sent to prison. In 1977, Gilberto Gil helped put her back on track, since when she's flourished as a not-overinspiring proponent of 'Rock Brasil'. Djavan, short for Djava Caetano Viana, emerged from Bahia in the mid-1970s and has done well in North America, where he cuts most of his records. My old chum Christian, now running a port firm in Portugal, was sent an album of Djavan's by a client, and said it was the most horrible thing he'd ever heard.

João Bosco, from Minas Gerais, is a child of the bossa nova. He is probably the most important figure in the 'MPB' generation after Chico Buarque, and is just two years younger.

With a distinctive voice and guitar-playing style, he arrived late on the scene in Rio, when both Chico and Nascimento were well established, and didn't have a big record sales success until 1982, with the LP *Commissão de frente (Parade Captains)*. His songwriting partnership with Aldir Blanc, a talented lyricist from Rio's Vila Isabel district – *sambista* Noel Rosa's home – has been one of the few musical success stories of the post-bossa, post-Tropicalismo era.

This success cannot be separated from the efforts of

one of the truly great figures of Chico and Caetano's generation, a woman from Pôrto Alegre in the south who sang and recorded dozens of Bosco-Aldir compositions in the 1970s: Elis Regina.

Elis came from a poor family, but made three successful recordings in Pôrto Alegre before she was twenty. She showed all the signs of a major interpretative talent, and had a deep feeling for the traditional music of Brazil.

She arrived in Rio in March 1964 brimful of ambition, in love with her own wide repertoire of non-bossa songs, and with a spunky personality.

'This gaucho girl is very provincial,' said Tom Jobim. 'She still smells of *churrasco*.' He included her on a record he was making at the time, *Pobre menina rica* (*Poor Rich Girl*), and Elis soon shot to stardom.

She was short, buxom, sassy, expressive, and sang not like an angel but like a street diva – open, sexy, direct, and with a more expansive vocal range and a deeper fund of styles and songs than any woman singer of her time.

Claus Schreiner (usually very dry in his assessments of Brazilian musicians) was bowled over by her: 'Elis Regina brought "show" back to the stage. She never gave a sterile concert. The first time I saw Elis in concert the frenzy and intensity of this woman took my breath away. It lasted 130 minutes, a non-stop programme interrupted only by a short announcement that we should not expect a break if Elis wanted to continue.'

She was also a blast of earthy vulgarity amidst the educated and *cultivé* bossa environs of Rio.

'She was considered,' writes Ruy Castro, 'ignorant, tacky and ugly' – though that at the outset only. Elis navigated Rio's and São Paulo's showbiz waters with an independence of spirit not entirely expected of a woman in so macho an industry. She was nicknamed 'Pimentinha' ('Little Pepper'), and hated it. If anyone used it in front of her, she replied with what Brazilians call a '*banana*' – a V-sign.

Her relations with men were tempestuous, and she amazed everyone when in 1967 she married the musician Ronaldo Boscoli, with whom she'd had a notorious bust-up in 1964. The marriage lasted until 1972, by which time Elis was a legend, as much for her unpredictability and indomitable spirit as for her voice. She should be a continuing part of this story. The reason she is not is because she was found dead of a drug overdose in 1982. She was thirty-seven.

Seven

Saudades *Hit*

There is something about the Piccadilly Line and Rio de Janeiro.

On my first trip there from London in February 1994, with Krim, we very nearly missed the flight. All Tube-users have had such experiences. See how my adventure compares.

Three different announcements from Holborn to Earl's Court gave three different sets of instructions about how to get to Heathrow, because, for no discernible reason, it seemed no Piccadilly Line train was going that far on this particular evening – a Friday – though Announcement Number Two had fleetingly suggested this train *might* get there. I figured: so, OK, perhaps the train will make it. If not, there will be buses and taxis available at Northfields, the station being cited, at Hammersmith, as the one that trains were likely to stop at. In the event, our train dropped us one short, and dumped us at South Ealing.

South Ealing is now etched on my memory like a course of ECT. I hate South Ealing more than any place on earth.

Just the words, when I see them from the Tube, or when I accidentally spot them looking at the line to count my stops, have me shaking.

Having hauled our cases off the train, now at a permanent halt, we awaited some kind and helpful words from London Transport as to how – having been advised to come this far – we should proceed. We might as well have waited for tea with Moses.

The station was shut. *Shut!* At eight p.m! There wasn't an LT person in sight. A man behind a taxi guichet at the station's entrance with little English said there were no taxis, and he certainly wasn't going to ring for one. He couldn't tell us about buses. Nor could anyone else. The one phone outside the entrance was broken.

So: no trains, no buses, no phone-taxis, no phones, and a distinct absence of black cabs in the piddly little road – I mean, it was *nowhere* – which South Ealing station gives on to, and a mere hour and a half till our flight left.

There was a bus stop on the other side of the road, though it was far from clear whether any bus that might happen to trundle by would take us an inch nearer Heathrow. I ran to a petrol station a hundred yards away to see if they could help: they had no idea about the buses, and no cab numbers they were prepared to try, let alone divulge.

I returned empty-handed to Krim and two other passengers who'd joined our quest, certain I knew how murderers feel just before they commit the crime which gives them their name.

After ten minutes, a bus did show up, and we clambered on, concerned only that it would take us *somewhere*. Anywhere that wasn't South Ealing had to be an improvement.

The driver, to his credit, didn't make us pay, and told us we should get out on the Great West Road and take another bus. And that one would get us to the right place to take another one which would take us to Heathrow.

The Great West Road. Another bus, and then another one. An hour and a bit to go. Does an air-traveller's desperation come more undiluted?

At the Great West Road, we trooped across the multi-lane tarmac under a flyover to the bus stop the driver had pointed at. The glass was broken and there was no timetable. In fact, there seemed to be no vehicles *at all* on the Great West Road.

I felt my brain go glassy. Smiling wanly, I looked at Krim, visiting England for just the second time, and thought: Hey, this is giving her *all* the ammo she needs to confirm once and for all that Britain has thrown it all away: Britain's like the former GDR. A fucking basket case.

An Esso garage up the road was the only solution. I ran to it like an ape on heat, and beseeched the man behind the counter to phone for a cab, any cab, black, white, pink. Phone Luton or Brighton if needs be, but please, get us a cab. He wanted a fiver. I demurred. No fiver, no call. I gave him a fiver. He called. Five minutes later, a man was loading cases from the glass-spattered pavement into the boot of his Audi. The garage man gave me back my fiver: honour was restored.

Fifteen quid got the four of us from the shattered bus stop near the Esso garage on the Great West Road to Heathrow in fifteen minutes. The other two politely split the bill with us, and we all swapped change, coins and so on, making sure no one was down.

It's amazing how reasonable and compliant complete strangers can be with each other in circumstances of whirling abnormality. We weren't under fire and hardly facing ultimate catastrophe, but the fact that what we were doing, something so normal and boring – taking the Tube to catch a plane – had become a nerve-crushing struggle every half-second somehow made the episode all the more unpalatable, particularly when the blame was attributable to one source, and one source only: the aforementioned pestilential company that runs that now infamous metropolitan underground railway system . . .

That's not quite the end of the story. On the plane, I linked up with an editor, Jessamy Calkin, who happened to be travelling to São Paulo (our flight's first stop) and, by a strange twist of circumstance, had commissioned me to do a piece for *GQ* on Caetano (hence my visit to Bahia).

How had she fared? Well, *she'd* got to Northfields! And? No buses or taxis, just hundreds of people wondering how in the name of buggery to get to Heathrow.

Jessamy had picked up her case and walked into the middle of the nearby motorway, and literally flagged down a black cab with no light on and commanded the driver to take her to Heathrow.

This is a woman who once road-managed the German rock group Einstürzende Neubauten. She learnt how to shoot handguns in the US for a *GQ* article. On this trip she was to research, for a British national, São Paulo transsexuals' calamities with silicone implants. She called her baby girl, born in early 1996, Alabama Rose. No London cabbie is going to mess with a lady like that.

★　　★　　★

February 1996

The fax arrived two nights before my departure for Brazil:

'Unfortunately, Bahiatursa can't give you any support due to the fact that the hotels in our city are overbooked.'

This helpful message came five weeks after I'd contacted Bahia's happy-happy-land office in Salvador. Their immediate (and only) message back before the above was: '. . . we from Bahiatursa can help oyu [*sic*] depending on your needs. Please, write us. We will be very happy to help you.'

So I did write. I faxed and I faxed, and I assumed the generously advertised 'help' would be forthcoming – particularly as these guys knew me from two years before. The fact that they decided not to help two days before I was due to visit them with a *GQ* commission in my pocket – this time on Salvador's Carnival – sealed the lid on Bahiatursa's competence as far as I was concerned: not quite as bad as London Underground, but they seemed comatose, drunk, illiterate or all three. I never sent them my fax bill.

I was flying to Rio, aiming to visit Salvador for Carnival, then spend a couple of days seeing friends and Chico back in Rio. In fact, I should have realised that Carnival in Bahia was doomed from the start: Bahiatursa's stupidity aside, it was proving impossible in London to organise any kind of transportation north from Rio – even the coach, which takes twenty-eight hours, was booked up weeks in advance. Flights were hopeless.

On the morning before my trip, I cancelled it. I'd made no contingency plans in Rio. Which meant forfeiting a London–Rio ticket, and therefore getting only a small refund. Such was my gloom I nearly wrote to the publisher of this book to say that I was returning the contract, along with the advance, and that would be that.

As morning became afternoon, I pondered my decision, slumped in my armchair. I *did* still have a ticket to Rio, goddamnit. Gloom turned into defiance. This propelled me back to the telephone.

First, Chico; then the writer, Ana Miranda, whom I'd met briefly on my first visit to Rio in November 1993. Messages for both: could they help?

Chico rang back. What was my problem? I explained. He said he'd do what he could. Then Ana: she'd be away for Carnival weekend, but was returning the following week. I could stay with her then, but the weekend – she'd do what she could, too.

Chico rang back an hour later. 'Come!' he said. Meaning something had been fixed. I didn't ask what; this was the answer I was after. Then Ana sent me a fax:

'We have a good place for you, here. A modest house, but where people (many girls) participate in Carnival. I think you'll like very much.'

This arrived at four o'clock on the day before my flight from Heathrow. I thus had just over twenty-four hours in which to undo my cancellation, reorder dollars, pay a few bills, ring my publisher, pack – and refocus on Rio, Rio, Rio . . .

With a flight at nine p.m., I settled on checking in about three hours in advance – being that early, there was always the chance of an upgrade. I'd managed it once before, to Buenos Aires.

At half-five, I was on the Piccadilly Line, Holloway Road to Heathrow, a route I've done dozens of times since moving to north London, and always with the greatest of ease – barring one notable exception.

And here, as so many pop songs have it, we go again.

At King's Cross, the train broke down. All passengers had to get out and wait ten minutes for another train. I thought: Zen, Zen, turn your eyes inwards, imagine you're on a cloud . . .

Now, the next part is not necessarily London Underground's fault. The actions of the IRA in Docklands on Friday 9 February 1996 were disgusting enough. Not to trivialise the negative impact of that bomb, for Underground abusees these actions proved equally disgusting. Or they did for me that Friday night a week later.

At Holborn (again), an announcement: a 'suspect package' had been found at Knightsbridge. No trains were stopping between Green Park and Hammersmith. The train didn't move. I held my breath. The doors shut. We moved on to Covent Garden – OK; Leicester Square – OK; Piccadilly Circus – slight pause, OK; Green Park – and then it came.

No trains were now proceeding from Green Park to Hammersmith. Everyone was asked to get out, and find 'alternative means of transport' (one of London Underground's slipperiest periphrases). I stared straight ahead of me, and started to sweat and shake.

I wasn't physically ill, of course: but the intensity of this development, recalling with the force of the most devastating nightmare the events of two years previously, swept through me like an attack of plague. Every dark

constituent of an appalling year until this moment –
money horrors, professional disasters, romantic misery,
failing friendships – all returned to haunt me at the very
second that announcement was made, at the same time,
in the fiercest detail, pricking brain and bloodstream.
Something, somebody, somewhere, did not want me to
reach Rio de Janeiro.

I summoned up sufficient self-control to remove myself
and my bags from the carriage without hitting someone
or screaming an obscenity. What I really wanted, what
I felt coming on, deep inside, in my very core, was
some pretty spectacular spontaneous combustion. I was
generating enough mental heat for it.

After the one-stop connection to Victoria, there was
barely room to stand on the District/Circle Line platform. The usual rush-hour crowds had doubled. A train
arrived; those who could crammed in, and those who
couldn't, like me, because we weren't near a set of
doors, inched forward, fuming. I was still sweating,
badly, and was tempted to turn to the woman behind
me and apologise if I exploded in her face, but would
she be kind enough to return the pieces to my parents,
at this address . . .

I got on the next train. I even got a seat, at Gloucester
Road. I could barely see, though usually there's nothing
wrong with my eyesight. I remember nodding my head
from side to side, like a madman. I was incredulous at the
inner narrative I found I was rehearsing to myself – which
came out as doggerel – and I was still sweating. 'Two years
ago to the day, Distressed I am to say . . .' If someone had
asked me what was wrong, I'd have collared them and held

their ear with my tale of woe and desolation, just like the Ancient Mariner pinioning the Wedding Guest.

At Hammersmith, which is not far from my brother and sister-in-law's, I nearly threw the towel in. Hell, I thought, who *cares* about Brazil, and why should I care? I'll take a taxi and go and see my little niece and nephew, read them a story, and talk of old times over a few bottles with Andrew and Jane.

A Heathrow train came within five minutes. I got on tentatively, as if I, it, the air around were made of porcelain, ready to shatter at the slightest touch. The carriage was not full. I sat down, quite still: think nothing, *be* nothing, for at least fifteen minutes. By Osterley, I had almost recovered.

At Terminal 4, I arrived three-quarters of an hour after my intended time, and there were no upgrades. The flight was packed. Eventually, I got an aisle seat which, for an overnight trans-Atlantic flight, is where you need to be, for both the leg space and most efficacious access to the drinks trolley.

After check-in, meanwhile, the angst of the previous two hours slowly subsided. I headed for the seafood bar I always treat myself to before flying out of Terminal 4. Never, ever have a half-dozen oysters and two glasses of white wine tasted quite so like heaven.

When Krim and I had arrived in Rio in 1994, we'd been met by a gaggle of the Prestons' friends, Darcy amongst them; their driver Paulo had taken us to João's in Leblon. The morning sky was bright blue, the heat immense. Everything about the city, about the weeks ahead, suggested tropical promise. The open-armed Corcovado seemed to welcome us personally, as it does all first-time visitors. This figure is central to being seduced by the city – if you can see it, which of course I hadn't been able to on my first foggy days in Rio in October 1993. I shall always remember Krim's expression of wonderment as we drove past the *favelas* of the North Zone, the main sight from the airport road, into the hills and high-rises of the South Zone – and then seeing the Corcovado, gleaming and magnificent. It was a stylish arrival.

This time, it was different. The fact that there is a $4.50 bus that takes you into the centre is not overadvertised at Galeão airport. Galeão is a long way from where most tourists go, the South Zone, so taxi drivers make a killing. Ana was going to try and meet me, as her husband Emir was arriving form Cuba at more or less the same time. But, as she'd written in her fax, 'If I lost you in airport, take a taxi': damned if I was – in the past, I'd thrown away far too much money I didn't have on Rio taxis. I resolved to tackle the bus option.

My flight in fact arrived three hours before Ana said she'd be there. The only flight from Havana was the only arrival about which there was no information; the only airline that had its computers up and running was Peruvian Airways, and they knew nothing. There is no seating in Galeão's arrivals hall. No shops and almost no refreshments. Galeão is, I discovered, a terrible place to be for three hours very early in the morning.

I missed Ana, or she missed me – as indeed she did Emir (I later found out), who'd flown in via Caracas and taken a taxi. Ana's plan, I have to say, wasn't shaping up too crisply.

I sat on a bent luggage trolley on the pavement outside the airport, and reflected that this was proving rather the inverse of my two previous Rio arrivals. I began to feel like the errant backpacker I'd been on Europe's trains in the summer of 1980: tired, unwanted, in the hands of the gods.

The $4.50 bus, which should have taken half an hour, took two and a half hours. This was par for the course. Everything was going wrong, so there was no need to expect a normal journey into the city, was there? It was the most grotesque bus ride I've ever had. The vehicle crawled down the coast road at the rate of a metre a minute. The traffic was solid, most of it made up of other buses, all of them full. I wasn't badly off, as mine was at least air-conditioned. The others had people hanging their heads out of small windows like dogs do out of car windows. It had been hot enough since my six-a.m. arrival. Now, at ten, it was frying-time. The scene resembled rush-hour Calcutta. I began to read a battered old Penguin edition of *Sense and Sensibility*.

It was the Friday before Carnival. Rather like that excellent decision taken by the Bahian authorities to dig up the whole of old Salvador at the same time, the Rio police had woken up that morning and thought it'd be a good thing to close off all the streets around the Sambadrome, kindly allowing Carnival floats to be manoeuvred through the city centre unimpeded. This caused total mayhem throughout the North Zone for the entire day.

I arrived in Botafogo at 11.30, five and a half hours after I'd landed. Ana had given mè the address (and phone number, along with two names, Márcia and Mimi) in her fax: rua Assunção, 53. I piled off the bus with my two heavyish cases and a camera, and practically fell over with exhaustion and heat.

The walk to rua Assunção, a small street running at the bottom of Cosme Velho, the Corcovado's hill, was infernal. Without cases, it'd have been baking; with, it was like walking through fire. I also felt exposed: this was one gringo just asking to be robbed.

First, I found a 53, but in the wrong street. Then, when I arrived in Assunção, the sweat pouring, there was (of *course*) no 53: a 59, a small, modest house behind a grille and shrubbery, and next to it a number 54, a swish, studio-like building made of modern red brick. From 54 it jumped to 45. I put my cases down, and felt like weeping.

There was nothing for it but to force my way into the studio. Mopping my face with the third handkerchief of the morning, I showed Ana's fax to a handsome woman in a yellow dress going through the gate, and begged use of the phone. My brief encounter with this emblem of style and sophistication was a study in incongruity: businesslike, cool *carioca* being approached by lost, jet-lagged Englishman in the wrong clothes, in front of the wrong building, and speaking the wrong language (I addressed her in my Portospanish) – was my Rio 96 going to continue like this?

The handsome lady was obliging, and led me into reception.

Air-conditioning! I could breathe again. To my astonishment, a thin and nervy girl behind the desk also seemed to know who I was. She had no English, and the Portospanish had been sweated out of me for the moment. So I smiled, and said, 'Márcia?' She smiled back, and told me to come with her through a door.

Márcia was sitting in front of a computer. She was black-haired, with ebony skin. She had great wide eyes, generous pink lips, almost too generous for the delicacy of her features, and long arms. She was wearing a thin cotton dress, and was completely flat-chested.

This angelic vision of tropical richness was almost over-powering; what I needed in my bedraggled if overheated state was an ice-cold shower, not a mulatto nymph.

Márcia spoke no English, but smiled broadly (stunning white teeth) and indicated that I should follow her. I shouldered my bags, while she took the camera. We left the studio, and I thought, Oh oh, here we go again, another hike through the inferno. We got as far as the small house behind the grille next door, number 59, and Márcia took a chain off the gate, which had a padlock on the end of it but did not actually lock the gate. Through a gap the gate allowed, we squeezed into the little garden, and then climbed a short flight of steps. From behind a black wooden front door appeared a lady in her dressing gown. I presumed she was the maid of the house.

She and Márcia struck up animated conversation, in which I heard the name 'Ana' mentioned several times, and I was shown to a small room with a mattress, a chest and a tiny chair. I put down my bags, and realised I was still sweating uncontrollably. Time for a soaking. The bathroom. Cold water. Quick. With a small towel in my hand, I went into the hall and bumped into a young black man who'd materialised from nowhere; he had magnificent dreadlocks, features not unlike Gilberto Gil's, and was wearing baggy striped trousers.

'Hello. I'm James.'

'*Bem-vindo ao Brasil*,' he sang. His name was Renavil. How did he fit into this house? It didn't matter. He took one look at me and realised I was in need of water. I followed him to the kitchen, just beyond a living room where a small boy was watching television. I said hello to him, uselessly, in English. The boy kept his eyes on the screen. Renavil poured me a glass of water from a jug taken from a huge 1950s fridge. I drank it in a second. He poured me another glass.

'*Obrigado*,' I breathed. Portuguese really shaping up. '*Banho?*' I tried next, which actually means 'bath'. He showed me a door between the kitchen and living room. I went in. There was a loo, a shower and a basin – and no lock on the door. The basin had one tap, out of which came one variety of water: tepid. I threw handfuls over my head, and very slowly began to cool down. I decided not to re-emerge until I had stopped sweating.

Five minutes later, Ana came on the phone. The maid gave me the receiver, and Ana said hello. She speaks English slowly, with a slight North American twang. I apologised profusely for missing her at the airport – from where she was now calling; she explained that she had also missed Emir, that the traffic was hell, and that it was just one of those days. She said she'd be over later that evening. And by the way, the lady who'd given me the phone was called Zuila. Ana asked to speak to her again. Though I could understand little of what she said, Zuila seemed to be on intimately conversational terms with Ana.

That Zuila was not the maid became clear when the real maid, Maria, from Bahia, emerged into the kitchen from a garden I'd spotted at the back. She was a huge mulatto woman, with treetrunk-like arms and legs, and a torso that consisted of folds of flesh undulating under a thin cotton dress, and enormous hips. She had thick grey hair, with a comb hanging out of it not doing anything noticeably useful, and thin, smiling eyes. She laughed a lot, and couldn't stop talking when I said I'd been to Bahia two years before. She looked both very kind and a bit of a walking disaster.

I had to lie down, so I made my excuses. In the room, I checked the cupboard for possible hanging space, and saw row upon row of female shoes. There were also some glittery jackets and silks and shawls, all of which had an antiquated look to them. Some kind of dressing room. I kept my clothes in the cases.

I stretched out on the mattress, and it was very hard. The pillow was a flat cushion. I put my towel and a pair of trousers under it, as I always need to have my head well elevated to sleep. Within minutes, Renavil put his head round the door and proffered an electric fan.

'*Sim, sim, por favor, muito obrigado,*' I wittered ('Yes, yes, please, thank you'). He plugged it in, it whirred, he smiled, and repeated, '*Bem-vindo ao Brasil,*' and vanished. I closed my eyes, tried to clear my head, and noticed how loud the television was. Where was I? Ana really had some explaining to do, as I seemed to be lodging in a doss-house.

The whirring fan was soothing. I dozed, picturing soft, downy pillows and a fall of Scottish water to jump under. I recalled the patios of dripping green plants at

João's flat from two years before (sadly, he was out of town). I thought of upgrades and chauffeurs. Oysters and champagne. I may have slept for ten minutes. I woke when a mosquito bit me on the cheek.

I rubbed the spot, and lay still for a further five minutes. It was 2.30. The TV was on. I *was* in Rio; it was, perhaps, time to bestir myself and celebrate.

I thought I'd start with a shave. This is never pleasant in tepid water, but as I am an inveterate leaver-of-battery-operated-razors-in-hotel-rooms I had no choice. After I'd finished, I noticed a large red weal in the middle of my left cheek where the mosquito had bitten me. Bloody marvellous.

Changed into shorts and T-shirt, I chatted briefly with Zuila – she told me the small boy from earlier was her grandson, so the plot was thickening – and then headed for the Garota de Urca, a restaurant under the Prestons' flat not far from the Pão de Açúcar where we'd had quite a few meals together in 1994. It was effectively their second home in Rio. I had a feeling I might find them there, as they were back for this year's Carnival.

I met Márcia outside the house and asked her how long it would take to walk to Urca. She looked at me as if I were barking mad. No one really walks anywhere in Rio, certainly not in this heat. It was a lesson I still had to learn. She told me to take a taxi, and helped me find one.

The taxi took eight minutes. Once there, I ordered a *caipirinha*, then another, with some *bacalhau* balls. I looked out over the modest bay, where people swim in not oversalubrious conditions. Sails shimmered on the white-hot water. To the left was Rio's pretty yacht club.

Beyond in the haze was the high-rise jungle of the Centro. For a moment everything stood still; casting aside the stress of the previous forty-eight hours, I let the memories flood back. Meals in the Garota. The Carmen Miranda parade. Chico in Gávea. The Canecão. Rehearsal at Mangueira. Carnival night. Krim. The tropical city by the sea: I was back, two years to the day . . . Had I changed?

I hadn't been at the Garota a quarter of an hour before Rachel and Roger pulled up in a car, and I snapped out of my reverie. They strode over to my table looking horribly well. We marvelled over the happy chance of bumping into each other like this and set about a loud if brief reunion. It was good to see them. This time, however, from the perspective of my shabby Botafogo lodgings, I felt them to be from a different world.

On my third *caipirinha* I told them about the fiasco with Bahiatursa, though spared them the new Tube story. I also said I was hoping to spend some time with Chico the following week. They told me about a New Year concert in honour of Tom Jobim given by Chico, Caetano, Gil and another Bahian, Paulinho da Viola, on Copacabana beach. The three major stars had apparently each been paid $100,000 to appear for fifteen minutes, da Viola just $35,000 for the same – and the 'scandal' had been raging in the press ever since.

A true black *sambista* such as da Viola would inevitably be discriminated against, ran his complaint. Er, Gil is black, and Chico a bit of a *sambista* himself, came the answer. Caetano alone had taken it upon himself to reply with a withering article about da Viola's attacks on him and the other two. Caetano is good at that sort of thing.

Chico, meanwhile, hadn't been receiving quite the same ecstatic praise for his new novel *Benjamim* as he had for *Estorvo*, objections including that it was all well and good for a superstar like him to get into print, but what about ordinary mortals? It was not a clever line to take, as it missed the point that Chico wrote and expected to be judged *as* a writer, of fiction, and not as a writer who also happened to be the 'A banda' boy. Envy again: the press in Brazil is evidently just as inept at making intelligent distinctions as the press anywhere else.

The Prestons had a predictably wild schedule ahead, though they were at least giving the Caprichosos a miss this year. We parted with promises to meet after Carnival, and I took a bus back to Botafogo. I spent the rest of the day drinking, first at a bar near Zuila's called Manolo's, then in the studio, which I now found out was a film-producing co-operative; a computer whizzkid there had an endless supply of bottled Brahma beer. As I worked on my laptop (I'm not sure it was 'work' – more looking up phone numbers, making the odd call and fiddling), I guzzled bottle after bottle.

I don't quite know what had got into me. Urgent relief at having landed after so many silly obstacles, certainly; thirst was no small part of it; a way of ensuring oblivion for the simple purpose of sleep, regular, calm doses of which, for reasons that lie outside this story, had for eighteen months become elusive. If I were to survive Rio for a week, and in this heat, I was going to need sleep above all. That afternoon's indulgence was a kind of necessary Mogadon.

There is also an expression in Portuguese: *matar saudades*

– to kill *saudades*. Over and above everything, I had a chronic case of them, as my daydream in Urca had suggested, though at the time I didn't know how chronic. One thing you should never do if you need to kill *saudades* is drink; it makes them worse.

In fact, you can never really kill *saudades*, any more than you can kill the blues, which is a pretty similar condition to *saudades*. Once they've struck, you'll live with them until you die. All you can do is ameliorate the pain, sometimes forgetting it by embracing new pleasures, sometimes facing it and trying to give it expressive shape. I'm sure one reason I was back in Rio was to see if I couldn't find new means and material to deal with my acute gringo *saudades*. It was a search in vain, as are all such searches to breach rifts in the soul.

I managed to sleep off the worst of the alcohol on my hard mattress. I awoke after three hours (that itching, inflamed mosquito bite on my cheek now feeling like a small hill) to a new voice from the living room. It was Ana's.

Ana is a beautiful woman. The photo on the back of the British edition of *The Bay of All Saints and Every Conceivable Sin*, her 1989 novel, makes her look like Bianca Jagger in a Calvin Klein studio. She later told me she thought the portrait ridiculous, as she doesn't look like that. I remembered her, from our brief meeting on the last night of my 1993 weekend in Rio, as a dark-skinned woman with long black hair, piercing dark eyes, and a cold.

She is beautiful in a simple way: unadorned, calm, composed. Dressed in a light, sleeveless dress, this was how she looked to me when I entered Zuila's living room. She embraced me, and said, 'Welcome.' She gestured towards Zuila, as if to ask whether we'd met properly, and I said of course. Then she dropped her bombshell: Zuila was her mother.

Ana smiled when she saw my amazement. I couldn't believe it, could not associate her grace with this Botafogo griminess. There was no resemblance between them apparent to my blinking eyes. Zuila smiled too, enjoying the joke.

Ana said this was a special house; it had been like this for years, and Zuila always kept it full of people, half-adopting some of them. People like Renavil came and went as they pleased. There was always a party in the offing. There'd be one the next day.

Márcia had been fully adopted over twenty years before, and the little boy was hers, which is why Zuila called him her grandson. Márcia's husband, no longer with her, was Israeli.

Ana didn't stay long. She'd come to say hello and make a proper introduction to her mother. She'd pick me up on Monday. We all went outside the house, and I was introduced to Dona Irene, a small, sparkling, grey-haired mulatta who worked for Ana in Leblon. Dona Irene was very excited at the prospect of the São Clemente samba school (junior league) processing through Botafogo the next night. She gave me a yellow São Clemente cap, and clapped her hands, and did a little dance. Ana had obviously brought her back from Leblon for the weekend. Ana then hugged me, climbed into her car and left.

It was still very hot. Courting recklessness, I wanted to carry on drinking. Zuila walked with me to Manolo's, and left me there. The drain on the terrace was oozing, and the smell was putrid: a mixture of ammonia, faeces and rotting wood. A puddle of metallic-grey sludge had settled under one of the tables, a fair distance from mine. I stayed put and had two beers, staring blearily into space.

Márcia appeared at 11.30, and summoned me away. We walked a few blocks, and back in Portospanish I was able to explain that I'd gone out with Mangueira two years before. I asked her whether she'd be going out for Carnival this year. She said she didn't know – maybe, maybe not, depending on her mood. I wondered who was looking after her son.

That was of limited importance. Márcia wanted to see some friends and hear some samba. We rounded a corner and came upon a heap of people. They were shivering round a café terrace like a shoal of fish working on a loaf of bread. A famous singer called Beth Carvalho was at the microphone: from the terrace she was conducting a pre-Carnival street party. I was, at last, in the mood.

We bought beers, and met Márcia's friends, Mossi and Fátima. Mossi was a short, good-looking, baldish *carioca* who'd spent years in Paris – in films – and spoke excellent English. He lived in Copacabana and was still 'in films'. Fátima was a big girl, and much younger than Mossi. He told me he'd been married four times.

Beth Carvalho was belting out the tunes, and then came a familiar refrain: the Mangueira samba from 1994. Everyone knew the words. Arms went up, and the crowd seemed visibly to tread air with 'Aplausos ao cancioneiro' . . . It was good to hear it. It was good to be back. Then the beer ran out.

Márcia said it was impossible to enjoy samba without

beer. I figured it was impossible to do anything in this heat without something cold in your hand. So we all wandered back to Manolo's. It was shut. The drain had now completely bust its gut and the terrace was awash with grey gunge. A police car parked next to the restaurant was clearly there to ensure that the place stayed shut.

A little bar opposite was still open, so more beers in plastic cups were bought. We idled in the street for half an hour. Eventually, Márcia, Mossi and Fátima, and the receptionist at the studio, twitchy and talkative, decided to go and find some more samba. That was my cue for bed. It was 1.45. I felt as if I'd been back for a week.

I awoke at three. I had nothing covering me; it was too hot. Something was crawling up my legs, slowly. It didn't hurt, simply tickled. All over. Mosquitoes. A whole pack of them. I was being eaten: piranha mosquitoes. As soon as I stopped scratching, the eating began again. They kept me awake for an hour. When I awoke, drenched, the next morning at eight, my legs and arms – and forehead, for heaven's sake – were smothered in bites. This was going to be a rough weekend.

It was Zuila's birthday. I didn't dare ask her age but guessed she was around sixty, maximum. We had a peaceful breakfast of fruits and strong coffee made by Maria, and my Portospanish was in good shape, even if my skin wasn't. Zuila had absolutely no English except 'five o'clock tea', but we got along fine. Then she went shopping for the party.

I fiddled once again on my laptop, rather to the aston-ishment of Maria, who thought I had my own tiny portable

TV set. At lunchtime, I decided to go for a walk and discover Rio's metro.

I suppose there is an anoracky side to every traveller. Mine concerns metros – and quite enough has been said about London's for the time being. But in general across the world, a metro system for a newcomer to a city (as I still felt myself to be in Rio) is one way of putting it on to the inner map, for orientation and assessing – if only in embryo – how the place works. A metro is the skeleton on which the flesh of a city hangs.

Le Métro in Paris is naturally the front runner, with its whooshing, speed, smells and names: Réaumur-Sébastopol, Marcadet-Poissonniers, Porte de Clignancourt, Miromesnil, Maubert-Mutualité, Lamarck-Caulaincourt, Sèvres-Babylone. One's mental topography of Paris rattles with this Babel of exotic words which make Le Métro far more exciting than it actually is. And the Paris most of us know rarely lives up to the promise of those titles we unavoidably stare at above the carriage doors . . .

On the other side of Europe, I remember my surprise at the gleaming efficiency of the metros in Prague and Budapest when I visited them in 1980: a clean metro and communism had seemed incompatible, I'm not sure why. Berlin's U-Bahn had been (still is) a delight to ride on, though of course in 1980, when I was there just before a hike through the Iron Curtain, the termini for the free were artificially positioned.

In the 1980s in Spain, it was a race between Madrid and Barcelona as to which metro would get air-conditioned trains first: Barcelona won, with years in hand. The 1992 Olympics were an inducement, and the Catalans are proud to be efficient and anything Castilians aren't: swift in business, 'European' in outlook and speakers of Catalan. Barcelona's is a great metro. In Madrid, they're still struggling to get their opera house open, closed since Franco's time.

In Washington DC's subway, it's *Star Trek* time. Never have I been more impressed in an underground than when lights buried in the platform below your feet start to flash with the imminent arrival of one of those luxurious trains. Back across the Atlantic, meanwhile, in Glasgow, you have to double over in order to enter its curious, bullet-shaped little carriages which seem to have been borrowed from a fairground.

In Rio, it's all back to front. The South Zone, the smart side of the city, has no underground system. It starts in Botafogo and, on a line which bifurcates two stops beyond the Centro's main railway station, Dom Pedro II, leads west and north-west into the unknown – the danger zone. You might therefore expect the metro to match the poverty and dilapidation it tunnels through. Not a bit of it. Rio's metro is one of the glories of Brazil.

I thought I'd go for a short stride, to Flamengo station. I'd never seen the central belt of the city close up, and felt I needed my eyes opening after the comforts of the South Zone.

There wasn't, all said, much to see: Botafogo beach to my right, palm trees, a loud road, the Pão across the bay; to my left, apartment blocks, some heavy-façaded mansions, more palm trees, more roadway. There were few pedestrians. The heat was overpowering. On my map of Rio ('Guia Schaeffer Rio de Janeiro, 24° Edição, 1993'), Flamengo station looked like a ten-minute walk, only a little further from rua Assunção than Botafogo station to the south, which is the beginning of the line.

My map was atrociously deceptive. Because of the shape and size of Rio, it's a problem to fit the city on to one sheet; but Schaeffer ingeniously solves it, at a scale of 1:27,000. Thus distances which are pretty immense look diminutive on paper. My stroll to the metro took forty minutes. I got lost twice. On both occasions, asking the way, I was told to 'be careful – Rio's dangerous'. That old saw.

I arrived at Flamengo metro in a state of unprecedented exhaustion. I could hardly stand. I undid the buttons of my drenched T-shirt, and let it hang casually off my back. (On Rio's buses, men often travel without shirts. I had once.) Inside the cavernous station, the entry system resembled Paris's: a ticket swallowed and then regurgitated by a metal unit allows you through a turnstile. Everywhere, it was clean, spacious – too spacious: why such a vaulting scale for a mere metro?—and uncrowded (it was Saturday), but hot.

As I descended the first flight of stairs, I heard a whistle behind me. I turned. A vaguely uniformed man indicated my shirt: do it up? I thought disbelievingly. That's exactly what he was after. So I did it up. This was a Rio I hadn't come across.

The platform was very long, and again clean. The silver-grey train that rumbled in looked like an inter-state express. The doors swished open. Inside, the ochre upholstery was spotless, as were the floors: not a trace of graffiti anywhere in the carriage. Best of all, it was cold – fridge-cold, ice-cream-cold, spine-tinglingly cold. After a couple of stops, the train zinging along with few bumps and meeting fewer bends, my T-shirt and my hair were almost dry.

Rio's metro was built in 1979. It remains a monument of fascist grandeur, with the structures of efficiency and cleanliness that can come with totalitarian enterprise still in place. The company which runs it today is private, and it is this, everyone told me later, that makes the metro safe, hygienic, comfortable and quite unlike any other public service in Rio. Closed-circuit cameras and privately employed security staff render crime almost non-existent; it's not a big network, so it's easy to maintain and run at a sensible profit – with more than enough room for investment in state-of-the-art technology: in other words, something of a South American miracle. And because of the desperate urban conditions all around – or above – it, the pleasure of using it is vastly heightened (which is typical of Rio, with its luxurious condominiums fenced off like castles from the bellicose streets below).

I spent a desultory couple of hours wondering around the Centro, getting hotter again. In the praça Floriano, on the edge of Lapa, a holiday atmosphere prevailed. Under café awnings, there wasn't an empty table: whole families squashed round plates of shrimp and bread-fried chicken and pork, drinking beer. There were loudspeakers all over the place. A market straggled across the square underneath the striking façades surrounding it on three sides: a Museum of Fine Arts, National Library and Municipal Theatre (modelled on the Paris Opéra). On weekdays, this area of Rio is thick with traffic and busy *cariocas* in suits; on normal weekends, deserted. Carnival weekend is abnormal, so imagine the City of London on a Saturday crammed to bursting with blacks dancing samba, beggars of all ages and pungent food stalls, and you have an idea of what Rio's Centro was like on this outrageously humid February afternoon.

On a similar afternoon two years before, I'd come to the praça Floriano with Krim. Our Carnival was over, as were the processions in the Sambadrome, so we thought we'd taste a bit of the street.

It was a curious sight. Swarming over the avenida Rio Branco, a long boulevard of skyscrapers and banks and glass-fronted offices, were Carnival devils, Carnival dancers, children guzzling ice-cream, men with drums hanging around their waists, women in feathers, and one fancy-dress merchant wandering around in a kind of excremental fantasy, including loo, loo paper, chain, his clothes covered in dollops of (imitation) Carnival shit. Hard to know exactly what his message was.

Towards evening a few processions began to parade – nothing major, but there was plenty of noise, singing and sweaty enthusiasm. It was tame compared to what we'd seen and heard over the previous two nights, and not easy to reconcile this little human riot with the forbidding architectural order all around. The Centro was once the site of Carnival proper; now, with the enormous controlling and commercial presence of the Sambadrome, this area was left for the tail-enders. Krim quite liked it.

'Thank goodness for a bit of street carnival,' she said. 'I'm missing it.'

Two years on, I was missing her. I felt in need of a companion for the travails ahead. Without one, my *saudades* were going to deepen. They were already deep enough. In the praça Floriano that afternoon, I seemed to have walked into the empty side of a mirror. I was forlorn. Half of me was lost back in Mangueira, February 1994. February 1996 felt like borrowed time. My *saudades* were an agent of ageing and loss. How was I going to re-find that Carnival spirit? Did I want to find it?

In the cold air of the metro back to Botafogo, I closed my eyes and tried to elevate reason over *saudades*: you can't be greedy. You can only have one great Carnival in a lifetime.

I knew something was wrong when the *caipirinhas* came out. I didn't want one.

Zuila's party had been going since mid-afternoon. Various friends had been filling her small living room since tea time – or red-wine time, as it turned out to be (at four p.m.), from a bottle brought by one of these friends. That was a mistake. In this heat, and feeling flattened after my trip to the Centro, to start an evening's boozing on red wine . . . Something had taken possession of me. I seemed to *want* to trash myself.

The friend who'd brought the wine was called Toni. He was by origin a Catalan, in his fifties, with a goatee beard, and very stylish cotton clothes, particularly his trousers, which were Arab-baggy. Like Mossi, he was in films. He lived with his wife Paula in Santa Teresa, and Paula, like most of the women now gathering in Zuila's living room, was very beautiful (so was this what Ana meant by 'many girls'?). Paula, with short hair and green eyes, perfect breasts and big hips, was Toni's third wife. How many wives, I wondered, does a man have to have in Brazil before he's happy?

Toni's neighbour in Santa Teresa used to be Ronnie Biggs. I was curiously depressed at the appearance of his name. This wasn't a Rio I particularly wanted to hear about – the Rio of sad old gringo ex-pats keeping their ends up on cheap rum and easy mulattas half their age, and havin' a pah'y. Toni said that Ronnie had had a wonderful swimming pool and thrown a lot of parties; Ronnie was a nice guy. I didn't doubt it.

Apropos nothing, I asked Toni about the sixty per cent illiteracy rate in Brazil. Wasn't that the country's biggest problem?

Toni's answer was fascinating:

'Why should it be? In much of the Amazon, for example, there's one person for every four square kilometres. In that situation, there's a particular kind of knowledge belonging to that person which is worth far more than literacy.'

This remains the wisest *aperçu* I ever heard anyone in Brazil proffer about the country.

Mossi arrived with Fátima. He had a mobile phone strapped to his waist like a gun. He was as ebullient as the night before, and as Toni and I were talking about Brazil he wanted to know what I thought of 'our President Cardoso'. I said I knew nothing about him, so asked Mossi to tell me what he thought.

'He's a good man,' he said, 'who will try and reconcile Brazil to itself. Brazil needs a unifier, not a ruler.'

Mossi and Toni then fell into a violent discussion about the state of Brazilian cinema.

It hadn't escaped my notice that amongst the women coming and going through the living room to the kitchen, one was wearing almost nothing. Márcia. She was decent, with a small, loose white top, but heavens above, a woman couldn't get more explicit about her female centre than Márcia had now managed: remember hot pants? Márcia was sporting a pair of white shorts so tight and curve-enhancing that they were, quite frankly, more concupiscent than if she were wearing nothing at all.

Márcia has a very taut physique, a blistering pair of legs and every reason to be proud of her body; but even nakedness compared with this garment would have seemed a bit tame. From bare belly-button to covered but uncensored mons veneris and buttocks of a shape for which English is not equipped, Márcia's display was a far, far greater Brazilian glory than Rio's metro (about which I had anorackily rhapsodised to Toni). I drank a lot of red wine as she ambled to and fro, eyeing her surreptitiously – more riveted than attracted. I wanted to know how she got away with it. Sad old gringos . . .

By nine, Zuila's house was full and spilling out into the garden. A chubby mulatto man was attending to a barbecue, carefully basting steaks, sausages, chops – serious *churrasco*. The man, whom everyone was calling José, wore shorts and flipflops and no shirt, and passed the meat around on plates. He looked forty plus. I was talking idly to Mossi, but was actually feeling ill. The food wasn't helping. I was introduced to a white-haired, somewhat raddled-looking fellow in his sixties: Ana's former husband. Later, Emir told me he lived in Niterói, across that enormous bridge, married to a much younger black woman. I could do no more than say hello. A wave of nausea swept through me. Renavil then brought out *caipirinhas* in globe-shaped glasses. I'd had enough, and headed for my mattress.

And thus, from ten p.m. on, I missed the core of Zuila's birthday party. I heard them all sing 'Happy Birthday' about an hour later, an event I had no strength to join in. The TV roared, children screeched up and down the corridor, and I lay sleeplessly with the fan whirring. I was completely de-energised, comatose with exhaustion. It served me right. *Saudades*-killing activities over the last twenty-four hours had managed only to insult my body and do nothing about the *saudades*. It felt like flu, fever and a hangover rolled into one. I was in appalling shape and had no one to feel sorry for me.

I got up to visit the bathroom, and was astonished to see Zuila hugging and kissing José in what was clearly more than a maternal fashion. Perhaps I was dreaming. Who was he? Who was Zuila? Who were all these people? What was I doing here? Why couldn't I sleep and why was I feeling so ill?

Carnival Saturday, Rio de Janeiro, 1996: I was as low as I'd been in a year.

Zuila was born in Cajazeiras, a small town in the north-eastern state of Paraíba, into a very poor family. She was the oldest of thirteen children.

Her father was an artisan who made leather bags at the outset of his career and who ended up as an engineer, building roads and bridges. He also had a taste for cards and darts. His fortunes fluctuated, and the family found itself constantly on the move from small town to small town. Zuila grew up closely involved in rearing her numerous siblings, and received minimal schooling.

One day in 1938, she met a rich man, also an engineer,

called Raul Miranda, from the rural sugar-cane aristocracy of Paraíba. He'd studied agriculture at university and was now engaged in irrigation-system building. Raul decided to marry Zuila, aged nineteen, but insisted she went to a Belgian school in Natal, in the state of Rio Grande do Norte, to improve both her literacy and her domestic skills – sewing and the like. He, meanwhile, went to Fortaleza, capital of the state of Ceará, also in the north-east, to establish a railway-building firm. Though wealthy because of his family, he started this from nothing.

In honour of Zuila, who was very beautiful, Raul built a house near Lima Campos in the interior, surrounded by fruit trees. Zuila was very spoilt, had all the clothes she wanted, and women attending her every need. It was a dramatic change from her itinerant and humble beginnings. She was gregarious, and loved having people around her, especially children. Droughts drove people off the land during the dry seasons, and many died; Zuila took in orphaned children when she could. For some reason, she was unable to have any of her own until the age of thirty.

In 1946, Zuila and Raul moved properly to Fortaleza. There, she led a hectic and glamorous life, and was on every party list. She wore split skirts and sparkling jewels. She owned an Oldsmobile 88, and zoomed from club to club on Iracema beach, Fortaleza's Copacabana.

Then disaster struck. The army nationalised Raul's firm, and he was ruined; he could keep his own opulent properties, as Brazilian law stipulated that a dissolved business could hold on to its private assets. Nobly, he sold the Fortaleza house where he and Zuila, and their two small daughters, Marlui and Ana, had lived in luxury, as well as the country house – Zuila's – in order to pay what he owed his employees.

He found new work under Israel Pinheiro, an engineer contracted by President Juscelino Kubitschek to build Brasília; indeed, Raul had already got to know the president quite well. Zuila, Marlui and Ana went to Rio de Janeiro, as there was nowhere to live in Brasília yet. From 1956–9, they lived in a modest apartment in Ipanema until the first houses were ready in Brasília. Neither Zuila nor Raul, it seems, functioned properly without the other. After his family joined him there, Raul lived and worked happily and in great comfort in the new capital for the rest of his life.

Zuila's lifestyle now altered dramatically. Instead of parties, cars and clubs, and beautiful clothes, it was the house and children (including Márcia, adopted in Brasília). Good mother though she was, Zuila stagnated – three or four maids did everything around the house, paid the bills and did all the shopping. Zuila barely had to get out of bed. This went on for ten years.

In 1969, Raul died. Ana had already left the family fold; Marlui stayed on with Zuila for a couple of years, then left too. Zuila saw no point in remaining, alone, in a well-appointed Brasília house, so she sold it – very badly. A dishonest buyer led to the deal going horribly wrong, including the loss of Raul's pension. Zuila ended up pawning her jewels to survive, and never got them back. She relied on friends and family to give her a roof over her head. She came to Rio with Márcia, and tried to live with Ana – in a house next to the one Zuila lives in today.

Ana was just starting out on her own life, and here was

her mother behaving as if she were *her* daughter; Zuila wasn't altogether balanced at this time, and didn't respect Ana's independence. The situation became intolerable. Ana had to do something. So she put Zuila in touch with a nun who sold beautiful things, clothes and furniture mainly, to rich *cariocas* for charity. Zuila had a talent for artisanship. Eventually, she moved into the house next door, Ana helping with the rent. And there, in rua Assunção, Zuila began a bazaar.

After two or three years she became very successful. TV producers and film-makers wanted her work. She built up a huge network of friends. People stayed over at the house, there were always parties, and she continued to 'adopt' people. Zuila was back in business.

Then, in 1990, she suddenly grew tired of it all, and threw in her lot with a young mulatto: José. José is absolutely in love with her. He's a hotel manager, and knows all about catering and cooking. Whenever there's a party at Zuila's, José provides the best food. He also helps her keep the house in order. He is, as I'd guessed, hitting fifty.

And then Zuila got cancer of the sphincter. It was malignant, and she underwent chemotherapy. She's quite unafraid of death, and often talks about it. She remarks that her own mother lived till the age of ninety-two.

So how many years were Zuila's friends celebrating when they sang her 'Happy Birthday' that Saturday night? She always said (so she told Ana) she wasn't sure. The year of her birth she'd now recently confirmed as 1918 (though her ID had long read '1925'). That made her seventy-eight. This was even more surprising than finding out that she was

Ana's mother, to say nothing of having a boyfriend thirty years her junior. Time has been extraordinarily generous to Zuila.

In the middle of 1996, her cancer was cured.

After a dismal night's sleep, I thought I'd cheer myself up and see if I couldn't find Sérgio, self-appointed protector of Jenny and Suzy in November 1993, in the hippie market in Ipanema.

The day was a humid, dreary grey. Half an hour's careful probing of the ersatz market stalls yielded no Sérgio. So I had an orange juice at the Garota de Ipanema, the bar where in 1962 Tom Jobim and Vinícius de Moraes had watched the fifteen-year-old Heloísa Pinto walk by, and were inspired to write the most famous bossa nova of all: 'Garota de Ipanema', 'The Girl from Ipanema'. Then the bar was called, curiously enough, the Veloso. Today, it sells 'Girl from Ipanema' T-shirts, and is full of Americans and Japanese. The Japanese I sat next to were baffled by the *cardápio*; the Americans nearby were loud and overenthusiastic.

Out on the street, the leisurely pace of Ipanema's bare stomachs and well-groomed flesh was in marked contrast to the selfish menace of the traffic. Bodies, fumes, noise, grey sky, sweltering heat: what an exhausting place Rio is, the least gentle city on earth. If you want to know it, you have to pay – with sweat, skin, sickness and bodily abuse. And where does that leave you?

In a jaded frame of mind, I had lunch back in Botafogo, at Manolo's. I wrote during the afternoon, at the back of the garden, and then watched some football. Finally,

Márcia suggested going to see the banda in Ipanema, and I thought, Well, yes, that has to be better than mosquitoes and a gaggle of Zuila's noisy women friends for the rest of the day.

Márcia was still in those shorts. She introduced me to Mimi, a history teacher who spoke Spanish and French, and not bad English. Mimi (the other girl Ana had mentioned by name in her fax) was quite large, very friendly and wanted to talk a lot, to find out about me. I wasn't into talking that day.

Márcia and Mimi insisted on sitting in the very back of the bus, where our bodies were shaken like soup in tins: more abuse and a darkening of my already dark mood. Once in Ipanema, where the banda began to parade at about 6.30, the sky turned black. It started to rain.

With beer cans in hand, the girls did a little dance-shuffle down the pavement parallel to the beach, and asked me why I didn't want to samba. I said I sort of had to be in the right mood ... Was I sure I didn't want a beer? they asked. Absolutely sure. The thud of the parade's music came closer. The crowds lining the beach road were thickening. Warm rain was falling fast. I positioned myself at the edge of the pavement, and watched the parade clamour forward. Márcia and Mimi stood behind me.

Simpatia Coisa de Amor is one of Ipanema's samba groups – very junior league. It always parades on Carnival Sunday. The first thing I noticed was a banner reading '*Entre o Gil y o Paulinho, eu ficou só uma grana*': 'Between Gil and Paulinho, I can see only dosh' – barbed commentary on the spat between the musicians in the New Year.

(Carnival is as much about speaking your mind as showing off your body.)

The parade was made up of Ipanema locals. Almost everyone clutched a can of Brahma beer. Some were very drunk. There was a lot of sweat, and a lot of leering. Simpatia Coisa de Amor seemed to be an excuse for a beery old jive. There was nothing startling in the costume department. A couple of guys dressed in skirts and wearing police helmets emerged from the ruckus, and pretended to patrol errant crowd members. A drag-queen in blue and white feathers danced elegantly around on roller-skates. The rain eased off a bit. The banda was a great success.

I was now wet and not enjoying myself. Mimi stood close behind me as the dancers moved on down towards Leblon.

'This is all about *alegria*,' she said matter-of-factly. Yes, I knew that; I smiled feebly at her. In fact, I thought the whole thing rather stupid. If anything, it was about the end of consciousness. There was Dois Irmãos winking in the damp twilight, there were the beach, the ocean, the humps of island silhouetted like whales, there were the insensitive façades of the overbuilt seafront, and I felt like nothing more than a lump of superfluous gringo.

Here passing before me was *alegria*: a procession of human nonsense revelling in its bouncing, frothy, sub-tropical silliness. I just didn't belong here. As my fly-by-night visit to Rio was proving to be, it all seemed utterly pointless.

Once I'd decided it was pointless, I perked up a little. We bumped into Mossi and Fátima. Mossi hailed me – a voice of normality: 'Hey, Jimmy!' He was shirtless, and wearing shorts. I apologised for disappearing so abruptly the night before; I hadn't felt at all well. He told me to think nothing of it.

'Did you enjoy the banda?' he asked.

'Not much,' I replied.

'Hey, Jimmy, cheer up! You're a friend of Chico Buarque's!'

Mossi then nodded his head towards Mimi and Márcia a few yards away. They were standing next to a parasol-covered stall, chatting to the young woman in charge. In front of her was what looked like a wooden handle, about eight inches high. I looked more intently at this device, and realised it was covered in tight rubber: a condom.

Smiling broadly, Márcia took a handful of square packages, and stuffed them into a little pouch slung round her waist. The stall was run by a Brazilian anti-AIDS organisation, and was dolling out free *preservativos*, as rubbers are known in the Iberian languages. Portuguese has a rococo equivalent of 'French letter': '*camisinha-de-venus*' – 'little Venus shirt'.

AIDS in Brazil has hit African levels of infection. It threatens to overtake illiteracy and drugs as the country's priority problem. Safe sex and Brazil are two ideas that haven't traditionally found much common ground. Which is why the government is now trying to make Carnival and condom ads as compatible as village cricket and pints of bitter.

'Be careful where you go in Rio,' warned Mossi as he hugged Fátima. I said I was careful wherever I went. Extricating himself briefly from Fátima, he slapped me on the shoulder. 'Hey, Jimmy, you're a good man!'

Mimi and Márcia wandered over to us. Mimi was determined to shake me out of my sullenness. She'd made it her mission for the evening. As a rule, I hate people with missions.

'What is typical British food?' she asked me. Roast beef, I told her. 'Like the American hamburger?' she asked. I said that this was not in my view an acceptable comparison. 'What about fiestas?' she persisted. I always find this a difficult one to answer, as apart from football and Guy Fawkes Night, Britain is lamentably short on public parties. So I tried a new line.

'We have a great tradition of theatre,' I announced.

'Is that like Carnival?' she asked. 'I mean, Shakespeare and things?' You tiresome woman, I thought, why are you asking me these questions? She went on: 'We have this tradition of homosexuals here, but in spite of what you might think, people are very conservative in Brazil about homosexuals. In the fields of jobs, finance, and so on.' She waited for me to agree or disagree, or simply show some interest. At this moment, I was not interested in Brazilian homosexuality or Brazilian finance. Frankly, I wasn't interested in Brazil, and now just wanted to be back in London.

She moved on to men in women's clothing. 'People love this at Carnival. Don't all men have something female in them that makes them want to do this?' I don't know why Mimi was insisting on extracting my gloss on so many Brazilian national pastimes, but insisting she was.

'Maybe,' I said, 'but it doesn't always end in drag.'

I looked towards a beach bar where quite a din had started up. A little band of people with drums and shakers and a guitar were knocking out a simple samba; a couple of guys were singing almost in tune. It wasn't the band or the music, however, that had caught my attention – and by God I was willing to have my attention kidnapped. It was a woman dancing.

She was tall, slim, white-skinned, with black bobbed hair. She wore tight black jeans and a red top; her chest was very sunburnt. She was dancing a samba out of all technical proportion to the music, with an ecstatic smile on her face. The sweat glistened on her chest and dampened her hair. The strong lamplight above the bar threw her litheness into sharp, irresistible relief against the sea behind her. Her face was out of Raphael, and never stopped smiling. Her legs and arms moved with frenzied elegance: she seemed to be in a state of total pleasure.

I hadn't seen anything like this since the mulatta at the Mangueira rehearsal. I was awestruck, tangibly enjoying her tangible enjoyment – for ten time-stopping minutes. After three days of endurance tests, the native gods had at last allowed me a brief sample of Carnival's sensual secrets; as I watched this Ipanema girl – and Mossi saw how absorbed I was ('Hey, Jimmy!') – I thanked them for fleetingly sending forth a vision of tropical Eros. This was worth suffering for.

It was now nine p.m. Márcia had to make a phone call, and Mimi had to go to the loo, so the three of us decided to leave Mossi and Fátima in the swelter-ing wet road, and find a restaurant. We went to one opposite the Garota de Ipanema. It was packed. Mimi and Márcia moved off to phone and ladies' room respectively, and I ordered a *chopp*, my first alcohol of the day.

When Mimi returned, I asked her about Márcia: how old was she? Thirty-two, said Mimi. And married? Four times, said Mimi. Four times married at thirty-two. I'd totally underestimated this national pastime of multiple matrimony. Aged thirty-five, the longest I'd held on to a girlfriend was three years. Ana, herself twice married, later told me that was the way Brazilians did things: they got married a lot.

Márcia rejoined us, and we had *chopp*s all round, and *frango a passarinha*, fried chicken in salt – so much salt that several *chopp*s in a row had to be ordered. I felt better. Márcia suddenly frowned and let out a yelp.

'*Ai, mi namorado!*' she said, putting a hand over her mouth, and muttering something very fast to Mimi. I looked at Mimi for help.

'She's just seen her lover,' Mimi said. Where? I asked. 'On a motorbike. They've been going about three months. She hasn't seen him all Carnival.' Márcia peered into the crowds now teeming through Ipanema, and sighed. Márcia was becoming more fascinating by the day.

She looked at me and said she would like to meet Chico Buarque. Chico was her favourite, she said. He was Mimi's favourite too.

'When are you going to see him?' they asked.

'I don't know exactly,' I said. 'For lunch perhaps on Wednesday.' I thought they were going to ask if they could come too.

'Please tell him how much we love him,' said Mimi.

I said of course I would. 'We'd love to meet him,' she added.

I paid for a taxi back to Botafogo, and we had more *chopp*s at Manolo's. We were joined by the receptionist, and went back to Zuila's. She was watching TV: live action from the Sambadrome. I sat with her and Mimi silently while the two other girls disappeared into the bathroom and chortled away together for a few minutes. What on earth were they doing?

Planning the rest of their night, apparently. Mimi eyed them both disapprovingly when, back in Zuila's front room, they brandished large quantities of condoms, the ones Márcia had picked up on Ipanema beach, and asked me whether I knew what they were. Zuila laughed out loud. So did I. Mimi looked embarrassed.

'It's Carnival,' she said. Yes, I said, I knew that; I said I knew something about Carnival. Mimi eventually retreated down Zuila's long corridor, and the girls noisily made their exit into whatever little-Venus-shirt-filled night on the tiles they'd plotted. I said goodnight to Zuila, went to my mattress, and closed my eyes to an image of a dancing girl by a beach who knows no unhappiness. I slept for ten hours.

Eight

Chico in Rio

Chico Buarque returned from exile in Italy to Rio de Janeiro in March 1970. He was immediately invited to appear on television, and released his fourth LP. This record, in the style of his previous three, had a conventional portrait of the twenty-six-year-old artist on the cover, and carried a line-up of songs he'd worked on before and during his exile in Italy. He still looked eighteen. In appearance, this was the Chico of 'A banda'; but his voice had thickened and sounded less ethereal, less feminine.

He'd also moved away from bossa nova pure. On 'Essa moça tá diferente' ('This Girl's Changed'), 'Agora falando sério' ('Speaking Seriously Now'), and 'Rosa-dos-ventos' ('Weathervane'), there were new rhythms, new melodic patterns, new textures, suggesting that Chico Buarque was a songwriter who wanted to move on and show that he was not merely the 'A banda' boy. His play, *Roda viva*, hadn't been given a fair outing – though many Brazilians might have preferred 'their Chico' untainted by controversy.

He'd just been in self-imposed exile. He'd been a

problem for the state. Perhaps he still was. For now, it was plain that his lyrics were getting sharper and more turbulent. 'Rosa-dos-ventos' is a picture of desolation: 'And from love the scandal grew/ From fear the tragic was born', it opens plangently. *Sturm und Drang* simmer. Violence isn't far away.

President Garrastazu Medici had turned Brazil into a nationalist theme park. 'Brazil, love me or leave me' read stickers in the back of people's cars – an ironic echo of Chico's predicament in 1968. A call went up for national pride and security. This meant new protectionism, conformity and xenophobia. It meant a hardening of censorship and a rooting-out of 'subversives'. It meant misery for millions, and smart offices and cars for the favoured few – those who admired the bully-boys.

So Chico wrote and released 'Apesar de você'. It managed to get past the censors, first time round, as some idiot had kindly suggested in print that the song was a 'homage' to Medici. Chico was asked in interview who the '*você*', the 'you', of the title was. 'A very bossy and very authoritarian woman,' he replied.

The single sold 100,000 copies in one month. Then the censors struck. The army closed the factory where the record was being pressed and had all existing copies removed from the shops. The song officially vanished until 1978, when it appeared as the last track on Chico's ninth LP. His struggle had just begun.

'Apesar de você'

Amanhã há de ser
Outro dia

Hoje você é quem manda
Falou, tá falado
Não tem discussão, não
A minha gente hoje anda
Falando de lado
E olhando pro chão, viu
Você que inventou esse estado
E inventou de inventar
Toda a escuridão
Você que inventou o pecado
Esqueceu-se de inventar
O perdão

Apesar de você
Amanhã há de ser
Outro dia
Eu pergunto a você
Onde vai se esconder
Da enorme euforia
Como vai proibir
Quando o galo insistir
Em cantar
Água nova brotando
E a gente se amando
Sem parar

Quando chegar o momento

Esse meu sofrimento
Vou cobrar com juros, juro
Todo esse amor reprimido
Esse grito contido
Este samba no escuro
Você que inventou a tristeza
Ora, tenha a fineza
De disinventar
Você vai pagar e é dobrado
Cada lágrima rolada
Nesse meu penar

Apesar de você
Amanhã há de ser
Outro dia
Inda pago pra ver
O jardim florescer
Qual você não queria
Você vai se amargar
Vendo o dia raiar
Sem lhe pedir licença
E eu vou morrer de rir
Que esse dia há de vir
Antes do que você pensa
Apesar de você

Apesar de você
Amanhã há de ser
Outro dia
Você vai ter que ver
A manhã renascer

E esbanjar poesia
Como vai se explicar
Vendo o céu clarear
De repente, impunemente
Como vai abafar
Nosso coro a cantar
Na sua frente
Apesar de você

Apesar de você
Amanhã há de ser
Outro dia
Você vaise dar mal
Etc. e tal . . .
La la la la la la . . .

'In Spite of You'

Today you're the orderer
You speak, no more,
No more discussion, no
My people today are
Cautious with their words
And, looking at the ground, see
You who invented this state
And invented it to invent
All this darkness
You who invented sin
Forgot to invent
Forgiveness

In spite of you
Tomorrow has to be
Another day
I ask you
Where will you hide
In the enormous euphoria
How will you stop it
When the cock insists
On crowing
New waters are rising
And people are loving
Without stopping

When that moment arrives
I will demand, I swear, for this
My suffering interest and more
All this repressed love
This contained shout
This samba in the darkness
You who invented sadness
Now, have the kindness
To un-invent it
You're going to pay, and double,
For each tear shed
In this my grieving

In spite of you
Tomorrow has to be
Another day
I'd pay any price to see
The garden in flower

Something you never wanted
You who'll be embittered
Seeing the day break
Without asking your permission
I'm going to die laughing
Because this day has to come
Before you could imagine it
In spite of you

In spite of you
Tomorrow has to be
Another day
You'll have to see
The morning reviving
And bursting with poetry
How will you explain
The vision of the sky clearing
Suddenly, and without punishment
How will you muffle
Our chorus singing
Right in front of you
In spite of you

In spite of you
Tomorrow has to be
Another day
You're going to have a hard time
Etc. and so on . . .

La la la la la la . . .

★   ★   ★

From now on, all Chico's songs had to be submitted to the state censor. Few escaped some form of doctoring. 'Samba de Orly', written with Vinícius de Moraes and Toquinho in Italy, had to lose a reference to enforced exile. In 'Partido alto' ('High Party'), from the 1972 film *Quando o carnaval chegar*, 'trash' had to become 'thing' and 'Brazilian' 'drummer' (to avoid potential cheapening of the national character). A love song from the same year, 'Atrás da porta' ('Behind the Door'), had to have 'hair' replaced unbelievably by 'breast' (singular), as the censor concerned was horrified at the possibility of capillary eroticism. In 1973, a wry first-person ballad about the life of a hooker, 'Ana de Amsterdam', had the word for 'randy' ('*sacana*') changed to an anodyne '*bacana*' ('great').

One of the more extraordinary acts of censorship occurred when Chico was performing his and Gilberto Gil's song 'Cálice' ('Chalice') in São Paulo, with Gil, in May 1973. The song is a powerful strike against repression, borrowing the image of Christ begging that the agony of crucifixion be taken away from him. The words had been printed in a São Paulo newspaper and weren't immediately banned by the censor.

Soon enough, however, the censors picked up the real message, and proscribed the song. In public, Chico and Gil decided merely to hum the melody, punctuating it with the word '*cálice*', which constitutes the refrain. Chico's company Phonogram, under pressure from the police, took fright and gradually disconnected the microphones. Hoping to keep '*cálice*' articulated, Chico moved from one mike to another, and each was disconnected until there was no sound at all. Recorded on television for posterity, this farce perfectly illustrated the song's complaint, and its hidden pun: *'cale-se'* means 'shut up'.

Chico wasn't going to shut up. Indeed, he'd already managed to produce under almost unendurable circumstances his greatest album and one of the classics of the era, in any culture. It appeared in 1971, and was not banned. It was called *Construção*.

This superbly crafted collection of ten songs was illustrated by something very new: the LP's green cover carried an oblong photo of a moustachioed Chico staring from some distance through what looked like the leaves of a tree. His left hand is on his hip, the other hidden by a blurred leaf. He's wearing an open-necked, slightly flowery shirt. His expression is one of uncompromising gravitas, almost threatening, perhaps tired. This is not only no longer the 'A banda' boy; this is a very adult musician who has some very adult messages to give his listeners.

What they heard was poetry: songs such as 'Deus lhe pague' ('May God Reward You'), a dark, frenetic, brilliantly parodic 'hymn' of thanks for wonderful social conditions, 'Cotidiano' ('Quotidian'), about the bleak lives of a working-class couple, and two of my personal favourites, 'Cordão' (see p.75), and 'Samba de Orly' – pure *saudades* for a longed-for Rio.

The LP's high point, however, perhaps the highest in Chico's career as a lyricist, occurs at the end of side one. The title song 'Construção' is a six-minute threnody on the last hours and sudden death of an unnamed builder. One morning, he says farewell to his wife and sons; having climbed the 'construction' (one assumes on a building site), he takes a rest, and falls. His crushed body disrupts the pedestrians on the pavement below, and the traffic. That is the song's narrative outline.

What is breathtaking is what Chico does with its verbal structure. Its complexity is dazzling, and demands analysis. It would be in vain to try and show here, in English, how the song works in Portuguese, so I have reproduced the words and Charles Perrone's translation in Appendix Two.★ Suffice it to say that the song's incantatory effect relies on an elaborate and subtly altered series of phrasal repetitions, which make it sound as though it is literally building itself as Chico sings. The song proceeds with an almost stately rhythm, starting on a lightly strummed guitar and swelling with orchestrated traffic noise as the drama of the builder's fall approaches.

'Construção' has been labelled a protest song. Chico has always denied that he wrote this or any other song with the specific idea of 'protest' in mind; but both 'Apesar de você' and 'Construção', written around the same time, clearly contain his poetic assessments of life under the generals – 'Construção' more obliquely than 'Apesar'.

★ See pp. 300–2. Perrone says: 'The text has forty-one lines of twelve syllables, all of which end in proparoxytone, that is, a word stressed on the antepenultimate syllable. A pattern of preterites organises the text as two series of quatrains and a sextain comprised of verses from each of the four quatrains, with both series and the sextain followed by an isolated single-line refrain. The strophes of the two series are differentiated only by the changing of the line-final word. Four new words are introduced in the second series, and the words used in the first now modify a different line. In the sextain, there is another substitution or switch at the end of each line.'

The triumph of both songs is that they rise easily out of their era; in 'Construção', we still hear a masterpiece of pop-musical image-creation which at that time had only been attempted by Bob Dylan in 'Subterranean Homesick Blues' and the Beatles in 'A Day in the Life' (by Caetano too, in his Tropicalista phase). Chico, however, is more considered in his writing than either Dylan or Lennon (and less fractured than Caetano), using a vastly more sophisticated verbal form to convey his strange, hypnotic, melancholy story. Yet his composition remains fundamentally accessible and direct. Twenty-five years on, every line and every note and every solemn beat make you want to listen, and understand.

In 1982, Chico told Adélia Bezerra de Meneses: 'It was no more than a formal experiment, a game with bricks. It didn't have anything to do with the problem of workers – of course you always open some windows . . . When I compose, there's no intention, only emotion. In "Construção" the emotion was in the wordplay . . . Now, if you put a human being in the word game, as if he were a . . . brick, you end up stirring people's emotions.'

Chico wasn't going to shut up. His problems thus multiplied. He lost faith in Polygram (the new name for Phonogram by the mid-1970s – both labels belonged to Philips), who were also probably in league with the censors, so he continuously sought ways out of his contract.

He suggested first, tongue only partly in cheek, that anything he wrote be recorded using his voice simply as a blueprint for orchestral versions of his songs: not accepted. Then he tried sabotage: he littered the master tapes with expletives. That didn't work either. The records continued to appear, from *Construção* in 1971 to *Meus caros amigos* (*My Dear Friends*) in 1976, under the Philips umbrella, with Polygram breathing noxiously down his neck. In 1980, he finally managed to change labels, from Polygram to Ariola.

Record labels have tended to be an albatross for Chico. The day he finished his first album for Ariola, *Almanaque* (*Almanac*), the company was sold – to Polygram.

In the early 1970s, Chico also clashed with TV Globo. It began with his and others' withdrawal at the last minute from the sixth and final International Song Festival in 1971, a protest more against censorship than against TV Globo. TV Globo nonetheless responded vitriolically and dropped Chico thereafter from its programming altogether. They didn't patch the quarrel up until the mid-1980s.

From this time, the early 1970s, he received more than twenty summonses to appear before state censors at the federal police and the army, which were deeply depressing and lost him a lot of sleep. Censors turned up at his live shows, and tried to invade his dressing rooms to lay down what he was and wasn't allowed to sing. They turned up at his house. In 1975, he composed a delicious upbeat ballad, 'Tanto mar' ('So Much Sea'), about the Portuguese revolution of 1974, the 'Revolution of Carnations': 'I know that you've had a party/ And I was happy/ And though I wasn't there/ I've kept a carnation for myself'. The song naturally was banned, or at least the words were.

The censors also ruined a project he'd started planning in 1972 with film-maker Ruy Guerra: a stage musical about a seventeenth-century mulatto from the north-eastern state of Pernambuco, who fought with the Dutch against the Portuguese colonisers. Domingos Fernandes Calabar, as he was called, was executed as a traitor in 1645. Chico and Guerra had the temerity to suggest that Calabar might have been a bit of a hero. They named their show *Calabar*.

First the censor passed it as 'suitable for persons over eighteen'. When Chico's script was resubmitted to the censors in late October 1973, another three months elapsed before the censor – a certain General Antonio Bandeira – declared the show could not appear with the name 'Calabar' anywhere. Moreover, he prohibited such a prohibition being made public.

The project had been shot out of the sky. Chico and Guerra lost $30,000. They managed to salvage some of the material for a show Chico put on later in 1974, and preserved some of the music for his first album since *Construção*, *Chico canta* (*Chico Sings* – not *Chico Sings Calabar*, as was originally intended). Even then, songs were doctored: 'Ana de Amsterdam' was reduced to an instrumental version, as was another, 'Vence na vida quem diz sim' ('Whoever Says Yes Will Win in Life'); 'Bárbara', a bittersweet love song, lost an implication of sexual coupling; 'Fado tropical', about the meeting between coloniser and colonised, lost the word 'syphilis'.

So it went on. These tamperings, and the demise of *Calabar*, were evidence to Chico that anything which had his name attached to it was doomed. For an artist of his calibre, such half-witted interferences, though not in themselves dramatic (the *Calabar* débâcle excepted), were continual, enervating and confidence-sapping. Chico had to find a ruse to beat the bureaucrats.

On his 1974 album, *Sinal fechado* (*Red Light*), there wasn't a single song composed by Chico Buarque. Other names were there: Caetano Veloso, Gilberto Gil, Noel Rosa, Toquinho, Vinícius de Moraes, Tom Jobim. Chico had made attractive arrangements of songs by the super-famous half-dozen but excluded himself. Side two opened with a song, 'Acorda, amor' ('Wake Up, Love'), which seemed to have been jointly composed: by Leonel Paiva and Julinho da Adelaide. These weren't exactly household names in Brazil. In fact, no one had the slightest idea who they were. But their song was unambiguous: 'Wake up, love, there's somebody unwanted at my door, call a thief to help me out . . .'

In September 1974, Julinho da Adelaide gave an inter-view to the São Paulo newspaper, *Última Hora*. He explained that he was the son of a *favelada*, Adelaide de Oliveira, one of whose husbands had been a German by the name of Kuntz. Julinho was thus proud to have a blond-haired half-brother called Leonel. Leonel had to be looked after and protected by Julinho, said the composer.

Talking of his work, he spoke of something he'd invented, called the 'samba-duplex', in which songs could have their meanings transformed: the samba 'Formosa', for example, could become 'Nationalist China', to allay any suspicions about communist leanings. Julinho's music had also, curiously enough, been performed by a number of famous singers, including Chico Buarque. The text of this interview carried a photo of a beautiful, smiling mulatta – Julinho's mother Adelaide from the era of the film *Orfeu negro*.

Julinho then faded from view, and the following year – lo and behold – Adelaide herself emerged into the press, contributing crossword puzzles to the *Jornal do Brasil*. This, she said, was consolation for the sudden death of her son, Julinho. The joke had run its course – the *Jornal* itself having conducted a report on censorship to discover that Julinho was Chico, and Adelaide and Leonel and Kuntz and the 'samba-duplex' wonderfully Surrealist hoaxes. (The photograph of the mulatta had been provided by Chico's father Sérgio.) To this day 'Julinho de Adelaide' is still technically the composer of three songs, 'Acorda, amor', 'O milagre brasileira' ('The Brazilian Miracle', from 1975 – Chico's sister Miúcha eventually recorded it), and a clattery rock number 'Jorge maravilha' ('Wonderful Jorge').

In 'Jorge maravilha' (1974), Chico sang, 'You don't like me/ but your daughter does'; this gave rise to a rumour that Chico had addressed his song to a high-ranking general, Ernesto Geisel, because his daughter was a well-known fan of Chico's. Chico said the last person he'd been thinking of was Geisel. The lines had been inspired rather by those visits from policemen who came to his house to take statements, and who used to ask him in the lift afterwards for autographs for their daughters.

By the mid-1970s, Chico Buarque was one of the most politicised and sought-after artists in Latin America. He had become as popular and as admired in Spanish-speaking lands as he was in Brazil. In interview, he was invariably asked not about music but about censorship, the government, the state of Brazil. The answers were, of course, all in his music, but he was too modest to say so. He used to joke that he was more applauded when he appeared on stage than when he left it.

At the height of his anti-establishment fame, *Meus caros amigos*, with its conciliatory title, was released, though as we shall see Chico had wrought a dramatic change on his career by 1976. The album had the usual difficulties with the censors, but featured three major songs: 'O que será' ('What Can It Be'), 'Corrente' ('Chain') and 'Meu caro amigo' ('My Dear Friend').

'Corrente' is a subtle dig at the mindless political optimism of Brazil's 1970s. Part of a government slogan, *'pra frente'*, 'ever and upwards', is echoed in Chico's ironic praise of his own samba, which apparently celebrates how 'good' everything is (recalling 'Deus lhe pague'). 'Meu caro amigo' is a spritely *choro* written as a letter from Brazil to a friend in exile: 'Here people are playing football/ There's a lot of samba, a lot of *choro* and rock 'n' roll/ Some days it rains, other days the sun beats down/ But what I really want to tell you is, things are black here . . .'

A version of 'O que será' was recorded with Milton Nascimento. Together, he and Chico mounted a massive outdoor festival in Nascimento's native state, Minas Gerais, at the time of the album's release. 'O que será' became quite an anthem, abroad as well as at home. It's a big tune of longing and hope. A *baião* – a dance from the north-east – the song also has a Caribbean swing, reflecting Chico's growing interest in music from Cuba, in particular: he christened the song a *'cubaião'*.

In February 1978, Chico made his first trip, with Marieta, to Cuba. Brazil had no diplomatic relations with the island,

and thus the singer became a kind of unofficial ambassador. His immediate interest was not in politicians, however, but in Cuban musicians, such as Pablo Milanés and Silvio Rodríguez, with both of whom he collaborated. On his return to Rio, Chico was detained at the airport, having books and records confiscated. This didn't stop him visiting Cuba many times until relations between the two countries were normalised in 1986.

Even if snooping bureaucrats hadn't finished their work in Brazil, by the end of 1978 the censors had. Chico's album of that year (called simply *Chico Buarque*) stormed into the charts featuring, among the eleven tracks, two previously proscribed songs: 'Cálice' and 'Apesar de você'. The record circulated without opposition. It was a turning point in Chico's career, and for Brazil.

Brazil was changing (Galeão's customs officers excepted). The '*Abertura*', or 'opening-up', was in full flight.

This process had begun as early as 1974, when the aforementioned Ernesto Geisel assumed the presidency, though without obvious or instantly tangible results: Geisel had promised reform, but it would, he added, be long and slow. By 1978, repression *had* loosened up, but not by choice of the generals. The year before, latching on to a mood of historical opportunity – to the possibility of workers' rights for the first time – a São Paulo metalworks union won unprecedented concessions for its members. The campaign was led by the charismatic Luis Inácio da Silva, universally known as Lula (Portuguese for 'squid').

Lula spoke for most Brazilians when he later observed that '1977 was a year in which various sectors of society screamed out to find a little bit of oxygen, to breathe a little more . . . we also had the consciousness that if the workers didn't speak out, nothing new would happen in the country'.

The following year, 1978, worker power not only made the headlines but – indeed – a massive difference to the future of Brazil. Lula engineered an all-out strike by the whole of São Paulo's metal and car industry, catching the military completely off guard. If Brazil's industrial belt ground to a halt, so would the country. The dictatorship was forced to negotiate. By late 1979, though there had been round-ups and interrogations and imprisonments of union members and leaders, a law had been passed to allow the creation of new political parties. One of these was the Partido dos Trabalhadores, the Workers' Party, under the leadership of Lula.

The strikes continued. Lula became a thorn in the side of the uniforms, and a national hero, a Brazilian Lech Walesa. Exiles began to return. The government was increasingly caught up in scandal and corruption. By the early 1980s, it had lost control of the economy and of the political status quo. Inflation began to soar – climbing by 239 per cent in 1983 – and mass opposition to the generals, so blithely underestimated in the ministries, signalled the end of a hated and destructive dictatorship.

The beginning of the *Abertura* coincided with an unusual phase in Chico's career. The pressures of the heroic status conferred on him by an adoring public, largely because of his stance against the generals, had got to him. Before live shows, he was drinking heavily – whisky, mainly – just in order to heave himself out of the wings. A terror of the dark crowd before him would strike each time he stepped before it: chronic stage fright.

So he decided to stop doing shows. He ducked out of the concert circuit for an entire decade. His last official appearance as a performer in the 1970s was with Maria Bethânia at Rio's Canecão, in 1975. Fans had to content themselves with a live album made of the show, which ended, poignantly enough, with a kind of silence: Chico's celebration of the 1974 Portuguese revolution, 'Tanto mar', in an instrumental version.

(In the summer of 1996, I took a short holiday in the north of Portugal, staying with my old friend Christian and his Portuguese wife Assunção. On my first day in Porto – hot, bright, the sky and sea a dazzling blue – I walked down to the beach from the suburb of Foz, and found a bar facing the Atlantic. Through speakers either side of the wide terrace came familiar voices: Chico's, and then Bethânia's. I hadn't heard the album properly before, snippets perhaps, but not the whole thing, as I now did. I doubt there's a better place in the world to experience 'Tanto mar' than on the Portuguese Atlantic. Yet I felt as frustrated as all those 1975 fans must have felt at the absence of the song's trenchant but sensitive words, and that mournful voice. It was easy, in 1996, to hear the point of censorship. Neither the sky nor the sea shone any the less blue.)

Between 1975 and 1984, Chico made public appearances only in the name of good causes, in Brazil and abroad. Good causes at home meant, of course, opposition rallies and benefits for strikers, which became more numerous as the *Abertura* speeded up. Abroad, Chico played in places as various as Nicaragua and Angola. He was not unkown in Europe, France and Italy especially: 'O que será' was picked up by radio stations as a summery tune for 1976; 'Essa moça tá diferente' had first become known in France as the theme for an ice-cream ad.

In Britain and the States, meanwhile, interest in Chico Buarque registered at a level somewhere between zero and a slightly bigger zero. (Latin American specialists might have had the odd record.)

With the lifting of censorship in Brazil Chico plunged into work. He composed the scores for a number of films, including one called *Bye Bye Brasil!*. Film was not new to him: *Quando o carnaval chegar* had been a hit in Brazil in 1972; *Joanna francesa*, starring Jeanne Moreau in the rôle of a bordello madam, had followed a year later. Chico was tongue-tied on meeting the actress in Paris to show her the music; Louis Malle's *Les amants* had been a seminal film for his generation. Still, Moreau adored the title song, the first verse of which is in French, and her version was included on the film's soundtrack, released only in Brazil.

Chico's major achievement in the late 1970s was *Opera do malandro*. This was an exuberant reworking of Gay's *The Beggar's Opera* and Brecht's *The Threepenny Opera*, set in Brazil's brave new world of the 1940s – President Vargas's 'Estado Novo'. One song, 'Homenagem ao malandro' ('Homage to the Hoodlum'), is a *carioca* 'Mack the Knife', and was enormously popular.

Malandro was first performed on stage in 1978, featuring Marieta in her singing début in 'O meu amor' ('My Love'), and a double album appeared in 1979. Ruy Guerra then turned the show into a film in 1983, and two further recordings of the *Malandro* music appeared on single LPs in 1985. It was a very Brazilian affair, highly original, witty and intelligent, as inventive as anything Chico has done. It has never achieved the international recognition it deserves.

By the end of the decade, Chico had reached a plateau. With Caetano in relative seclusion in Bahia and Gil exploring his roots outside Brazil, Chico was now without doubt the most popular musician in the country, if not in Latin America. With the police off his back, he was cruising. He was a family man, with a stable marriage and three daughters – Silvia, Helena and Luisa. He loved football, and had his own Rio team, Politheama, which he still plays in. He was rich – he had his own house built in Gávea at the edge of Rio's forest in 1980 – but he was without airs. Chico related as easily to people in the street and to *favelados* as he did to the educated élite: he was loved across all classes – as demarcated in Brazil as they are anywhere in the world.

The return to democracy and Chico Buarque were waiting for one another. It was inconceivable that he would not join in the party. Indeed, he was active in the great '*diretas-já*' – 'elections now' – campaign of 1983–4, when millions of Brazilians took to the streets to demonstrate their support for the end of dictatorship, and vocal in his espousal of the opposition candidate, Tancredo Neves.

Chico's lasting contribution to the party was the record he released in 1984 in anticipation of the new era: 'Vai passar'.

What other pop singer has produced one of his greatest songs, his most irresistible melody and his most glorious chorus approaching forty? 'Vai passar', in structure and procedure really a Carnival *samba de enredo*, is somehow the essence of Brazil: extroverted, full of desire and generosity, drivingly rhythmic, and tinged with melancholy – the song shifts at chromatically crucial moments through major and minor keys, but always lands back in its dominant, drunken major.

Like 'Apesar de você', 'Vai passar' is a public song. Its singer celebrates visceral release from narrowness and enforced restraint. Chico being Chico, he declined at a peak of musical triumph to take the limelight. Just three lines into the second verse, on the word *'memória'*, a chorus of female voices enters, and builds and builds throughout the remainder of the song, drowning Chico, until it sounds as if the whole of Brazil is singing.

And it was. At a moment of historical truth, no one who was there can separate the dawning of freedom from this felicitous samba offered by the nation's favourite troubadour. In a way he never had before, Chico Buarque was singing for the hopes of millions. He would never have to do so again.

Ana Miranda and Emir Sader live on the top floor of a modern high-rise in the heart of Leblon. The dizzying view over the Lagoon on one side and the roofs of Leblon towards the ocean on the other is similar to that seen from João's flat nearby. Ana has known Chico for many years; they also share the same publisher. Emir, a slim, handsome intellectual with a forbidding grasp of international affairs, was at university with Chico in São Paulo in the late 1950s.

Ana had rescued me from Botafogo on Carnival Monday. In the car on the way she'd asked me what I was *really* doing in Rio. Fair question – I hadn't taken part in Carnival, after all. I explained the business about Bahiatursa, my Rio ticket, and so on. Also, that I had to see Chico.

After a late lunch, I walked over to Ipanema beach for a swim. I thought I'd better wash out the weekend's cobwebs. The beach was jam-packed. The sky was also slightly overcast. For some reason, nobody looked beautiful. No nubile New Yorkers today. No Krim. When I peeled off my T-shirt and shorts, I saw that I too was part of the ugly club: my pasty skin was pockmarked with mosquito bites. I looked horrible.

I crept into the sea, swam, floated, and played in the waves for ten minutes: and then began to experience that churning sensation I'd had when swimming in Salvador – the water was full of poison, gunk, Carnival detritus. I did not want to be here, and there was no point pretending otherwise. I left the water, dressed hurriedly and abandoned further thoughts of enjoying Rio as an ocean resort. The ocean had suddenly become as nasty as the city's murders.

The next day at lunchtime, I was sitting with Ana and Emir in their small kitchen eating spaghetti and drinking red wine, tiny glasses of it. We were talking about John Updike.

Updike visited Brazil for an author tour, lasting a week, in 1992. On the basis of that tour, he wrote his novel *Brazil*. What did I think of it? Well, the brevity of the tour seemed to have had a pretty severe impact on the quality of the writing, I said, throwing back the wine and hoping for some more.

'I think it's quite dreadful. In fact, I've never really liked Updike. For me, he's a show-off.'

Ana paused. Emir smiled. Ana now told me she was a friend of his and admired his novel. She'd met him during that tour and they'd been corresponding ever since. He's also published in translation by Luiz Schwarcz's Companhia das Letras. Ana found Updike quite delightful.

Oh God. That's what I said. *Heck.* I'd managed to be obnoxious on my first full day with my Leblon hosts. 'Oh God. I'm so sorry. I mean . . .' Well, what did I mean? Exactly what I'd said. I thought John Updike's *Brazil* was pure garbage, though I was *sure* too that he was a very nice man. Ana was perfectly sweet about it.

'It's because he was writing about *your* territory, no?' she said, with a very slight smile. No answer to that. We laughed.

Ana and Emir wanted to know how I'd first met Chico. I told them.

'Who do you think speaks better English, Chico or Caetano?' asked Emir. I said, Caetano, probably. There was a postcard of Chico from 'A banda' days pinned on the wall above the table. Ana had already pointed it out to me, with a sigh. 'Chico is our idol,' Emir now said, with rather surprising urgency.

The phone rang. It was Chico, calling from Petrópolis, where he'd spent Carnival. How were *os ingleses*? he asked Emir. Emir winked. *Os ingleses* were fine, he answered. They chatted for a few minutes, and then Emir hung up.

'Chico suggests dinner tonight,' he said. Fine, I said. We

chatted on. An hour later, I excused myself for a brief rest. Shortly after lying down, I heard the phone ring. Emir came into my room – his five-year-old daughter Bebel's, in fact – a few minutes later. 'Chico is now saying lunch tomorrow,' he said. Fine, I said. The phone went again five minutes later, and Emir came in once again. 'Chico is going for a walk down Ipanema beach, and suggests we join him. Shall we go?' he said.

'What, now?' I asked, rubbing my eyes.

'Sure,' said Emir.

'*Fine*,' I said. Good grief.

It was very, very hot outside. At three o'clock, it couldn't be anything else. Ana had put on a light dress and donned a wide straw hat. Emir was wearing shorts and a T-shirt, as was I. But I'd had a little debate over my footwear before leaving. Should I put on my battered but thick-soled moccasins – the same ones which had travelled with me on my first trip to Rio two and a half years before – or should I stick to the espadrilles I was wearing? Espadrilles, I decided. It was only the beach. Major error.

Fifteen minutes later, we emerged on to the busy coast road that runs from Leblon up through Ipanema to Copacabana. We looked around. Chico was striding off down the pavement that runs alongside the beach, on the other side of the road. He was in shorts, trainers and a white vest. We crossed the road, and Ana called out his name. He was about fifty yards away but he didn't hear. She tried again. No response. He was walking fast. Perhaps he thought Ana was a fan. I ran after him, and tapped him on the shoulder.

He grinned broadly, and shook my hand.

'Hey, James,' he said, in his unmistakable gruff voice. Emir and Ana caught up, and Chico hugged Ana. Emir, who doesn't give much away, was visibly delighted to see him.

We set off down towards Ipanema. The sun was behind us. The pace was cracking. Terrifying. I looked down at Ana's and Emir's feet, and realised they were both wearing 'sensible' walking shoes: Ana trainers and Emir thick-soled moccasins. They'd obviously done this before.

After three minutes, the usual: sweat had soaked my T-shirt. After five, my neck was getting burnt. Worse were my feet. The concrete under the espadrilles was bashing out a callus at every step. Oh fuck, I thought. Blisters and sunburn. It's going to happen *again*. In the name of Chico, Rio de Janeiro, literature, music, I'm going to end up crippled with heatstroke and bleeding feet. What was it about this city?

The talk was as furious as the pace. Ana had already warned me that if Chico and Emir weren't separated quickly, they'd spend the entire time talking about football. Which they nearly did, until Ana managed to insert herself between them, and we got talking about books – Chico's new novel, Ana's current project, Luiz Schwarcz in São Paulo, Liz Calder in London, the death of Giovanni Pontiero.

We were now at the southern end of Ipanema beach, and there were a lot of people around. I was struggling to keep up. My soles were weeping with pain. Then, as a group of young men approached, I realised I was going to have to veer way off to the right to avoid them in order to stay level with the other three. They saw Chico, talking

animatedly with Ana, and looked – questioningly, I thought
– at me: 'who *he*'?

I did my veering. Back next to Chico the other side of
the group, I turned and saw all of them gawping at us.
Yes, I *was* part of this foursome, with Chico Buarque, no
less, right in the middle of us. My head swelled. I cheshired
back at them. Then my feet reminded me who I was.

A little further on, a black girl saw Chico and came up
behind us.

'Chico,' she called plaintively, 'I love your music, I have
all your records.' He turned, hugged her to him and planted
a kiss on her head.

'*Ciaou*,' he said, as we walked on. The girl sat down on
a concrete bench and put her head in her hands. Soon she
was surrounded by friends and others who probably weren't
friends but soon would be. 'What happened?' 'I was kissed
by Chico Buarque.' It was enough to make her the star of
an entire neighbourhood.

We continued to the top of the beach. Chico took his
shirt off. He was brown, lean, almost adolescent-looking.
At fifty-one, he was fitter than I'd been at twenty.

We got used to the stares – part of daily life for Chico.
A lot of people simply greeted him: 'Hey, Chico!' Chico
always turned his head with a brief smile but never stopped.
I wondered whether he kept up this speed to avoid being
mobbed. We halted finally at a drinks stall, and Chico
bought coconuts for us all. I felt in need of about eight. We
talked about Dois Irmãos, bright green and sharply outlined
against the brilliant afternoon sky. Having demolished my
cocount water in seconds ('very nutritious,' said Ana, 'and
very fattening'), I asked Chico where the song 'Morro Dois

Irmãos' ('Two Brothers Mount', from his 1989 album) had started, and what various words in it meant.

'It was after a night of samba in the *favela*,' he said, 'when the music stopped. I could hear the music, and then the silence. There's that line about the instruments being laid down, you know the one?' I did. I'd been trying to translate the song that very morning. Chico indicated the two fingers of green rock. 'Don't they look great today?' They did.

And then I thought: how on earth, when I first heard those beautiful, bittersweet opening bars in October 1992, could I have anticipated that one day I'd be standing on Ipanema beach admiring with Chico Buarque the very piece of nature that had inspired the song? Dois Irmãos is truly one of the most evocative shapes in the southern hemisphere, but this moment was almost preposterous. Yet, it made the pedal misery of the last twenty minutes, and the moral misery of most of the previous weekend – and of the whole of the year until then – somehow worthwhile.

After signing a couple of autographs, Chico took off again. Greetings from the beachside bars were now continuous. Smiles of recognition positively littered the pavement. He and Emir were back to football. Ana and I let them go slightly ahead, and she said quietly, 'He's an athlete. I can't keep up.' We laughed, and I pointed at my espadrilles, and grimaced. 'You're also getting burnt,' she added.

'Quite normal,' I replied.

We came alongside the footballing chat a few minutes later. I admitted to Chico that my knowledge of the game, England's or anyone else's, was minuscule, but I did want to know something about the current Brazilian

scene. Weren't there two major teams in Rio, for instance
– Flamengo and Botafogo?

'OK,' said Chico. 'Who are the current Brazilian cham-
pions?' I looked blank. Emir laughed. 'James,' Chico
continued, gesturing vividly with his hands, 'if you remember nothing else about Brazil, get this name: Flu-mi-nen-se.
Fluminense. Best in the world, OK?' I wasn't about to
disagree. For Chico, supporting Fluminense is tantamount
to religious faith.

There is plenty of football in Chico's work. As long ago
as 1969, he'd addressed a song celebrating the birth of his
daughter Silvia to a famous Brazilian singer, Ciro Monteiro,
who'd sent the baby girl a Flamengo shirt: Chico's song
explained how Flamengo's colours could and should be
changed into Fluminense's. First-born and football: same
thing really.

Chico had grown up in the era of Brazil's almost
supernatural dominance of the international game. Aged
six he would have seen what many regard as the greatest
national side ever; the 1950 World Cup was held in Rio,
but Brazil unfortunately lost 2–1 to Uruguay in the final.
This was put right in 1958 – the start of the Pelé era – when
Brazil won in Stockholm. In 1962 they won in Santiago de
Chile and then, of course, in 1970 in Mexico, when they
beat Italy.

Another quarter of a century would pass before Brazil
did it again, once again against Italy, in America in 1994,
launching the likes of Romário and Juninho on to the
global stage. It was a ropy final, and mean though it is to
detract from Brazil's success by recalling that it came after

a mistake made by Italy's top striker in a penalty shoot-out, that's exactly what happened. It didn't stop Brazil going mad, and there was at least some poetic justice in the country's triumph given the trauma experienced after the death of racing driver Ayrton Senna two months earlier. A week after the final, in a fax I sent to Chico about his forthcoming visit to that year's Frankfurt Book Fair, I added a PS of congratulations.

We approached Leblon. I told Chico I was shortly moving to Berlin. It was a place he was interested in visiting. What was it like? he asked. A mess, I told him, a fascinating mess, but a mess. East and west were like oil and water – chalk and cheese. Chalk and cheese? Chico looked at me quizzically. He's always quick to pick up on linguistic oddities. This one caused immediate problems. What was the Portuguese for chalk? *Greda*. But why cheese? Two things that don't go together. Chico laughed. In Portuguese it made no sense whatsoever.

I urged him to come and visit. Come and do a show. His riposte was firm.

'No shows,' he said. 'No more shows. But I'd like to see the city.'

I'm still waiting.

We drank a final coconut, and all agreed to have lunch at the end of the week – three days hence. Then, Chico and I would talk. I would have much to ask him.

That evening, with Carnival over, Rio was engulfed in a tropical storm. At least, that's what I thought it was. The black sky cracked with neck-crunching thunder, lightning ripped past the Corcovado and into the Lagoon below, the rain cascaded down like liquid bullets. It was the loudest, wettest, most ballistic storm I'd ever witnessed.

I stared in amazement from Ana's living-room window, saying this looked 'pretty serious to me'. A news headline the week before I left England had stuck vividly in the back of my mind; in certain Rio *favelas*, hundreds had died and ten thousand been made homeless when mud had simply smothered houses and swept them away after days of heavy rain: one of those catastrophes that one tends to hear about from Bangladesh or China. Was it going to happen again?

'Oh, it's just a *chuva de verão*,' said Ana. Was that all? Not even a *tempestade*, a storm: just a nonchalant *chuva de verão* – summer rain, a heavy shower? I wondered what a real storm looked like in Rio: the end of mankind presumably.

The next day, still grey after the previous night's downpour, I decided to take the metro north again. Emir's children by his first wife, Bebel and two-year-old Miguel (so: another minimalist Brazilian marriage), were due at the flat some time over the next two days. Now that Carnival was over, Dona Irene had rematerialised to clean and cook, and Ana – who'd already admitted that her finest dish was spaghetti – heaved a sigh of relief. She also politely suggested that I should make myself scarce while things got back to normal under Dona Irene's iron fist, and particularly if the children were around.

I left towards midday. First stop on the bus was Botafogo. I wanted to visit the Museu Villa-Lobos and the Museu Casa de Rui Barbosa, both quite near Zuila's house.

Heitor Villa-Lobos is Brazil's most famous composer;

in fact, it would be fair to call him Brazil's only known composer of so-called classical music. He died in 1959 aged seventy-two. He wrote huge quantities of music and was a good friend of Darius Milhaud. Given that the great Brazilian produced five symphonies, five operas and a number of large-scale symphonic poems, it would also be fair to say that he's lamentably underperformed, at least in Europe.

European audiences have a problem facing classical music from outside Europe. I sometimes think if we bothered to stretch our ears beyond Continental confines, a lot of European junk from the last two and a half centuries would disappear, and people like Villa-Lobos would attain their rightful position in concert halls – and not just, in his case, with *Bachianas brasileiras*, wonderful though they are.

Rui Barbosa was a statesman from Bahia, born in 1849. He was a liberal, critical of Brazil's monarchy (which finally collapsed in 1889), and spent two years in exile in the 1890s – in Argentina and England – for his stern opposition to the bombastic dictatorship which succeeded Dom Pedro II. He founded a newspaper, *A Imprensa*, became a senator in Bahia, and twice tried to become president in the first decade of the century, without success.

His great bequest to his nation was his library of 35,000 books, two hundred of which are by Barbosa himself. They remain more or less as he left them at his death in 1923, housed in the building that became his in 1893, on the avenida São Clemente, just south of rua Assunção. During my weekend at Zuila's I'd noticed this tidy, incongruous structure, locked away behind wrought-iron gates. With its pale-yellow façade and white shutters, it was without doubt the prettiest building in Rio de Janeiro.

However, both it and the Villa-Lobos Museum were shut. Of course. It was *quarta-feira de cinzas*. Ash Wednesday. I'd forgotten. I cursed, and got hotter. During my walk from the bus, my T-shirt had come off. It stayed off as I headed back towards Botafogo station. I stopped just before the entrance and rubbed myself down with a handkerchief. I then made myself metro-respectable for a journey north.

I went to praça de Onze. This is the stop for the Sambadrome. With culture out of the question, I thought I'd have a further taste, a little reminder, of the high of two years before. I also thought there might be something to see. There wasn't. There wasn't even a *praça* – a square. It was a wasteland. Hills and *favelas* were visible in the near distance. Traffic on a main road thundered past the metro station. Grey concrete was everywhere. There wasn't even a pavement to walk on: the geographical centre of Rio de Janeiro.

I headed eastwards for the avenida Presidente Vargas and found myself in a shanty town. Stalls and makeshift dwellings spread out for about three acres over what might otherwise have been a car park. Radios blared, and a few people idly swept water away from in front of their entrances. Cardboard, cloth and some corrugated iron constituted the principal building materials of this curious inner-city agglomeration. There seemed to be little life; it was as if all who inhabited these gimcrack hutches were comatose with heat, damp and collective hangover. Dead perhaps.

I crossed an empty road. Looking left, I sensed a certain familiarity. Looking right, I saw why. I had stumbled into the top end of the Sambadrome.

I'd only seen it at night, full of floats, paraders, colour and madness. The shanty dwellings were obviously overspill from Carnival nights, providing back-up services – beer, food, cassettes of the year's sambas, condoms – for the punters. Now, under a leaden sky, two lines of grey seats leading to a concrete arch a kilometre away, the finishing post for the *desfiles*, were empty, and grim. There wasn't a soul in the Sambadrome. Bits of streamer and costume were all that remained of the most extravagant party on earth. The sambas had been sung, the *desfiles* cheered, the thousands and thousands of bodies displayed – and the cleaners had done their work. The place would lie unused for another year. It looked like a mausoleum.

I returned to Leblon. The Prestons had given me the name of someone who would show me a *favela*. I phoned him and we made an appointment for the next day.

When I arrived at the Museu Villa-Lobos the next morning, a young black policeman quizzed me at the entrance. Who was I? What was my business? What was my name? I thought he might ask me to stand to attention. No museum anywhere else in the world has greeted me with such an interrogation. I showed him my press card. He ordered me to follow him into the lobby, and punched a few numbers into a phone.

'Jain Woodaww is here to see you,' he said. Good Lord, was I expected to make an *appointment*? I was about to turn on my heel when the policemen said, 'Go on in.'

So I did. The museum was dull. There were some photographs, a few scores, and Villa-Lobos's cigar case. I thought things might improve in the library, and was shown the way by another policeman. I was met by a thin lady in her fifties who was very keen to describe to me the museum's collection of books, mainly in Portuguese, and mainly facsimiles of scores, and a good deal of music criticism too. The lady insisted I fill in a form with my London address and pressed on me a book about Villa-Lobos in French, and an LP, a live recording of a Villa-Lobos music competition from 1984. I shook her hand and smiled gratefully, and as I left thought I must have been mistaken for someone who *had* made an appointment, poor chap. Either that or I was the first person to have visited the museum in a year.

The Museu Casa de Rui Barbosa was enchanting, its well-tended gardens not least of all. There were roses and lilies and clipped hedges. Grass was being sprayed by sprinklers. Mothers trundled prams down the polite gravel pathways, and old folk sat chatting on benches. It was almost European, an extraordinary sight to come across in Rio, particularly this area of it, which had all the charm of Dalston. I'd found my first *carioca* oasis.

Inside, many of Barbosa's possessions were intact, and every room, named after a different stage of his career, was full of books and ornaments. But if the Villa-Lobos house was a touch jumpy about security, this place was a study in organised paranoia. Every room was also full of police: three or four of them in each, male and female, all about twenty, all in smart uniforms and all armed. They were all friendly, and all said hello. I was one of about three visitors in an hour. The uniforms didn't follow me around exactly, but I ran into most of them at least twice.

A museum whose security staff outnumber the public by ninety to one could only belong to a city like Rio de Janeiro.

I recalled Chico's dry comment about my first attempted use of Rio's buses. Perhaps he'd say the same about my cruise of its museums. I genuinely felt they needed some attention. Samba and Carnival and the beach were fine, and always on show. I'd had my fun. The museums, as with many aspects of the city's non-musical culture, were hidden and completely unadvertised, as if Rio were ashamed of them. I wanted to see one more before I left.

The skies had cleared and the temperature risen again. Diving into the metro at Botafogo was becoming a ritual pleasure. Márcia had been right to regard me with incredulity when I'd suggested walking to Urca. If you want to enjoy walking in Rio, you have to pay with blood and body water (or be as fit and as famous as Chico Buarque).

I travelled the twelve cooling stops to São Cristovão at the foot of the North Zone. Not far from the station is the Quinta da Boa Vista, a lush park once owned by the Jesuits, who grew sugar here. In 1808, the land and the neo-classical mansion in the middle of it passed into the hands of Dom João VI. Today this former country seat of the royal family has become the Museu Nacional. Unlike the Casa Rui Barbosa (which was bought and is still maintained by the federal government), the Museu Nacional looks as though it hasn't been painted since the royal family abandoned it in the late nineteenth century.

There are supposed to be a million exhibits in the

museum's twenty-two rooms. About ten were closed for refurbishment. Being a very long ride from the South Zone also renders even the museum's open rooms pleasantly empty of tourists. Of the half-million exhibits on offer, most were scientific specimens, stuffed birds, fish and insects.

The collection is ramshackle and themeless: next to a display of Eskimo clothing is a mummified head from Ancient Egypt; Indian artefacts and pre-Columbian pots and pans are thrown together with no regard for date or location. The Museu Nacional, officially a scientific institute, is really a zoological and ecological bazaar, an excuse to have countless bits of antiquity in storage in semi-opulent surroundings. Calling it a 'museum' is like calling my kitchen a brasserie. It is immensely confusing and rather fascinating – a rambling, subtropical Pitt-Rivers in a forgotten patch of royal green, the last vestige of *carioca* civilisation before the desert of the North Zone.

I spent two hours there, agreeably absorbed in a room full of preserved parasites which cause horrendous diseases, before taking the metro back down to Catete. This is an area just north of Botafogo, old, residential, tattered. It was here that I had my last duty in Rio to perform: a visit to a *favela*.

Favelas had been on my mind since I'd first seen Rio. As they make up a substantial portion of the city's population, it had been impossible to ignore them. Their human contents are evident everywhere on Rio's main streets, often as piles of sleeping bodies curled up without covers or bedding in shop entrances, sometimes as figures sprinting away from cries of 'Stop him!' in Copacabana, handbag or camera flailing behind the fugitive; generally, though, *favelados* stay at home, plying their motley trades from the front rooms of their hutches.

Most *favelas* are frankly dangerous unless you know exactly what you're doing, or go into one with someone who has the right contacts. It seemed to me a failure of nerve not to visit one while in Rio, given their pervasiveness and the urban myths that have grown up around them: drugs, cheapness of life, daily shoot-outs with the police, great music and yet more drugs. I had no real *entrée* into any of the big ones, but I did have a way of getting into the one above Catete.

The Prestons had given me Bob Nadkarni's name during our lunch in Urca the previous Friday. Nadkarni is a film-maker who's lived in Rio for years. Roger wasn't sure if he'd be around or whether he still lived in a *favela*, but gave me the number anyway. When I rang him after my visit to the Sambadrome, I heard a thick-voiced, cordial fellow who said any friend of Roger's was a friend of his. He had a London accent, and was recovering from some tough days' filming over Carnival.

'Come at what we call the *caipirinha* hour,' he told me. 'When you get to the *favela*, ask for the "*casa de Bobby*".'

The *caipirinha* hour was not something with which I was familiar. I suspect it was an invention of Nadkarni's: it apparently meant any time from midday on. I got there at two. He'd given me instructions to line up at the bottom of rua Tavares Bastos along with anyone else who was going to the *favela*, and to take the communal VW van up the windy street for half a real.

As the van reached the start of the *favela* – where the official street stops and the hillside muddle begins – a black boy with appalling teeth asked me, '*Casa de Bobby?*' I nodded. We got out and he showed me the way up a tiny passageway threading through dwellings of breeze-blocks and corrugated iron and wood.

At the entrance to Bob's house, I had to pull a bell. Through a gate at the top of some stairs appeared a hulk of a man. Bob has a thick mane of grey hair tied in a ponytail, a huge stomach and fat legs. Asian features – Indian perhaps – would explain his surname. He was wearing a sweaty blue T-shirt and shorts. He told me to push the gate open, which I did, and welcomed me into his house.

The main room was very large, with a stone floor and heavy beams across what looked like a multi-layered ceiling; up beyond it was a warren of smaller bedrooms, reached by a makeshift staircase. Just beyond the stairs, behind a solid wooden screen, was a small, compact and elaborately equipped kitchen. Leading off one corner of the living space was a cheese-shaped room, a study, where two boys – one of them Bob's son – were playing on a computer.

The house was like a cross between a student hovel and Aladdin's cave. The only thing that could possibly remove this structure was a meteorite landing on it.

The main feature of the living room was a big glass window and door which led on to a wide, long veranda. Over the edge was a precipitous drop to some mean houses below. Bob's veranda offered a view of Rio I'd never seen before: a breathtaking panorama over Guanabara Bay, from the Pão de Açúcar on the right, over hills, islands and ultramarine-blue sea to Niterói and the curve towards Gloria, just north of Catete, on the left.

White sails dotted the bay, and the sun blazed off the water. Rio de Janeiro from this angle was a sea symphony, a shock of natural blue no postcard or brochure could ever capture – a painter, perhaps. This was the *cidade maravilhosa* so often spoken of, the beautiful city spread out like a giant Canaletto. I could see why Bob had decided to live here.

He sat me down on the cushioned banquette under the window and said a ton of beers were in the freezer outside on the veranda, and would I mind waiting? Of course not – and looking round I noticed the walls were hung with enormous canvases plainly imitative of Francis Bacon. I switched on my tape recorder.

Bob's father was Indian. He'd come to England in the 1920s, got into Oxford where he took a degree in Greats, and was determined to join the ministry. He became a vicar, fetched up in the parish of Harrow, and married Bob's mother, who was pure English, from Buckinghamshire. Nadkarni *père*'s career didn't flourish, as he was caught playing around with one too many of his female parishioners.

Bob arrived in Brazil for the first time in 1972 on the rebound from a break-up with a well-known model. Someone told him: 'Don't just get on a plane, take a ship, get over it slowly; otherwise you'll be back.' He was going to go to Ecuador, but the ship got stuck in Salvador da Bahia. So he disembarked and took a taxi, not knowing it was the middle of Carnival, not knowing anything *about* Carnival. The taxi-driver wasn't a real one and didn't know where he was going. They got lost. Someone opened one door of the taxi and threw a bucket of water over the passenger. The other door opened and a young girl was thrown in next to him.

'Brazil seemed like a fun place,' Bob said. 'So I bonked her for the next two months, and eventually made my way to Rio. I was deported after nine months in Brazil.'

In London he became a cameraman, then a film-maker, and returned to Rio in 1981. He learnt his Portuguese from Brazilian girls during 'many nocturnal conversations'. He ended up living in Catete, and one day someone said, 'There's a spot on the hill, why don't you go and investigate?'

He did, and this house was the result: about ten years' worth of building. As I'd seen, the principle was building out rather than up.

'It's all about claiming space: that's what you have to do in a *favela*. Going up makes your dwelling tall and thin. Going out, bit by bit, is what gives you space.'

Bob had some trouble when he first arrived. There was a crazy guy who wanted him out. He said he'd try anything to do it. And he did. Bob couldn't think what to do. One day, when Bob was going to be married – to a much younger Brazilian woman – the crazy told someone he was going to rape Bob's fiancée so that she'd be 'used goods' when he married her.

Bob snapped. He went down to a bar not far from the house and confronted him. He found himself surrounded, and then on the floor: the very position he'd meant his antagonist to be in. Bob still had to do something. He'd made a film about an execution squad and they said after he'd finished it that they'd always be at his disposal. So he called them, and they came round and beat up Bob's foe very, very badly. Thereafter the crazy got himself into all sorts of trouble and apparently knows that if he returns to Rio he's a dead man.

'Couldn't have happened to a nicer man,' Bob added with a twinkle.

Life in a *favela*, he continued, was tough, though this was by no means the worst of them, nor was it big. The biggest have upwards of 200,000 inhabitants; here, there were about 6,000 – a hamlet by comparison with Mangueira, for example. Bob tries to help wherever he can. One day, a man suddenly deserted his wife and small children, not far from Bob's house, and literally left them in the street. Bob took pity on them and sheltered them in a bit of his house that was vacant – told them they could stay there until they got themselves sorted out. Eventually, they did so, and one of the boys ended up in a drugs death-squad: armed *favelados* who eliminate those who don't pay for their fix. The boy had told Bob that if ever he needed his help, Bob just had to call. He hadn't needed to so far.

Bob stays clear of drugs completely. All the *favelas* dealt in drugs and everyone knew it. The police were a nightmare, corrupt and easily bought off, and, Bob claimed, didn't know what they were doing most of the time. They occasionally made raids into the *favelas*, but the worst ones were no-go areas even for the cops. They once forced their way into Bob's house, just because it was in a *favela*, and he confronted them: what right did they have to enter private property? He told them he'd report to the station if it were required, but he wasn't going to cooperate for a second until they got out of his house. They backed off. They had nothing on him.

'If you're a gringo and think you can deal in drugs here,' Bob mused, 'you'll end up dead. I knew a young French guy called William – I don't know why he wasn't called Guillaume – who used to sell innocent things on the beach. One day he reckoned that if others could make good on drugs deals, so could he. He got involved in a *favela* ring and ended up on a rubbish dump with eighty stab wounds.'

I asked Bob if he missed Britain.

'I don't feel any need to return to Britain, ever. This is my home, all my friends are here, and anyway I'm trying not to do any more filming. I want to paint. Plenty of people come up and visit me here. Alan Parker was sitting just a few nights ago where you are, very pissed, and Stephen Frears has come by too. Here, I'll just go and check the beers.'

We had a few. I liked Bob. He was coarse, unsubtle and had something of a one-track mind; he was also generous, frank and unpretentious. He'd gone completely native, and was clearly both very capable and much liked – if not feared – in the *favela*. No one in his right mind would want to cross a man of his physique. Beautiful though the view was (and Bob's ranks as the best I've ever seen anywhere), living in a *favela* required highly developed survival skills. Bob, I saw, had them in abundance.

He heated up some spicy beef stew with potatoes and manioc flour for a late lunch. After, I persuaded him to take me on a stroll through the *favela*. It was much neater than I'd imagined. The dwellings, compared to Bob's, were tiny. There was little sign of dirt or misery, and there were plenty of televisions: televisions are *favelados'* lifelines. Brazil's interminable soaps, '*tele-novelas*', are a signal of human life. Beyond the dead end of a *favela*, a material world of leisure and money and negotiation is possible: fictions in Brazil, certainly in a *favela*, are often to be preferred to fact. Owning a TV in total poverty is perhaps proof that you're alive.

We came to a small football area, which no one's allowed to build on. At one end of it was a yellow Telerj phone box being used by a beautiful mulatta. Bob explained that there was a strong sense of community here; people helped each other, found the most efficient ways of getting by, were driven to sustain the *favela*. One of the underlying processes of *favela* life, ensuring its continuance, he told me, is the manner in which families and whole networks of *favelados* call upon their like in some distant corner of Brazil, and bring them into the urban fold. It's a form of colonisation, and is both the problem for the cities where *favelas* proliferate and the reason for their curious success – violent and deprived though life in them can be.

We arrived back at Bob's gate. Overhead was a labyrinth of bare wires, a mad spaghetti of metal and plastic splaying out in all directions. Opposite his house was an open socket, and a plug hanging limply next to it: an emergency electricity supply if needed? I thought of the recent rain.

'It's all intended,' said Bob, chuckling. 'Nothing goes wrong.'

He walked with me to where the VW shuttle would arrive.

'Property is a big issue here. It's all about what you can get your hands on, what's free. If your plan fits the evolution of the *favela*, building can sometimes go ahead. The biggest problem is stuff that doesn't belong or threatens the integrity of a bit of *favela*. Look, down there' – he pointed at a patch of green below us, clearly on the border of the *favela* – 'we're fighting to preserve that; but developers want it, and the *favela* wants it, and we must keep it for what might be useful for the *favela*. We need it more than they do.'

He stopped, and gestured at the strangely eloquent shacks and roofs behind us. 'Believe me, in a hundred years' time, these *favelas* will be like Hampstead.'

We shook hands. Bob lumbered off up towards his other world. In one way, I envied him. In another, I couldn't think of anyone I'd less like to be.

Lunch with Chico took place in an empty Italian restaurant called Arlecchino, in Leblon. As Emir and I had already communicated in Spanish in the flat, we continued to do so at moments during lunch, when Ana and Chico were talking together. Chico overheard.

'You speak Spanish?' he asked, looking at me in some amazement. I thought he knew. 'No, no – and after our conversations in French and English, we could have been speaking Spanish all the time!' We would, I decided, make up for it.

Since the fall of the military, Chico has produced five albums: *Francisco* (1987), *Chico Buarque* (1989, the one I'd searched for for so long and eventually found in London), *Chico Buarque ao vivo* (1990, a live recording of a concert in Paris), *Paratodos* (1993) and *Uma palavra* (*A Word*, 1995) – new arrangements of fourteen old songs. His decision to turn to novel-writing has inevitably slowed down the musical flow, and he's happy to admit it. He understands the tremendous public pressure on him to keep composing and performing, but today Chico does everything in his own time.

'I always thought I'd be a writer,' he told me in his Gávea living-room looking out on the Tijuca forest – and we were, at my suggestion, speaking in Spanish – 'but music came and kidnapped me. When I made my first album, it was very hard to know what to include, as I had thirty songs to choose from. When you start, you always have masses of material, but I think there's a tendency in all of us authors of popular music to diminish the quantity. It's a great mystery. Painters go on painting, writers go on writing; in music, I don't know . . . It's a lot to do with fashion, showbiz, youth and so on. There was so much enthusiasm twenty, thirty years ago – more enthusiasm than reflection. In your twenties, it's spontaneous creativity, whereas in your fifties . . .'

I wanted in particular to hear his thoughts on two major themes of that era, when he shot to fame: Caetano Veloso, and so-called 'MPB'.

'I remember very well the first time I met Gilberto Gil, but not Caetano exactly. In 1966 and 1967 I saw Caetano many times in both São Paulo and Rio. We spent many days together in the house of another musical poet, Torquato Neto. Caetano and I had a really close friendship at this time, though we were more distanced when Tropicalismo came along. Brazil was divided between Tropicalistas and non-Tropicalistas, and I was an example of non-Tropicalismo . . .

'Caetano shows above all a lucid spontaneity. He's a thinker. He thinks about Brazil, about the world, and he's not limited either by Brazil or by music. He's very attentive to all the arts: cinema, literature, music. He's a great critic and could be – but isn't – a kind of cultural commentator. He *is* one of the fundamental intellectuals of our culture.

'Though both he and I are supposed to be part of it, MPB is not something *I've* ever talked about. It was a term created by the press, a category that came along with bossa nova, and was there to simplify comprehension in the newspapers. It was also used to distinguish what we were doing from rock, but there is rock in MPB. There always was.

'If we speak of Pixinguinha, a great maestro from the 1920s: he was accused of being a jazzophile, an Americanophile, because he played the saxophone. Saxophone? people asked. What is this instrument? Brazilian music was supposed to be just guitar and piano. But Brazilian music above all has this characteristic: it can assimilate anything that's around it.'

In 1989, the first free elections for three decades took place in Brazil. The slick, youthful ex-karate champion Fernando Collor de Mello was voted in as president by a small margin. His opponent, Lula, won the majority of the vote in the big cities; the vote of the conservative landowning classes nonetheless ensured the left was kept out of office. Lula wasn't helped by a revelation shortly before the vote that he'd offered a former lover money to have an abortion. Chico had openly supported him, and along with Caetano and Gil performed free during his campaign rallies and on TV shows.

It was not enough, and Brazil soon hit disaster again. Inflation ran riot. Collor was arraigned on charges of massive corruption and removed from office in 1992. Itamar Franco took over, and was considered a provincial liability until he presented to the country his '*Plano Real*' – the first attempt since the 1960s to put Brazil's economy right. It looked as though it might work.

Franco's finance minister, Fernando Henrique Cardoso, was voted in as new president in 1994; once again Lula was beaten, and once again Chico had supported him – even throwing a party for him in his house in Gávea. Collor's impeachment, meanwhile, in December 1994 – much looked forward to by Brazilians – ended in the playboy's acquittal.

By early 1995, Cardoso's economic plan had led to Brazil's new currency, the real, being pegged to the US dollar, thereby controlling inflation. If Brazil's economy can be calmed, then there is a chance, just a chance, the country might start to add up; but land, poverty, mass migration, violence, drugs, AIDS and the environment are bleeding wounds. Brazil, possessing the potential for the greatest success in the world, could work. Equally, it could carry on failing miserably.

Chico seems jaded about politics these days. When I asked him how close he felt to the pulse of contemporary political life, he was as emphatic in his negatives as he was about 'no more shows':

'Listen, I don't like politics. During the military dictatorship, the rôle we musicians had was extravagant. To assume such a political rôle had little to do with music. But music *did* have this importance because of the struggle against the dictators, for democracy. Afterwards, music returned to its original and natural state. I can't deny that the political burden we carried around *was* my life then, but today I feel freer, more integrated, than I did in those times. When democracy came, I was able to go back to what artists have done for all time.

'Art in Brazil, in Latin America in general, has served as an instrument of struggle. And it doesn't please me that this is so – for art. I don't deny that at the time I had to submit my art to something extremely important. But now, for my art – my books, my songs, my music – it's better not to have to.

'I feel perfectly happy as I am, as a novelist. I know it's very difficult for you to understand this: to make a connection between someone known for his music and his becoming a novelist. There are sympathisers and non-sympathisers. I write a song or a book, and they say, Here's this guy who for twenty years was deeply involved in this political story. I say, It wasn't to my liking, it doesn't interest or attract me now, this political stuff. I don't want to take up cudgels against the government – I *used* to want to. Today, no.'

Chico Buarque is a child of Rio de Janeiro. It is this city, far more than politics or MPB, with which he has to be identified, and which explains him. He is the reason I had travelled there. He will continue to be so. He will never leave it. Nor will Rio leave him.

'Rio has changed like any of the great cities down here in the South. It's grown too much, from inside. What characterised it in the 1950s came with the romanticisation of films such as *Orfeu negro*. There was some truth there.

The proximity of the different classes made everyone close, and offered a possibility of co-existence. But what could have been ideal has been transformed for the worst. It has encouraged great tension between the classes, a very violent and acute one; the great *difference* between the very rich and the very poor has become emphasised because of this proximity. And at each step the physical space between them becomes smaller and smaller.

'The clearest example of democracy in the 1950s and 1960s was the beach. It was free, open. Everyone was together. Today, it's as if it's from one to ten, this section for one sort of person, this for another. Each day it's more compartmentalised. It never used to be like this, this closure of the middle-classes behind their condominiums, in their cinemas, theatres, shopping centres and so on. The streets are public but the middle-classes stay away from the public cinemas unless they're in the middle of a shopping centre with their own security.

'I remember as a boy in swimming shorts climbing a hill to the top of a *favela* to look at Rio, which I loved. I could see the whole city. It was the same view as in *Orfeu negro* – from the hill in Leme, at the end of Copacabana. Today, there's no boy who'll climb a *favela* to see this, it's impossible to imagine! I regret the decline in the quality of life, and it's the same in São Paulo. Here, in Rio, it's the loss of this ideal, this possibility, this co-existence. The *cidade maravilhosa* is a *cidade dura*. Think of the rain that's just wiped out ten thousand homes. It's a problem of the terrain, with all the people coming here. Rio just can't take any more.

'That said, I couldn't live anywhere else. I lived in Rome, which is a beautiful city. I can go to Paris for twenty days in a month, but then I must come back. Rio is important to me as an artist. Even if I live in this upper-class condominium, I'm not considered upper-class – because I'm an artist. The violence we have here can happen to no matter who. There *are* still more transitional possibilities here, a crossing of barriers. I couldn't walk down a street in São Paulo as I did in Ipanema on Tuesday. In Rio, they're used to seeing artists. Remember, this city is my childhood.'

'Morro Dois Irmãos' (1989)

Dois Irmãos, quando vai alta a madrugada
E a teus pés vão-se encostar os instrumentos
Aprendi a respeitar tua prumada
E desconfiar do teu silêncio

Penso ouvir a pulsação atravessada
Do que foi e o que será noutra existência
É assim como se a rocha dilatada
Fosse uma concentração de tempos

É assim como se o ritmo do nada
Fosse, sim, todos os ritmos por dentro
Ou, então, como uma música parada
Sobre uma montanha em movimento

'Two Brothers Mount'

Two Brothers, when it's late at night
And at your feet the drums are laid down
I learn to respect your bearing
And to suspect your silence

I think I hear the desultory beat
Of what has been and what it will be in another
 existence
It's as if the dilated rock
Were a concentration of times

It's as if the rhythm of nothing
Were, indeed, all the rhythms on the inside
Or, if not, it's like a still melody
Over a mountain in movement

Nine

A Simple Brazilian Song

Chico and Caetano and Gil are three of the planet's most enduring pop musicians. They are in fine physical shape. They sing as well as they did in 1966–7, when Brazil first began to love them. They are still the repository of the diverse hopes of millions of their countrymen. They carry around with them an exotic species of Latin American intelligence. They were born with rare gifts, and have not squandered them. Each in his early fifties, they have attained an enviable serenity. They will not stay young forever, but of them it could truly be sung, adapting Bob Dylan's words of 1964: 'They were so much older then, they're younger than that now.' They are wise.

For me, an Englishman, the reason for their appeal is found in a rude question. Why are our pop heroes so awful and our poets so dull?

★　　★　　★

Gil was stretched out in his dressing room in the Royal Festival Hall in London. It was a hot July afternoon in 1995, and he'd been rehearsing. He was dressed in vest, shorts and sandals. He looked very calm, and unperturbed at the prospect of the concert ahead. He'd granted one interview while he was in London, and his promoter had fixed it for me. I felt honoured, but it felt right too: the magic triangle was incomplete without at least a stab at conversation with Gil in person.

Of the three, Gil is the least shy. He is the most cosmopolitan, and the most able to be un-Brazilian in his music-making. In chats with Gil, you come across names such as David Gilmour and Alan Watts and Stevie Wonder and Youssou N'Dour. He knows the Italian and French music scenes as well as he knows the American scene. He tours a lot. He seems indefatigable.

His relationship with Bahia is almost mystical, and it's there in his songs. 'I never feel like being in Salvador,' he told me in early 1994, 'as being in Salvador is just being.'

One of Gil's more impressive traits is his sense of responsibility: being black and being very much in the public eye, more so than Chico or Caetano, he's aware of how he can speak up for Brazil's blacks, particularly the murderously impoverished ones of his home town.

He tried his hand at local politics in 1987. In the new situation in Brazil, and fascinated by what Gorbachev seemed to be achieving in the Soviet Union – by a climate of liberation in various corners of the globe – Gil became chairman of a Salvador cultural institute, the Fundação Gregório de Matos (named after a roguish, seventeenth-century satirical Bahian poet). Gil was elected a city councillor in 1988, and pursued keenly the interests of Salvador's blacks, as well as trying to deepen links between Bahia and Africa.

He thought about running for the mayorship but dropped the idea. Politics proved to be a dirty game – really dirty in Brazil if you're black – and he knew he was better at getting his message across through music. He remains tied to his city and vocal in standing up for blacks' rights in Bahia, though the appalling conditions in which so many of them live are unlikely to improve even with Gil's good vibes. He knows as well as anyone that the country has to change.

Speaking fluent English in a light voice, Gil told me a little about his friendship with Caetano, his exile in London, his admiration for Chico, his international collaborations. His grace and charisma were almost overwhelming.

I wanted to know one thing above all. During our conversation by phone in 1994, Gil told me he'd bought his first electric guitar, a Gibson 335, in a shop in Shaftesbury Avenue in 1969. I wondered whether he still had it.

'It was inside a van on tour in Brazil, and someone broke in and stole it. It happened ten years ago. I've been back to the shop, but guitar styles move on. Now I buy mine mainly in New York. I was very sad.'

Gil was smiling when he said this.

Caetano Veloso's critical stance towards the music and the culture in the air of his time, both native and alien, have underpinned his artistic evolution. At every stage of his career, his music has been accompanied by, if not infused with, a kind of running commentary, pricking his own and others' pomposities, poking fun at the establishment (musical and social), and not flinching from waspish social comment.

This status as radical commentator, a persona in this respect less friendly, more prickly, than Chico's, marks him out from most other international musicians of his generation – with the exceptions of Frank Zappa, Dylan perhaps, and probably John Lennon, though Caetano is more coherent than the frequently idiotic Beatle. If one wants to be pat (to condone for a moment his own 1994 comparison!) he is Lennon, to Chico's Dylan; yet the equation doesn't really work. Both Brazilians are musically more interesting.

In August 1994, Caetano Veloso sat on the stage of the Queen Elizabeth Hall. He was dressed in a grey linen suit, his slight figure bathed in a discreet spotlight. Accompanying himself on an acoustic guitar, he sang for forty-five minutes, and ended with an exquisite 1978 ballad, 'Terra' ('Earth'), about a journey through space, and the relationship of self with land: a tender, questioning reflection on who we are and on who he is.

The Brazilians in the audience, as always, knew the refrain, and sang the words with him. They translate: 'Earth, Earth, no matter how far away/ The errant navigator should stray/ Who could ever forget you?' Caetano smiled quietly when he heard his compatriots join in.

That smile was the song and the song was the singer: as unforgettable as the earth whose strangeness and wonders he was praising. Whether he's in London, New York, Hamburg or Bahia, something unique in the spirit of the earth is singing when Caetano Veloso sings.

*   *   *

After our lunch in Arlecchino, Chico had driven me to his house in Gávea. On the way, he told me he was about to be a grandfather. His second daughter Helena was pregnant by the Bahian samba-reggae star and drummer, Carlinhos Brown. The baby was due in the middle of the year. He lit a cigarette as he told me this, and smiled. I almost laughed out loud, but congratulated him instead. I shot a sideways look at him: Chico Buarque, the youngest man in Brazil, a grandfather!

Things might therefore be changing for him, but he was the same man I'd met in October 1992 on a cold night in Paris, and the same man millions had known since 1966.

He had to stop at a cash dispenser. As he got out of the car, he was noticed by a woman pushing a pram, and another woman at her side. The mother's face broke into a broad smile, and she nudged her companion. It was a small, unostentatious gesture, and Chico didn't see it.

It's the gift of smiling that stays with me: Gil's, Caetano's – and with Chico, that smile all over Rio of instant recognition. For Brazilians everywhere, just catching sight of him can transform a dull day into one of light.

How dare these men be so beautiful.

'Coração vagabundo' (1967)

Meu coração não se cansa de ter esperança
De um dia ser tudo o que ser
Meu coração de criança
Não é só a lembrança
De um vulto feliz de mulher
Que passou por meu sonho
Sem dizer adeus
E fez dos olhos meus um chorar mais sem fim
Meu coração vagabundo
Que guardar um mundo em mim

'Vagabond Heart'

My heart doesn't tire of having hope
Of one day being all it desires
My heart of a child
Isn't just the memory
Of the sweet figure of a woman
Who passed through my dream
Without saying farewell
Making of my eyes an endless weeping
My vagabond heart
Which guards the world within me

Glossary of Terms

Abertura	literally, Opening-Up: period from mid-1970s in Brazil when political repression began to ease
ala	wing; section of Carnival parade
alegria	happiness, joy
bacalhau	cod
baiana	woman from Bahia; member of section of samba-school parade consisting of women wearing distinctive costume modelled on traditional Bahian dress
baião	dance-rhythm from Bahia
bateria	drums; drum section of Carnival parade
bichero	'animal-banker'; samba-school bigwig furnishing school with illegal earnings, invariably won from drug deals

bicho	illegal lottery played on Brazil's street corners with images of animals
bossa nova	musical form relying on sophisticated syncopation and unusual modulation, invented by composer Tom Jobim and guitarist João Gilberto in late 1950s
cachaça	distilled sugar-cane spirit
caipirinha	cocktail with *cachaça* base, mixed with lime chunks and crushed ice
camisinha-de-venus	condom
candomblé	form of religious worship in Brazil's north-east combining basic tenets of Catholicism with ritual devotion to African gods
cardápio	menu
carioca	native of Rio de Janeiro
cavaquinho	miniature guitar
chopp	draught beer
choro	north-eastern dance-rhythm
churrasco/churrascaria	barbecue/restaurant specialising in barbecued meat

cinema novo	Brazil's New Cinema in early 1960s, corresponding roughly to France's Nouvelle Vague
cordão	chain; Carnival procession
cruzeiro	Brazil's currency until early 1995
desfile	Carnival parade, procession
favela/favelado	Brazilian shanty town/shanty-town inhabitant
feijoada	Brazil's national dish, made of black beans, pork, sausage, served with rice and *farofa* (manioc flour fried with onion and egg)
frango	chicken
locutor	song-leader during samba-school rehearsal
MPB	Música Popular Brasileira, term coined in early 1960s to describe new Brazilian musical rhythms, eventually used to bracket together musicians such as Chico Buarque and Caetano Veloso
orixá	*candomblé* god
praça	town or city square
quadra	warehouse-like space where samba schools rehearse

quilombo	renegade slave communities in seventeenth and eighteenth centuries
real	new Brazilian currency introduced in early 1995
samba	originally a dance and rhythm from Bahia, developed into an idiosyncratic song-form by black migrants to Rio in early decades of twentieth century
samba-canção	name given to bossa novas before they became bossa novas
samba de enredo	part of samba-school parade which tells a story, illustrates a theme
sambista	composer of sambas
saudade	untranslatable term laid claim to by Brazilians and Portuguese; combines nostalgia, heartache, hope
sertão	Brazilian backland
suco	natural fruit juice
terreiro	community of Brazilian blacks, especially in Bahia

Appendix One

Excerpts from Reviews of the Four Bahians in London, 1 June 1994

'Fab four in feathers', Robin Denselow
The Guardian, 3.6.94.

For Brazilian music fans, this was an extraordinary, if infuriating, event. The country's four great heroes from the sixties – each with the status of a Bob Dylan, John Lennon or Joni Mitchell – were not just appearing on the same stage but were actually performing together, like some veteran supergroup. And yet they were doing so as part of a Brazilian Musical Extravaganza which attempted to recreate the colour and sensuality of the Rio Carnival in the Albert Hall. As a result the historic reunion became swamped in a sea of wild and befeathered samba dancers just as it was beginning to come to light . . .

Every Brazilian in town seemed to have turned out for [the Bahians'] first performance together here in twenty-three years, and there were crowds massed around the hall, hoping for a £40 ticket. Inside there was a carnival atmosphere even before the feathers appeared, although the subtlety and variety of the performance went far beyond good-time Latin dance themes.

Maria Bethânia, a million-seller back home who has never appeared here before, started with a series of powerful romantic ballads that showed she could have been a major star in the West if she didn't sing in Portuguese. Then she was joined by Veloso, now a thoughtful besuited middle-aged troubadour, accompanying his relaxed and intimate ballads on solo guitar, with a gentle charm that eased across the language barrier.

Gal Costa, dressed as a Brazilian dance queen should, with red dress and red rose in the hair, was also making her first appearance here, but didn't have quite the power to make the most of her stomping Latin funk.

Gil, the Brazilian star best known in the West, provided the greatest variety of all, shifting from a soulful bluesy falsetto ballad about his exile in England (the only song in English all night), through to powerful Latin/rock dance pieces and gentle passages where he backed his three famous friends on solo guitar. These easy, lilting close-harmony pieces, in which all four sang together, were a real delight and made this a very special event – or would have done if they'd been allowed to go on for longer.

'They sambaed in their seats', Trevor Grove
The Daily Telegraph, 3.6.94.

How do you raise the roof of the Albert Hall when it's not the Last Night of the Proms? You pack it to the gods with

Brazilians and let them hear music from Bahia and Rio. To play it, bring together four of Brazil's most popular singer-composers, all of them in their late forties . . . and you have the tropical equivalent of a concert teaming Bob Dylan with Joan Baez and the Rolling Stones. Except that none of them, not even the Stones, could have got several thousand people sambaing in their seats and swivelling their bottoms so alluringly that one was as gripped by the audience as by the performances. Even the Duchess of Kent, guest of honour at the Brazilian Musical Extravaganza on Wednesday night, was swaying to the South American sound (if I interpreted the royal *moues* correctly) entreating encores.

It started off quite quietly. Gal Costa wore a Tabasco-red dress and sang romantic ballads. The enormous audience sighed with expatriate appreciation. Maria Bethânia, another local heroine, took over, performing a popular duet with her brother Caetano Veloso. But it was with the Aznavour-ish Caetano on his own that the Brazilian beat really began to assert itself. He held bossa nova dialogues with his guitar. There were pleasing echoes of João Gilberto. I couldn't understand most of the words, but they sounded witty and sweet. My Portuguese-speaking companion translated a line here and there. 'You are beautiful – and your breasts have muscles.' The audience sang along with these interesting lyrics.

By the time the other main performer, Gilberto Gil, had got into his stride, aided by at least four drummers with at least four bits of kit per drummer to drum on, the Albert Hall was throbbing . . . Rock 'n' roll has vigour and aggression. This music has sexiness and . . .

well, you just had to look at that girl undulating in the next aisle . . .

'Exiles go wild for the Bahian beat', Antony Thorncroft *The Financial Times*, 4.6.94.

Imagine Elton John, George Michael, Shirley Bassey and Kate Bush sharing a stage and you get some idea of the excitement frothing around the Albert Hall this week when the Four Great Bahians, Gilberto Gil, Caetano Veloso, Gal Costa and Maria Bethânia, collectively gave the Bahian Festival a celestial climax . . .

You expect Brazilians to stand up and samba at the tap of a drum; you do not expect them to know every word of every song. It is distinctive music. Unlike Spanish Latin American music, with its sensual brass obligatos, the music of Brazil is drum driven – very African. To outsiders the singers often seem to sing across the musicians; it has no easy appeal – it is a national ritual . . .

Gil was exuberant; Caetano wistful; Costa and Bethânia full-throated.

Romantic ballads and plangent songs of home nestled alongside rousing chants, in which the audience hurled back as echoes the Amazonian caws of the singers. There was no interval and the bars stayed open.

There was also the overpowering sight of Mangueira, the Manchester United of the samba bands, sashaying its way on to the Albert Hall stage. First the percussionists, dressed like camp centurions; then the poseurs, arrayed like gigantic birds of paradise, parading plumage tails

15ft wide; finally the dancers, quivering every inch of their bodies.

Once the balloons had fallen, the audience had danced itself dry; the flags had been fluttered; the fever had died down, the Four Bahians returned for their own encore. It was both a personal event yet also a national occasion, a vibrant nostalgia for home. It was no place for a foreigner to be.

While the Rio carnival might now be a tourist attraction Bahia hugs its local identity and for one night the heart beat of Salvador, its capital, was in SW7.

Appendix Two

'Construção' (1971)

Amou daquela vez como se fosse a última
Beijou sua mulher como se fosse a última
E cada filho seu como se fosse a único
E atravessou a rua com seu passo tímido
Subiu a construção como se fosse máquina
Ergueu no patamar quatro paredes sólidas
Tijolo com tijolo num desenho mágico
Seus olhos embotados de cimento e lágrima
Sentou pra descansar como se fosse sábado
Comeu feijão com arroz como se fosse um príncipe
Bebeu e soluçou como se fosse um náufrago
Dançou e gargalhou como se ouvisse música
E tropeçou no céu como se fosse um bêbado
E flutuou no ar como se fosse um pássaro
E se acabou no chão feito um pacote flácido
Agonizou no meio do passeio público
Morreu na contramão atrapalhando o tráfego

Amou daquela vez como se fosse o último
Beijou sua mulher como se fosse a única
E cada filho seu como se fosse o pródigo

E atravessou a rua com seu passo bêbado
Subiu a construção como se fosse sólido
Ergueu no patamar quatro paredes mágicas
Tijolo com tijolo num desenho lógico
Seus olhos embotados de cimento e tráfego
Sentou pra descansar como se fosse um príncipe
Comeu feijão com arroz como se fosse o máximo
Bebeu e soluçou como se fosse máquina
Dançou e gargalhou como se fosse o próximo
E tropeçou no céu como se ouvisse música
E flutuou no ar como se fosse sábado
E se acabou no chão feito um pacote tímido
Agonizou no meio do passeio náufrago
Morreu na contramão atrapalhando o público

Amou daquela vez como se fosse máquina
Beijou sua mulher como se fosse lógico
Ergueu no patamar quatro paredes flácidas
Sentou pra descansar como se fosse um pássaro
E flutuou no ar como se fosse um príncipe
E se acabou no chão feito um pacote bêbado
Morreu na contramão atrapalhando o sábado

'Construction'

He loved on that occasion as if it were the last
He kissed his wife as if she were the last
And each of his sons as if he were the only one
And he crossed the street with a timid step

He climbed the construction as if he were a machine
In the stairwell he built four solid walls
Brick on brick in a magic design
His eyes numb with cement and tears
He sat down to rest as if it were Saturday
He ate rice and beans as if he were a prince
He drank and wept as if he were shipwrecked
He danced and laughed as if he heard music
And stumbled in the sky as if he were drunk
And floated in the air as if he were a bird
And ended up on the ground as a flaccid bundle
He agonised in the middle of the sidewalk
He died on the wrong side of the street disturbing the
   traffic

He loved on that occasion as if he were the last
He kissed his wife as if she were the only one
And each of his sons as if he were the prodigal
And he crossed the street with his drunken step
He climbed the construction as if he were solid
He built four magic walls in the stairwell
Brick on brick in a logical design
His eyes numb with cement and traffic
He sat down to rest as if he were a prince
He ate rice and beans as if he were the greatest
He drank and wept as if he were a machine
He danced and laughed as if he were his fellow man
And stumbled in the sky as if he heard music
And floated in the air as if it were Saturday
And ended up on the ground a timid bundle
He agonised in the middle of the shipwrecked sidewalk

He died on the wrong side of the street disturbing the
    public

He loved on that occasion as if he were a machine
He kissed his wife as if it were logical
He built four flaccid walls in the stairwell
He sat down to rest as if he were a bird
And floated in the air as if he were a prince
And ended up on the ground a drunken bundle
He died on the wrong side of the street disturbing
    Saturday

Some Books

All titles published in London unless otherwise stated

Buarque, Chico, *Turbulence* (Bloomsbury, 1992)

———*Benjamin* (Bloomsbury, 1997)

Castro, Ruy, *Chega de saudade: a história e as histórias da bossa nova* (Companhia das Letras, São Paulo 1990)

Cleary, David, Jenkins, Dilwyn, Marshall, Oliver and Hine, Jim, *Brazil: The Rough Guide* (Harrap Columbus, 1990)

da Cunha, Euclides, *Rebellion in the Backlands* (Picador, 1995)

Guillermoprieto, Alma, *Samba* (Bloomsbury, 1990)

Perrone, Charles A., *Masters of Contemporary Brazilian Song: MPB 1965–1985* (University of Texas Press, Austin 1989)

Sader, Emir and Silverstein, Ken, *Without Fear of Being Happy: Lula, the Workers Party and Brazil* (Verso, 1991)

Schreiner, Claus, *Música Brasileira: A History of Popular Music and the People of Brazil* (Marion Boyars, 1993)

Werneck, Humberto, *Chico Buarque: letra e música 1* (Companhia das Letras, São Paulo 1993)

Now you can order superb titles directly from Abacus

☐ The Land of Miracles: A Journey Through Modern Cuba	Stephen Smith	£7.99
☐ Three Moons in Vietnam	Maria Coffey	£7.99
☐ Travels in a Thin Country: A Journey Through Chile	Sara Wheeler	£7.99
☐ Bad Seed: The Biography of Nick Cave	Ian Johnston	£8.99

Please allow for postage and packing: **Free UK delivery**.
Europe; add 25% of retail price; Rest of World; 45% of retail price.

To order any of the above or any other Abacus titles, please call our credit card orderline or fill in this coupon and send/fax it to:

Abacus, 250 Western Avenue, London, W3 6XZ, UK.
Fax 0181 324 5678   Telephone 0181 324 5517

☐ I enclose a UK bank cheque made payable to Abacus for £...........

☐ Please charge £........... to my Access, Visa, Delta, Switch Card No.

☐☐☐☐☐☐☐☐☐☐☐☐☐☐☐☐

Expiry date ☐☐☐☐   Switch Issue No. ☐☐

Name (Block Letters please) _____

Address _____

_____

_____

Post/zip code: _____   Telephone _____

Signature _____

Please allow 28 days for delivery within the UK. Offer subject to price and availability.
Please do not send any further mailings from companies carefully selected by Abacus ☐